A HISTORY

OF THE

REIGNING FAMILY OF LAHORE

A HISTORY

OF THE

REIGNING FAMILY OF LAHORE

WITH SOME ACCOUNT OF

THE JUMMOO RAJAHS,

THE SEIK SOLDIERS AND THEIR SIRDARS;

EDITED BY

MAJOR G. CARMICHAEL SMYTH

GYAN

Published by

Gyan Publishing House
5, Ansari Road
Daryaganj, New Delhi-110002
Phone: 011-47034999, 9811692060
E-mail: books@gyanbooks.com

Distribution Network
gyanbooks.com
India, USA, Canada, UK, Australia

ISBN: 978-93-6433-841-7 (HB)
First Published, 1847

2nd Impression 2024

Printed at: Gyan Press, Delhi.

A HISTORY OF THE REIGNING FAMILY OF LAHORE,...
EDITOR: MAJOR G. CARMICHAEL SMYTH

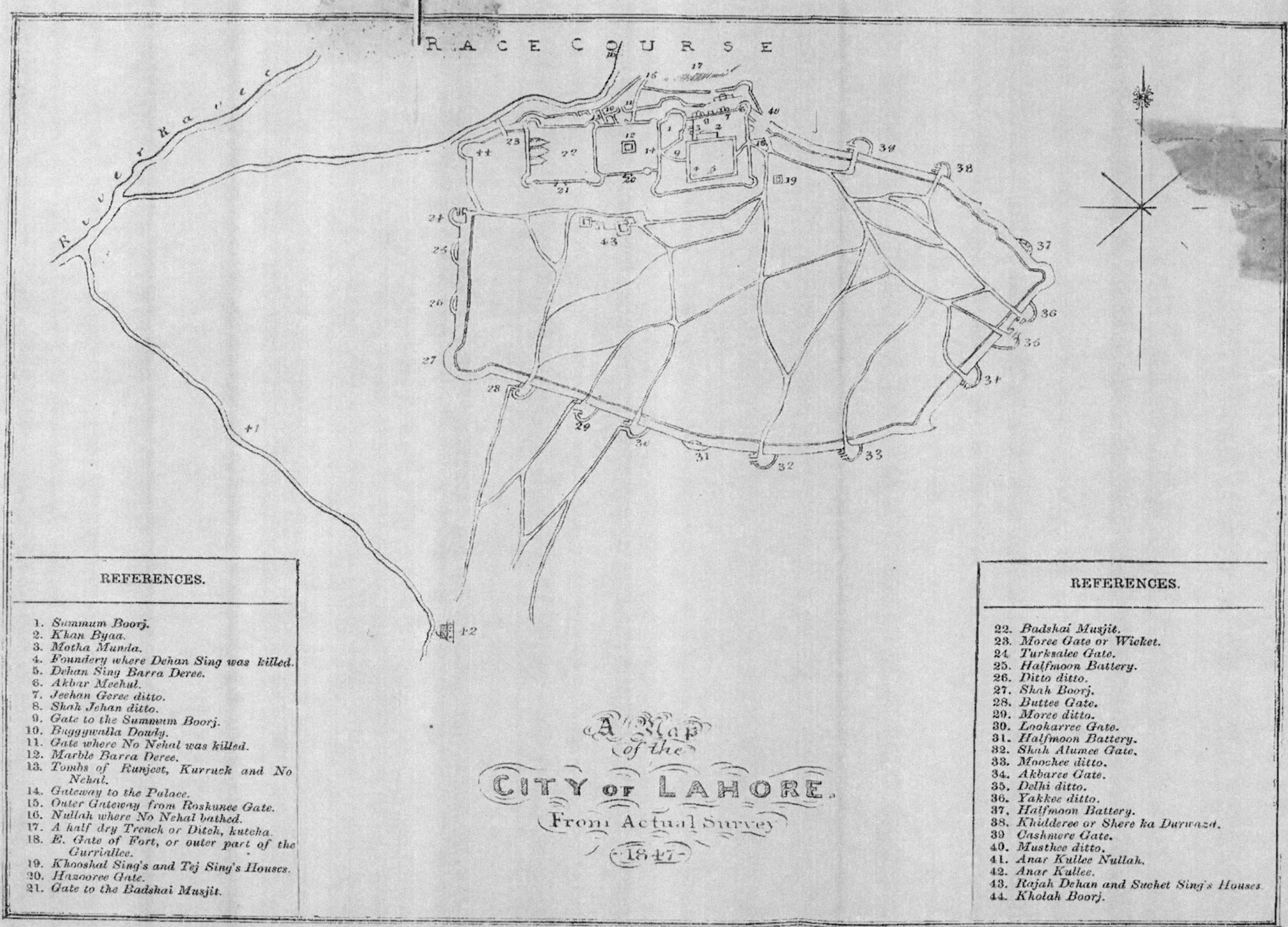
RACE COURSE
River Ravie
A Map of the
CITY OF LAHORE.
From Actual Survey
1847
REFERENCES.
1. Summum Boorj.
2. Khan Byaa.
3. Motha Munda.
4. Foundery where Dehan Sing was killed.
5. Dehan Sing Barra Deree.
6. Akbar Meehul.
7. Jeehan Geree ditto.
8. Shah Jehan ditto.
9. Gate to the Summum Boorj.
10. Buggywalla Dowdy.
11. Gate where No Nehal was killed.
12. Marble Barra Deree.
13. Tombs of Runjeet, Kurruck and No Nehal.
14. Gateway to the Palace.
15. Outer Gateway from Roskunee Gate.
16. Nullah where No Nehal bathed.
17. A half dry Trench or Ditch, kutcha.
18. E. Gate of Fort, or outer part of the Gurridlee.
19. Khooshal Sing's and Tej Sing's Houses.
20. Hazooree Gate.
21. Gate to the Badshai Musjit.
REFERENCES.
22. Badshai Musjit.
23. Moree Gate or Wicket.
24. Turksalee Gate.
25. Halfmoon Battery.
26. Ditto ditto.
27. Shah Boorj.
28. Buttee Gate.
29. Moree ditto.
30. Lookarree Gate.
31. Halfmoon Battery.
32. Shah Alumee Gate.
33. Moochee ditto.
34. Akbaree Gate.
35. Delhi ditto.
36. Yakkee ditto.
37. Halfmoon Battery.
38. Khidderee or Shere ka Durwaza.
39 Cashmere Gate.
40. Musthee ditto.
41. Anar Kullee Nullah.
42. Anar Kullee.
43. Rajah Dehan and Suchet Sing's Houses.
44. Kholah Boorj.
Bullen's Lith Press 7 Mission Row

A HISTORY

OF THE

REIGNING FAMILY OF LAHORE,

WITH SOME ACCOUNT OF

THE JUMMOO RAJAHS,

THE SEIK SOLDIERS AND THEIR SIRDARS;

EDITED BY

MAJOR G. CARMICHAEL SMYTH

THIRD BENGAL LIGHT CAVALRY;

WITH NOTES ON

MALCOLM, PRINSEP, LAWRENCE, STEINBACH,
McGREGOR, AND THE CALCUTTA REVIEW.

CALCUTTA:
W. THACKER AND CO.—ST. ANDREW'S LIBRARY.

1847.

NOTICE.

UNFORESEEN and unavoidable circumstances and the great distance from Calcutta at which the Editor has been stationed, to whom constant references were made, have delayed this work long beyond his expectations.

TO

THE MEMORY OF

MAJOR BROADFOOT, C. B.

LATE

AGENT TO THE GOVERNOR GENERAL

OF

India

ON THE NORTH WESTERN FRONTIER,

THIS BOOK IS

DEDICATED,

BECAUSE THE MORAL COURAGE OF HIS COUNSEL
WAS ONLY TO BE EQUALLED
BY
HIS UNDAUNTED CONDUCT

IN THE FIELD.

PREFACE.

A Dedication is generally addressed to a great man, or some one to whom the author has been placed under obligations; it is either as a debt of gratitude, or as a loan, which the writer expects will be repaid to him with Hebrew interest, most praiseworthy in the first instance, most paltry in the second.

The expressions, flowing from a grateful heart, will ever be read with admiration; but the foul flattery of a Parasite is beneath contempt, and generally as false as it is foul.

My dedication, however, is neither as a debt nor as a loan; and, if the name of one who was great, and would have been greater, has been mentioned, it is—because he has departed; for, notwithstanding this book was undertaken at his suggestion, when we last met at Loodiana, still it would never have been presented to the living man, though offered now "to his memory."

G. C. S.

PREFACE

CONTENTS.

MISCELLANEOUS NOTICES.

APPENDIX.

GENEALOGICAL TABLES AND A MAP OF LAHORE.

LIST

OF

SUBSCRIBERS.

Nos.	Names and Rank.	Corps.	No. of Copies.
1	Abercrombie, J. Lieut	Horse Artillery	1
2	Abbott, J. R. Captain	12th Regt. N. I.	1
3	Alexander, C. B. Lieut. Col.	Horse Artillery	1
4	Alexander, H. Ensign	55th Regt. N. I.	1
5	Angelo, J. Lieut. Colonel	3rd Lt. Cavalry	1
6	Aratoon, Mr.	Merchant, Loodianah	1
7	Ashburnham, C. B. Lieut. Col. ..	62nd Queen's	1
8	Baring, S. D. C. Lieut.	55th Regt. N. I.	1
9	Baring, E. A. Ensign (Unposted)	D. D. 51st N. I.	1
10	Barclay, C. Esq.	Hallyford, Middlesex	1
11	Barr, Captain	Horse Artillery	1
12	Barnwell, Lieut. Colonel	H. M. 9th Foot	1
13	Becher, A. M. Major	Assistant Qr. M. General....	1
14	Becher, J. R. Lieut	Engineers	1
15	Beller, R. B. Lieut.	50th Queen's	1
16	Belli, W. H., Esq.	C. S. Calcutta	1
17	Berrill's Hotel	Allahabad	1
18	Biddulph, E. Lieut. Colonel	Horse Artillery	1
19	Birch, R. J. H. Lieut Colonel....	J. A. General..............	1
20	Bird, W. W. Cornet	9th Lancers	1
21	Blagrave, T. C. Lieut	26th Regt. N. I.	1
22	Blake, M. T. Capt. Commanding	2nd Inf., Sindiah Contg. ..	1
23	Boileau Ensign, N. C.	27th Regt. N. I.	1
24	Bodle, G. Lieut.	H. M. 80th Foot	1
25	Book Club	1st Bengal Fusileers	1
26	Book Club (Officers)	2nd Light Infantry	1
27	Book Club (Officers)	Horse Artillery	1
28	Book Club	69th Regt. N. I.	1
29	Book Club	H. M. 21st Fusileers	1
30	Book Club	29th Regt. N. I.	1
31	Book Club	26th ditto ditto	1
32	Book Club	68th ditto ditto	1
33	Book Club	20th ditto ditto	1
34	Book Club	1st ditto ditto	1
35	Book Club	61st N. I.	1
36	Book Club	46th N. I.	1
37	Book Club	Juanpore	1
38	Book Club	Mussoorie	1
39	Brigs, H. C. Lieut.	9th Lancers	1
40	Britten, C. Captain	60th Rifles	1
41	Brown, E. Lieut.	1st Bengal Fusileers	1
42	Budd, G. R. Lieut.	3rd Light Cavalry.........	1
43	Bunbury, A. C. Ensign	34th Regt. N. I.	1

Nos.	Names and Rank.	Corps.	No. of Copies.
44	Burke, J. Ensign	36th Regt. Foot	1
45	Butler, J. Major	3rd Regt. N. I.	1
46	Bunny, A. Lieut	Artillery	1
47	Burn, J. Ensign	40th Regt. N. I.	1
48	Bruce, R. R. Lieut.	Horse Artillery	1
49	Byng, E. Lieut.	A. D. C.	1
50	Burten, J. A. Lieut.	3rd K. O. Lt. Dragoons	1
51	Balders, Lieut. Colonel	3rd K. O. Lt. Dragoons	1
52	Boxer, B. H. Lieut.	H. M. 80th Foot	1
53	Cameron, T. M. Lieut.	55th Regt. N. I.	1
54	Campbell, Lieut.	60th Rifles	1
55	Campbell, Sir E. Lieut. Col.	Late 3rd B. L. Cavalry	1
56	Canora, Colonel	Seik Service	1
57	Caley, Lieut Colonel	64th Regt. N. I.	1
58	Carnegy, Lieut. Colonel	27th Regt. N. I.	1
59	Carmichael, Sir J., Bart.	London	1
60	Carmichael, C. M. Lieut. Col.	3rd Lt. Cavalry	1
61	Cheap, Captain M. of B. Neemuch	51st Regt. N. I.	1
62	Christie, J. Major	9th Irregular Cavalry	1
63	Christie, Major E.	Artillery	1
64	Charde, D. Esq.	Meerut	1
65	Clarke, Captain	1st Bengal Fusileers	1
66	Clarke, Mr. S. M.	Tailor, Meerut	1
67	Clarke, Stanley, Esq.	Civil Service	1
68	Clifford, B. W. Cornet	10th Light Cavalry	1
69	Colquhoun, Dr.	3rd ditto ditto	1
70	Corfield, C. Major	47th Regt. N. I.	1
71	Coombe, Captain	1st Bengal Fusileers	1
72	Cortlandt, Lieut. Colonel	Late H. M. 31st Foot	1
73	Cookes, C. H. Lieut	Artillery	1
74	Costley, Brigadier	Barrackpore	1
75	Craigie, G. Surgeon	H. Artillery	1
76	Cunningham, J. D. Captain	Engineers	1
77	Cureton, C. B. Lieut. Col.	Adjt. Genl. Q. Troops	1
78	Coxen, Captain &. P. M.	66th Rifles	1
79	Cullen, W. Major General	....	1
80	Davidson, C. T.	Civil Service, Tirhoot	1
81	Dawson, J. Ensign	1st N. I.	1
82	Day, E. F. Major	Horse Artillery	1
83	De Montmorency, R. E. Lieut.	60th Rifles	1
84	Dewar, A. C. Capt. Commanding	1st Cavalry, Sindiah Contg.	1
85	Dempster, J. Surgeon	H. M. 21st Fusileers	1
86	Dixen, C. G. Major	Artillery	1
87	Douglass, Major	H. M. 9th Foot	1
88	Douglass, Captain	60th Rifles	1
89	Drummond, Major	3rd Light Cavalry	1
90	Drummond (C. B.) Lieut. Col.	Dy. Q. M. General	1
91	Dorin, H. A. Lieut.	Commissariat	1
92	Dunlop, J. Lieut	12th Regt. N. I.	1
93	Donaldson, A. S. O. Lieut	45th ditto ditto	1
94	Edwards, H. B. Captain	1st Bengal Fusileers	1
95	Edwards, W.	Under Secretary G. G.	1
96	Elliot, A. J. H. Cornet	G. G. Body Guard	1
97	Faithful, R. W. Surgeon	9th Irregular Cavalry	1
98	Fast, Major General	Calcutta	1
99	Farquharson, G. Major	8th Regt. N. I.	1

Nos.	Names and Rank.	Corps.	No. of Copies.
100	Ferris, J H. Captain	12th ditto ditto	1
101	Fisher, Mrs.	Europe	1
102	Follett, Captain (Major of Brigade)	Kurrachee	1
103	Forbes, W. Lieut.	27th Regt. N. I.	1
104	Forrest, M. S. O. B. Lieut.	12th ditto ditto	1
105	Forrest, J. H. Captain	11th Hussars	1
106	Frank, Lieut. Col.	H. M. 16th Foot	1
107	Fraser, A., C. S	....	1
108	Frith, Lieut.	Artillery	1
109	French, J.	Indigo Planter, Tirhoot	1
110	Fulleron, Lieut. Col.	9th Lancers	1
111	Flyter, J. Captain	64th Regt. N. I.	1
112	Galloway, A. S. Lieut.	3rd Light Cavalry	1
113	Galloway, S. C. C. Lieut.	10th Foot.	1
114	Garden, Col. Q. M. Genl.	Head Quarters	1
115	Gifford, J. Captain	2nd Grenadiers	1
116	Gibbs, J. J. Lieut.	68th Regt. N. I.	1
117	Gilbert, Sir W. Major General ..	Comg. Sirhind Div.	2
118	Gilberts, F. M. D. Lieut & Adjt .	2nd Gren.	1
119	Gilmore, J. F. Lieut.	Artillery	1
120	Gorle, J. T. Captain	10th Foot	1
121	Gordon, P. Major	Loodianah	1
122	Gough, Lord, C. C. in India	Head Quarters	2
123	Gough (C. B.) Lieut. Col.	H. M. Troops in India ...	1
124	Gordon, J. Captain	3rd Lt. Cavalry	1
125	Graham, J. Surgeon	H. Artillery	1
126	Graydon, W. Lieut.	16th Grendiers	1
127	Gray, W. J. Lieut.	Artillery	1
128	Grey, Sir John K. C. B. Major Genl	Comg. Meerut Div.	1
129	Greville, S. Lieut.	1st Bengal Fusileers	1
130	Grant, (C. B.) Lieut. Col.	....	1
131	Gubbins, J. P., C. S.	Adjt. General	1
132	Gundry, C. B. Lieut.	12th Regt. N. I.	1
133	Hamilton, C. V. Lieut.	45th Regt. N. I.	1
134	Handscomb, J. H. Lieut. Col. ..	26th Lt. I.	1
135	Hammersley, H. Cornet	6th Light Cavalry	1
136	Hardinge, Lieut.	80th Queen's	1
137	Harvey, F. Esq. Seharunpore ..	Civil Service	1
138	Harvey, Lt. Col.	52nd N. I.	1
139	Havelock, H. (C. B.) Lieut. Col. .	Bombay	1
140	Hawkes, Lieut. Col.	9th Lt. Cavalry	1
141	Hardinge, C. S. Esq	Private Secretary	1
142	Herbert, Captain	9th Light Cavalry	1
143	Hissen, E. H.	56th Queen's	1
144	Hathern, H. V. Lieut.	18th Regt. N. I	1
145	Hopper, A. Q. Captain	24th ditto N. I.	1
146	Hoste, W. D. Lieut.	55th ditto ditto	1
147	Honig Berger, (D. Martin)	Seik Service	1
148	Howard, Esq.	Profr. of Music, Umballa ..	1
149	Huish, A. Captain	Artillery	1
150	Hutchinson, W. C. Lieut.	Horse Artillery	1
151	Hoyden, T. Lieut.	Artillery	1
152	Hughes, W. T. Lieut.	2nd Irregular Cavalry	1
153	Hughes, E. J. Lieut.	57th Regt. N. I.	1
154	Innis, P. R.	1st Bengal Fusileers	1
155	James, C. P.	50th Queen's	1

Nos.	*Names and Rank.*	*Corps.*	*No. of Copies.*
156	Jameson, W. Dr.	Shaharunpore	1
157	James, T. Captain	Kotah Contingent	1
158	Joseph, Mr. Merchant	Loodianah	1
159	Keer, J. Ensign	60th Regt. N. I.	1
160	Keiller, D. C. Captain	6th ditto ditto	1
161	Kennion, Lieut.	Horse Artillery	1
162	Kirke, H. Captain	12th Regt. N. I.	1
163	Knowles, Captain	50th Queen's	1
164	Kyroff, Mr., Merchant	Lahore	1
165	Lamb, W. Captain,	Major of Brigade	4
166	Lawrence, (C. B.) Lieut. Col.	Agent, Lahore	1
167	Lawrence, G. St. P. Major	11th Light Cavalry	1
168	La Touche, Brigade Major	Nusserabad	1
169	Lawrell, H. Esq.	Late 3d Bengal Cav. London	1
170	Lambert, G. C. Lieut.	1st Bengal Fusileers	1
171	Lee, E. Lieut	10th Foot	2
172	Leeson, J. Major	2d Irregular Cavalry	1
173	Library	Kurrachee	1
174	Library, (Officers')	86th Queen's	1
175	Library, Soldiers'	86th ditto	1
176	Library, Soldiers'	28th L. Infantry	1
177	Library	Gwalior Contingent	2
178	Library	80th Queen's	2
179	Lindesay, H. Capt.	3rd Light Cavalry	1
180	Littler, (Sir John) Major Genl.	Comg. Punjab Div.	1
181	Liptrap, Capt	42nd Regt. L. I.	1
182	Lindam, C. Lieut	10th Foot	1
183	Loch, H. B. Cornet	3rd Light Cavalry	1
184	Lovette, Captain	28th Queen's	1
185	Long, Major	50th Queen's	1
186	Loyd, B. P. Lieut	Loodianah, Regt.	1
187	Low, A. Major	Late 16th Lancers	1
188	Louther, Civil Service	Allahabad	1
189	Lugard, E. Major	Head Quarters	1
190	Macdonald, Lieut. and Adjt.	7th Regt. Sindiah Contingent	1
191	Macleod, D. J. Ensign	12th ditto N. I.	1
192	Macleod, W. B. Supery. Surgeon.	Dacca	1
193	Macleod, D. Esq.	Tirhoot	1
194	Macdermott, W. Vey. Surgeon	8th Light Cavalry	1
195	Macgregor, G. H. Major	Artillery	1
196	Macgregor, W. L. Surgeon	1st Bengal Fusileers	1
197	Manning, H. D. Lieut.	19th Regt. N. I	1
198	Mainwaring, C. Captain	Commissariat Dept.	1
199	Mackenzie, J. Captain	8th Lt. Cavalry	1
200	Mackenzie, Colin, Capt.	Loodiana	1
201	Marsh, H. Captain	3rd ditto ditto	1
202	Maginn, Ensign	69th Regt. N. I.	1
203	Mande, Lieut.	Artillery	1
204	Maloney, Surgeon	50th Queen's	1
205	Mess, H. M.	9th Foot	1
206	Mess, H. M.	10th ditto	1
207	Mess, Officers	8th Regt. N. I.	1
208	Moore, L. G. Cornet	3rd ditto Lt. Cavalry	1
209	Momet, T. De, Ensign	68th ditto N. I.	1
210	Monteath, T. Brigadier	Comg. at Umballah	1
211	Menteith, W. S. Capt.	Brigade Major	1

Nos.	*Names and Rank.*	*Corps.*	*No. of Copies.*
212	Money, E. K. Lieut.	Artillery	1
213	Monro, A. Esq.	Edinburgh	1
214	Mulcaster, W. E. Capt.	Fort Adjt. Chunar	1
215	Muller, E. C. Lieut.	50th Queen's	1
216	Murray, B. H. Lieut.	43rd Regt. N. I.	1
217	Napier, Sir Charles, Lt. General..	Governor of Sindh	1
218	Newton, The Rev.	Loodianah Mission	1
219	Nunn, Major	80th Queen's	1
220	Ogston, Ensign	34th Regt. N. I.	1
221	Oldham, J. A. Lieut	86th Queen's	1
222	Ormsby, Captain	80th Queen's	1
223	Palmer, C. O. B. Lieut.	1st Bengal Fusileers	1
224	Palmer, Brigadier	Delhie	1
225	Palmer, Captain	60th Rifles	1
226	Parsons, (C. B.) Lieut. Col.	Depty. Comry. General	1
227	Paterson, A. H. Lieut.	68th Regt. N. I.	1
228	Pearson, A. Lieut.	Artillery	1
229	Polwhele, Major	42nd Regt. Lt. I.	1
230	Philips, Vety. Surgeon	Saharunpore Stud	1
231	Plunket, J. Lieut.	6th Regt. N. I.	1
232	Prendergast, W. G. Lieut.	8th Lt. Cavalry	1
233	Rajah Mahtab Chund, H. H. The	Burdwan	1
234	Renney, G. A. Lieut.	Artillery	1
235	Reid, B. T. Lieut.	1st Bengal Fusileers	1
236	Reid, A. T. Lieut. Col.	12th Bom. N. I. Allan Deffell..	1
237	Riley, A. W. Capt.	80th Queen's	1
238	Richardson, R. Lieut.	3rd Regt. Lt. Cavalry	1
239	Robbins, W. P. Captain	15th ditto N. I.	1
240	Robinson, Lt. Col. Pol. Agent.	Mewar	1
241	Ross, A. H. Capt.	42nd Lt. I.	1
242	Rowcroft, Major	1st Regt. N. I.	1
243	Russell, E. S. Lieut.	12th Bombay N. I.	1
244	Russell, W. C. Lieut.	Horse Artillery	1
245	Rubie, P. Lieut.	40th Regt. N. I.	1
246	Sale, Lady	Europe	1
247	Salter, Lieut. H. F. Col.	11th Light Cavalry	1
248	Salmon	60th Rifles	1
249	Seaton, D. Major,	1st Bengal Fusileers	1
250	Siddall, J. Vety. Surgeon	11th Light Cavalry	1
251	Sidley, J. H. H. B. Major	86th Queen's	1
252	Sim, George, Lieut	Engineers	1
253	Scott, P. G. Lieut.	12th Regt. N. I.	1
254	Simpson, A. Lieut.	Artillery	1
255	Skinner, S.	Delhi	1
256	Smith, (Sir H.) & Major Genl..	Europe	2
257	Smith, Captain	9th Lt. Cavalry	1
258	Smith, R. A. Lieut.	19th Regt. N. I.	1
259	Smyth, Carmichael, Captain	H. M. 32d Foot	1
260	Smith, R. M. Lieut.	54th N. I., Ferozepore	1
261	Snow, T. R. Lieut	9th Lt. Cavalry	1
262	Stewart, D. Asst. Surgeon	10th Foot	1
263	Stacy, L. R. Brigadier	Comg. Mewar Field Force..	1
264	Studdy, T. B. Captain	8th Lt. Cavalry	1
265	Sutherland, J. Lieut. Col.	2nd Bombay L. C.	2
266	Swetenham, E. Major	Mussooree	2
267	Syers, J. D. Lieut. Col	59th Regt. N. I.	1

Nos.	*Names and Rank.*	*Corps.*	*No. of Copies.*
268	Tabor, J. Captain	7th Light Cavalry	1
269	Taylor, R. G. Lieut.	11th Light ditto	1
270	Taylor, Ens. with 16th Grenadr.	Dinapoor	1
271	Thackwell, Sir J. Major Genl.	Comg. Cawnpore Div.	2
272	Thorpe, D. B. Clerk Adjt. Genl.	Office H. M. Troops	1
273	Thompson, W. A. Lieut.	9th Light Cavalry	1
274	Tombs, H. Lieut.	Artillery	1
275	Trevelyan, M. Captain	60th Rifles	1
276	Trower, F. C. Lieut.	9th Lancers	1
277	Tulloch, C. B. Lieut.	12th Regt. N. I.	1
278	Templer, H. J. Ensign	6th ditto ditto	
279	Tudor, Major	46th ditto ditto	1
280	Trewlaney, Lieut. Col.	Europe	1
281	Tweddell, H. M. Surgeon	Garrison Surgeon, Chunar	1
282	Vansittart, H. Esq.	Jullender	1
283	Vincent, Major General	Mussoorie	2
284	Vincent, G. V. Merchant.	Meerut	1
285	Wallich, G. C. (M. D.) Doctor	2nd Irregular Cavalry	1
286	Ward, G. Cornet	8th Cavalry	1
287	Watson, Major General	Allahabad	2
288	Watt, Major	27th Regt. N. I.	1
289	Warburton, R. Capt. Comg.	2nd Comp. Arty. Sindia Contg.	1
290	Wedderburn, J. Lieut.	69th Regt. N. I.	1
291	Welman, H. T. Lieut. and Adjt.	80th Foot	1
292	Wood, Lieut. Col. Mily. Secy	Governor General	1
293	Wood, A. Surgeon	Artillery	1
294	Wood, A. Captain	29th M., N. I.	1
295	Wyndham, C. Cornet	9th Light Cavalry	1
296	Wollaston, C. Captain	8th ditto ditto	1
297	Woodington, H. P. T. Lieut.	21st Fusileers	1

INTRODUCTION.

INTRODUCTION.

The following pages have been compiled partly from native manuscripts, and partly from information collected from Seik Sirdars, and European officers in the Seik service; but chiefly from the notes of a Captain Gardner of the Seik Artillery, who has for several years past supplied important information to the British Government without betraying his own,* as all the intrigues he brought to light were those of the Jummoo family, and their coadjutor the Pundit; and there is every reason to believe Captain Gardner could give further information, and prove that the Dogra chiefs were at the bottom of the Cabul insurrection! An insurrection, which, in all probability, never would have taken place, had Lord Auckland followed the suggestions of Sir William Macnaghten regarding the Punjaub, on the death of No Nihal Singh; for then it was the Envoy declared the tripartite treaty at an end, as Sheer Sing who had usurped the rajh, could not, by the most forced construction, be considered the posterity of Runjeet Sing; and all those who had made themselves acquainted with the History of the Punjaub must have been aware of this, as Suda Kour's attempt to pass off the two children (Sheer Sing and Tara Sing) on the Seik chief, as the twin sons of her daughter, Metab Kour, is stated in Mr. Prinsep's Life of the old Maharajh; and I might bring forward the authority of many others, well informed upon the subject, from General Ventura to Mr. Vigne; but it is useless discussing this point, for it is as well known that Sheer Sing was *not* the son of the Maharajh, as it is that

* To give an idea of Captain Gardner's knowledge of Seik affairs, I may mention that Major Lawrence, in writing to me from Katmandoo, observed, "If I was in Broadfoot's place I should like to have Gardner at my elbow."

Heera Sing was the Alexis, the *delicias domini:* I do not mean to assert, however, that Dulleep Sing is the offspring of the old impotent sinner, but he certainly is his mother's son, and that may give him some small claim to the Guddee.* I think it is in Don Juan, Byron says of the Emperor Alexander of Russia,

> "Oh mighty Alexander, if you be,
> Your mother's son, that's quite enough for me;"

and had Sheer Sing been the son of Metab Kour, it would have been quite enough for the British Government; and Sir William Macnaghten would never have asserted that he could not by the most forced construction be considered the posterity of Runjeet Sing.

Our connection with the Lahore Government, it is supposed, was much the same as our connection with Bhurtpore;† the Rajah was independent, but we were bound to support the reigning family, and yet, when Sir David Ochterlony *(clarum et venerabile nomen)* had the moral courage to come forward, and convince the Indian community that even a petty Prince might rely on the fulfilment of a Treaty entered into with the paramount authority, he was rebuked and disgraced by the Members of the Government at the time, with the exception (according to his own statement) of Sir Edward Paget; for this high-minded man has no paltry feelings; he is as little acquainted with jealousy as with fear, and would have been delighted if Sir David Ochterlony had taken Bhurtpore, and obtained the Peerage ‡—but the unjust treat-

---

* Dulleep Sing's mother, Mai Chunda, was *not*, however, one of Runjeet Sing's wives; he was only married to two women, Metab Kour, the daughter of Suda Kour and Mai Nekee, the mother of Kurruck Sing; and he only performed even the Chadardalna with three women, namely, the two widows of Sahib Sing, of Guzerat, and Gool Begum, a Kunchenee of Lahore.

† See Agra Guide and Gazetteer.

‡ Ochterlony's military reputation was established, and he had no wish to wade through carnage to a Coronet; but on the contrary was a *peacemaker*, like the able and amiable Metcalfe; his letter to Lord Amherst shews he would have

ment of the Resident at Delhi may have been borne in mind by the Envoy at Lahore.* The Bhurtpore Usurper after a time, however, was deposed, but Sheer Sing was allowed to end his days in possession of the rajh. Lord Amherst plucked up courage after a short time, but Lord Auckland (notwithstanding his love for legitimacy) remained timid to the last, though he refused to acknowledge Sheer Sing until he stood in need of his assistance; so that we may suppose he only objected to support a woman's rule in the Punjaub, having himself so completely failed in his attempt to keep an old woman on the throne of Cabul. But I believe the real fact is, Sheer Sing was considered the Louis Philippe of Lahore, "The King of the People," and the rajh was supposed to be as safe in his hands as it had been in old Runjeet's; though, if such was the case, how little did our Government know of the intrigues of that arch hypocrite, Dehan Sing, a Sejanus to Runjeet, who merely placed Sheer Sing on the guddee to destroy him, knowing he was too ambitious and too powerful to be passed over; for there is not the least doubt that the Minister and the Prince had arranged matters, even before the death of the one-eyed monarch, as Sheer Sing spoke to Colonel Skinner on the subject of his succeeding to the guddee, when Lord Auckland and Sir Henry Fane were at Ferozepore with the "Army of the Indus," though Kurruck Sing was only a few years his senior, and No Nehal Sing

---

settled every thing at Bhurtpore without firing a shot!—proving, that as a diplomatist, as well as a military man he was superlatively great. Sir David was born at Boston, New England, in 1758, so that in 1825 he was only sixty-seven,—younger than most of our Indian generals.

* It appeared to be the wish of the Indian Government to add insult to injury, and to forget who had conquered the Nepalese and defended Delhi, while the panic that had so often prevailed within the Mahratta ditch was their only excuse for this gross piece of ingratitude: indeed they were so much alarmed that they not only ordered Sir David *not* to depose Doorjun Saul, but to prepare to *act on the defensive!* which even brought a smile on his lips in the midst of his anger.

was then quite a young man.* It was to bring forward all these facts, that chiefly induced me to undertake this History of the Punjaub; for since Mr. Prinsep's "Life of Runjeet Sing," no work of importance has appeared except Major Lawrence's "Punjaub Adventurer," which, although it gives, generally speaking, a very correct account of the Seiks, still, as will be seen by the Appendix to this work, it contains a few errors, and it was written before all the disgraceful scenes of slaughter had taken place, of which I profess to give the true version. My work also includes the History of the Dogra family and their iniquities, with which but few people are acquainted; though, after the account given in these pages of Goolaub Sing's atrocities, the public will, I dare say, be greatly surprised at the British Government entering into a treaty with such a monster; † but, when a political measure is to be carried out, I verily believe we would make friends with the Old Gentleman himself,—for I have now been twenty-six years in India, and during the whole of my sojourn in the East, I have never heard of so infamous a miscreant as the Rajah of Jummoo,‡ though I am acquainted with the

---

* The *Calcutta Review* for August, 1844, states, that Sheer Sing, actually consulted with Mr. Clerk regarding his *opposing* no less a person than Kurruck Sing, the *only son* of the old Maharajh.

† It has been generally asserted, that making Goolaub Sing a Maharajh was a mockery, and giving him Cashmeer, was in keeping; that the justice of the act and the policy were on a par. The "Rose-water" Rajah's life has been spent in the enjoyment of very different feasts to "the feast of Roses," and he would soon reduce "the sweetest that Earth ever gave" to the state to which Cabul's hundred gardens were reduced by our "Incendiary Generals," as Lord Brougham called them.

All those who have heard, and "oh! who has not heard of the Vale of Cashmeer," must have observed that every traveller who has visited that place since it fell into the hands of Runjeet Sing, has heard the unfortunate inhabitants cry out against the oppression of the Seik chieftain, and now their falling into the power of Goolaub Sing is like escaping from Scylla into Charybdis.

‡ See "*Punjaub Adventurer*," *Chap. XIII. p.* 75, *Note* 1st.—"Goolaub Sing is the elder brother, and, in the family pact, he has charge of their conquered territories in the hills: while he manages those of Dhyan Sing, he yearly adds to his

evil deeds of such wretches as Kam Ran and Yar Mahomed, his Vizier, with whom the British Government, to their cost, at one time, were connected.

Regarding the Punjaub war; I am neither of opinion, that the Seiks made an *unprovoked attack*, nor that we have acted towards them with *great forbearance;* my opinion is, that we should, as the paramount authority, long ago have adopted coercive measures with the Seiks, and have assumed what kings call "a commanding attitude,"* but if this policy was disapproved of, no half measures should have been pursued, no middle course should have been taken; for, if the Seiks were to be considered entirely an independent

---

own by conquest, or by the terror of his name. He has overrun the whole district between Kashmeer and Attok; and inflicted such terrible vengeance on the people of Sudan, (a large district south-east of Mozaffarabad,) cutting up, maiming, flaying to the amount, is is said, of twelve thousand persons, that the men of Dundi and Satti, two adjoining territories, sent in their submission, but begged *not to see his face.* Of course, the brothers must unite in this barbarous policy, though it is difficult to believe such horrors of either, seeing their mild and winning demeanor. They are alike too in their boundless ambition and fathomless duplicity; as wary as they are daring, as little disposed to use force where cunning will succeed, as they are unscrupulous in the employment of violent measures where such seem called for. Of Gulab Singh I have heard tales which I can hardly believe myself, and therefore, will not task my reader's credence with. His information, like that of his brother, is considerable; and though not a very accurate geographer, nor with clear ideas as to the direction in which his lieutenant, Zorawar Sing, went to push his conquests, he has a good estimate of the wealth and products of China, as well as of Europe. In manner, Gulab Singh is highly mild and affable: his features are good, nose aquiline, and expression pleasing, though rather heavy. Indefatigable in business, he sees after every thing himself; hardly able to sign his name, he looks after his own accounts, and often has the very gram for his horses weighed out before him. Since the death of Runjit Singh, the Rajah has been in bad odour with the *durbar*, for holding out against the present monarch; and with the army, from the numbers killed in his famous defence of the *Suman-burj*, in the commencement of 1841, as well as from the summary punishment inflicted on the mutineers in Kashmir. Both Gulab Sing and his brother are, therefore, always surrounded by regiments of their own *Dogur* clan, who serve them in fear and trembling, having their families in the Rajah's hands, and knowing that any dereliction from duty would entail torture on them."

* Surely after having deposed Dost Mahomed merely because Captain Vickovitch paid him a visit, we need not have stood upon such ceremony with the Seiks.

state, in no way answerable to us, we should not have provoked them !—for to assert that the bridge of boats brought from Bombay, was not a *causa belli*, but merely a defensive measure is absurd; besides, the Seiks had translations of Sir Charles Napier's speech, (as it appeared in the *Delhi Gazette*,*) stating that we were going to war with them; and, as all European powers would have done under such circumstances, the Seiks thought it as well to be first in the field. Moreover, they were not encamped in our territory, but their own; and, although the second article of the treaty of 1809 states, "the Rajah will never maintain in "the territory, which he occupies on the left bank of the "Sutlej, more troops than are necessary for the internal "duties," still the third article states, "in the event of "a violation of any of the preceding articles, or of a de-"parture from the rules of friendship on the part of either "state, the treaty shall be considered as null and void."

We have been told that the Seiks violated the treaty, by crossing the river with their army; but the question is, Was not the treaty null and void when they crossed? To expect a native power to make a regular declaration of war is too ridiculous; and I only ask, had *we* not departed *from the rules* of *friendship* first? The year before the war broke out, we kept the island between Ferozepore and the Punjaub, though it belonged to the Seiks, owing to the deep water being between *us* and the island.†

We either had or we had not a treaty with the Seiks;

---

* "If they (the robber tribes of Scinde) were allowed to remain undisturbed while Scinde was quiet, they would become turbulent and troublesome *when the British Army was called on to move into the Punjaub*."

† "Claims to islands in rivers between two Manors, and to alluvion are determined by what is called the 'Kuchmuch' or 'Kishtie bunna,' which practice or rule assigns the land to the proprietor of the 'bank or main,' upon which the alluvion is thrown, and from which the water has receded."—*Prinsep's Life of Runjeet*, p. 203.

my opinion is that we had none, and I have heard one high in the political department on the north western frontier state, that no treaty existed with the new Government. If then no treaty existed how can we call the Seiks the breakers of treaties? But if on the other hand the treaty of 1809 is said to have been binding between the two Governments, then the simple question is, who first departed from the "rules of friendship?" I am decidedly of opinion that we did; but as I am also of opinion that no treaty existed, I think, as I have before said, we ought long ago to have adopted coercive measures with the Seiks; and the reason assigned for our not doing so, "the helpless state of the young Maharajh,"* won't exactly go down with the public. The real cause must be apparent to all, and it was this, "what will they say at home if we interfere with the Seiks?" This "what will they say at home," is the great bugbear in the present day; and we certainly should not have been in India now, if Lord Wellesley had troubled his head about what they would say at home.

With the Seiks for several years past, in fact ever since the death of Runjeet Sing, we have been playing the fable of the "Shepherd Boy and the Wolf." The Papers and the Politicals had constantly been crying out "*The Seiks are coming!*" until at last we would not believe them; consequently the Seiks came, and we were, as events proved, quite unprepared to receive them. And yet, surely, defensive measures might have been adopted, and every thing might have been ready at Umballa, if not at Ferozepore, without disturbing the "perpetual friendship," which, I suppose, it was expected would last, like Paddy's love, "to the end of the

* "He (the Governor General) has shown on every occasion the utmost forbearance from consideration to the helpless state of the infant Maharajh, Dulleep Sing, whom the British Government had recognised as the successor to the late Maharajh, Shere Sing."—*Proclamated 13th December*, 1845.

world, and after O!" However, I don't stand forward myself as one of the "prophets of the past" and say, "I told you so;" but on the contrary, am willing to confess I never thought for a moment the Seiks would have crossed the River, though Captain Gardner always informed me that they would; but when I mentioned this to one who it was said knew them well, he wrote me word, they were not quite such fools as to think of that. However, few people appear to have known them; they were generally described as boasters and cowards; but we at last discovered (what I never suspected) that they were brave men and good Soldiers,* though like many other *fine troops*, they were sadly in want of *good Generals;* and never before did two armies so singularly prove the truth of Sir Charles Napier's assertion that "War is a series of blunders!"

The first great fault the Seiks committed was in not attacking Ferozepore and destroying that place; and when Runjoor Sing found he was allowed quietly to cross the Sutlej near Loodiana—turn our right flank—and get in our rear,† he ought certainly to have marched direct upon Delhi instead of entrenching himself, first at Buddawal, and

* A great deal has been said of the gallant bearing of Moreau (the "Arch Traitor," as Hazlitt called him) when he lost both his legs at the Battle of Dresden, where he was engaged with the allied powers *against France;* but I doubt much if the General bore his misfortune with the stoic courage of a Seik Sergeant, who had both his legs taken off by a round shot at the Battle of Aliwal! I conversed with him for about ten minutes, during which period not a muscle of his countenance indicated that he was in pain; and he spoke out boldly, like a Spartan, smiling at the idea when I told him one of our Surgeons would save his life, and remarking, he had no wish to live without his legs: he then asked for water, and, after washing his face, gave a silver ring with a ruby in it to the water carrier, and requested some of the men of H. M.'s 31st, who were standing by, to put an end to him with their bayonets. He was a fine, handsome looking man, between 50 and 60 years of age, with a grey beard covering his chest.

† Had General Grey been permitted to march when he was *first ordered*, he might have been present at Ferozshah or at Moodkee, and would have superceded the necessity of bringing Brigadier Wheeler's force away from Loodiana; or, had General Grey been ordered to Loodiana when he *did march*, he would have prevented Ranjoor Sing from crossing the River.

afterwards on the banks of the river; his Cavalry might have laid waste the country, and his army would have increased like a snow-ball, and easily have got possession of a portion of the siege-train, which was on the road without proper ammunition, and unprotected.*

But while *we* had a contempt for the Seiks, it is evident the native army had a great idea of their prowess; it was, therefore, most fortunate that with this army there was a large body of Europeans; for, after the war was over, a Foreign officer in the Seik service observed to a friend of mine, "If it had not "been for your European soldiers, we would have driven "you from Ferozepore into the sea;"—and I must confess, I could only painfully acknowledge to myself, the truth of his remark; for, as it was, the troops under their excellencies Sir Hugh Gough and Sir Henry Hardinge had but dearly gained a victory over a portion of the Seik army when Sir John Littler came to their rescue!—and, after his arrival, from all that I can learn, the Europeans had almost formed as high an opinion of the Seik soldiers as the natives; and it was long undecided whether we were to be the victors or the vanquished. The 62nd affair now must ever remain a mystery, and though no excuse can be made for the military faults of Colonel Reid, some credit may be given to him in coming forward to sacrifice himself, for the honour of his regiment, he having acknowledged that *he* ordered the retreat, when General Littler was present who had ordered the advance. He had every reason to expect he would be brought to a Court Martial for such "culpable conduct," as the Commander-in-Chief himself termed it.† However, it must be acknowledged after all

* It was most fortunate for the poor Recruits who accompanied the siege-train that it was *not attacked* because they must have been sacrified to a man, as they could only have fought like the Irishman at Donnybrook Fair, who declared that he had *nothing in his hand but his fist!*

† General Littler certainly shewed great forbearance in not placing Colonel Reid

the Seiks were but a contemptible enemy, as all troops must be who are without discipline and without leaders: and therefore had we only conducted things properly, and received proper information, we should, as Count Edward de Warren expected, have terminated their existence in a single action.

Their Artillery certainly did great execution, and from their strength in this arm, and from the way the Khalsa troops fought, and even their Hindostanee sepoys, of whom only six came over to our camp, notwithstanding every attempt we made to induce them to desert.* It must be seen that our

---

under an arrest, as soon as he became aware of his "culpable conduct:" but whether he acted right, in a military point of view, or wanted the moral courage, is another question.

* Hindostanee Proclamation—"Whereas the English Government is anxious to reward the bravery and fidelity of the Poorbeas, by raising a Regiment of them—it is hereby proclaimed, that any non-commissioned officer or soldier of the Lahore Government who shall present himself before His Excellency the Governor General, shall be immediately rewarded with the accustomed liberality, and shall have the benefit of invalid pension; and, if engaged in a law suit in a British court of justice, his case shall be immediately decided before any other. In fact, every opportunity of favour and cherishment shall at all times be kept in sight by the Government. However, it is reported that Tej Sing has given out, that if any sepoys of the Lahore army go over for service to the English Government, the officers of this Government will cut off their noses and ears and kill them. This is altogether an infamous falsehood—for the customs of this Government were never of such a description, and never will be—therefore let such a falsehood not enter their head; but let them feel assured that if they come here they will be well rewarded."

(A true Translation.) H. MARSH, *Bt. Captain,*

Interpreter and Quarter Master, 3d Cavalry.

After this proclamation, however, a Serjeant of the Seik Artillery, who was I believe the first to come over, and who was taken to Colonel Havelock, Persian Interpreter to the Commander-in-Chief, and sent also to the Under Secretary to Government—got nothing!!! and I had to feed him and clothe him at my own expense; and it was merely owing to the kindness of Major Lawrence, who at the time had other business to attend to, that the man at last got into one of the new Regiments as a corporal: his name is Mahomet Alli, he is or was in Mr. Edwards' Ferozepore Regiment, and, being a smart fellow, can tell his own story.

Cabul expedition was far more quixotic than ever it was supposed to be; for had the Jummoo Rajah only combined with "the Wallace of Cabul,"* which it is well known he intended doing, if the Affghan troops could have checked the advance of General Pollock, for Goolaub Sing was too knowing to think of attacking the British until they were repulsed. Had such an event, however, taken place, it is quite evident that Pollock, attacked in front and rear, must have been destroyed with his whole army; and Dehan Sing, with the army at Lahore, would have been too much for the force under Sir Jasper Nicolls; and without the special interference of Providence, the Seiks would even have destroyed "the Army of Reserve," though headed by "the Brumegem Napoleon" himself. But weak as we were in undertaking the Affghan campaign, we were not quite so weak as we were wicked. The war was not so impolitic as improper, and the hope of being able to reinstate Shah Soojah was certainly not quite so absurd, as to expect that the rajh of Runjeet Sing would last.

Major Lawrence said it would end with the "old Lion," as the Maharajah has been called; though, perhaps Mr. Thackeray's appellation of "the old Robber" would be more correct.

In the "Punjaub Adventurer" Dehan Sing is made to speak like Cassandra, and foretell the destruction of the rajh, and all the bloodshed that ensued.

What a country the Punjaub was then to have between

* Of all the names that have been applied to Ukbar Khan, Mr. Roebuck's appellation of "the Wallace of Cabul" was the most happy; for, be it remembered, that although the Scotch Hero was a Christian, and a much better educated man than the Cabul chief, even he commenced his career as a murderer; and I have never read that he repented of the deed; yet I believe to this day it is the opinion of the best informed, that to secure the person of the Envoy, was the *extent of the treachery intended* by the Dooranee Patriot.

us and Cabul! What a nation to form an alliance with,—who were on the brink of a revolution, and whose Government depended on the life of a decrepit debauchee!

How could we look to such people for support?

How could we expect succour from the Seiks?

Regarding this nation, I observe in *Frazer's Magazine* for April, 1846, some account of their rise and progress; and the writer, I perceive, has not only followed the erroneous statements in Major Lawrence's book, and Colonel Steinbach's, for the death of No Nehal Sing, but has taken quite a false view of the cause of Sheer Sing's death! He says, "The refusal of Sheer Sing to fall upon the rear of General Pollock's army, and cut off its convoys, cost that individual his life." Now the Sirdar who put Sheer Sing to death,—and it must be remembered that he was not employed by Dehan Sing, but, on the contrary, proposed the thing himself to the minister, and made all the arrangements!—this very Sirdar, so far from wishing Sheer Sing to fall upon the rear of General Pollock's army, gave information to the British Government, that such was the intention of Rajah Goolaub Sing! I happen to be aware of this, as Ajeet Sing sent a confidential servant of his own to me at Kurnaul, to inform me that the Sirdar had received intelligence from Peshawar of the greatest importance; and also to let me know he was anxious I should communicate the same to Mr. Clerk, with whom, he was aware, I was intimately acquainted. I replied, that if it was of such consequence, I thought it would be much better for the Sirdar to give his information to the magistrate, who would then write a public letter to Mr. Clerk upon the subject. The Sirdar objected, however, to make his appearance at the house of the magistrate; but, when I proposed that Mr. Woodcock should come to my house, he agreed, and there gave the evidence I have stated, which Mr. Woodcock communicated to Mr. Clerk;

and when Ajeet Sing took leave of me, not long after this, I am convinced he had fully made up his mind to take his "wild justice," as Lord Bacon calls it, for he observed, "*Lord Sahib kooch keeah nuheen, lekin hum be kooch kurringa.*" "The Lord Sahib has done *nothing*, but I will do *something*," and had it not been for his too hasty proceeding, he would, in all probability, have been minister at Lahore; but though he had enough of the cunning, he had not the courage of his uncle, Bhood Sing, to carry him through his daring intentions.* But the writer in *Fraser's Magazine* has fallen into a third error, when stating, "No Nehal Sing's death was announced to the minister;" for it so happened, it was the minister who announced the young Maharajah's death to the people; he, and he only having witnessed the last moments of his expiring Prince, refusing admittance even to his mother, and pushing aside Lena Sing Majeeteea, and some others of the chief Sirdars who were anxious to see what injury their sovereign had sustained. From that moment every thing became a mystery, and the *real cause* of the Maharajah's death was only known to the minister and his Maker; and scarcely was his death made known to the public ere Sheer Sing arrived, post haste, at the capital, an express having been sent off for him by Dehan Sing; but the Chief Sirdars declared they would not allow the son of a Washerman to sit on the throne of Runjeet; and Chund Kour claimed the rajh as her right according to the Seik custom. I am not aware that No Nehal Sing's widow was mentioned at the time, though she certainly was '*enciente*,'†

---

* Runjeet himself, I have been informed, was even afraid of Bhood Sing, who was not killed at Peshawar, as stated in the *Calcutta Review*, but died at Lahore, report says, of the cholera morbus, though his family declare that he was poisoned by the Dogra faction.

† It was reported to our Politicals that Chund Kour was the lady in this state, but if so, what reason could there be for her concealing it? and why declare it was her son's widow? as the child of either would have been the heir of Kurruck Sing; and of course, Chund Kour's power would have been greater as mother than as grandmother!!!

as I ascertained from Colonels Mouton and Lafont; and from Colonel Skinner who always had the best information,* and from many natives at Lahore; I learnt that she had a still-born male child soon after Sheer Sing succeeded to the guddee, the fact, however, is of little importance.

I have now only to apologise to my subscribers for the great delay that has taken place in bringing this History to a close; and yet it is not by any means so complete as I could wish, and had intended to make it, for having been requested by Major Lawrence, when at Lahore, to send him a portion of the work, I did so, on my return to Meerut, the first week in May, but owing to that officer's being constantly on the move, having great press of business, and also suffering from ill-health, the papers were not returned to me until the end of September; and, having previously despatched several manuscripts to England, had I forwarded the remainder of the work there, or recalled what I had despatched, my subscribers would not have received their copies for the next twelve months: I trust, therefore, I shall be pardoned for sending forth this work so imperfect; and though it was at Major Broadfoot's recommendation, as I have already stated, that I first thought seriously of undertaking the task, I ought here to mention, that it had been previously suggested to me by my much valued and high gifted friend, Dr. Archibald Gordon, who, I am confident (knowing the great opinion entertained of him by Mr. Clerk,) had he remained in the Political Department, would have succeeded to the appointment of Envoy at Lahore.

G. C. S.

Jullunder, 5th January, 1847.

---

* When I sent Mr. Clerk an account of the death of my ever to be lamented friend, in answering me he observed:—

"Poor Skinner! No man knew the natives and *every thing that took place at their* "*Courts*, and their feelings towards us, so well as he did: we have no Secunder now."

HISTORY

OF

RUNJEET SING'S FAMILY.

ABOUT the year of Christ 1470, lived a Hindoo Ját of the Varaich caste, named Kauloo. His family had for three generations dwelt at the village of Pundee Buttee, otherwise called Butt, forty or fifty miles south-west of Lahore; whence Kauloo, who was born and continued to reside there for some time, was generally styled Kauloo Buttee. The people of his native village were notorious for their wild and predatory habits; but Kauloo is said to have been a peaceable man, working hard for an honest livelihood. Having, while yet at an early age, had some quarrel with his friends at Buttee, he took with him his wife, and wandering away from the village and the low country, after some time settled at the small village of Sanseree, near Rajah Sansee, the present patrimonial jaghire of the Scindawalla family, and lying about four or five coss west of Umritsir. This place was the resort of hordes of Sansees, a wandering race of low caste, noted for their addiction to plunder, and moving about in parties of from one hundred to a thousand, dwelling in tents or huts made of reeds. Here however the self-exiled Kauloo dwelt safely, though surrounded by these Sansee bands. It happened on a time, that his wife, then far advanced in pregnancy, had occasion to go to some distance from home, and on her return, being suddenly seized with the pains of labour, was forced to take refuge in a Sansee tent. Here she gave birth to a son, and being kindly and hospitably treated by the Sansees, did not return to her home in the village until the end of forty days. The child she bore was considered by the Sansees as an adopted son of their race, and though he was named Jaddoo Maun Buttee, they gave him the designation of Jaddoo Sansee, by which he was generally known to his dying day. This is the commonly received account of the way in which Jaddoo received the cognomen of Sansee; but Scandal whispers another tale, to the effect that he had a still better claim to the appellation, as being really the son of one of the tribe, and not of the simple Kauloo his reputed father.

About the year 1476, Kauloo, with his wife and only child, removed from Sanseree to the small village of Sund (afterwards called Sceende,) about a coss and a half from Drownkell, and about four coss from Wuzeerabad. Here Kauloo died, sometime about the year 1488. His reputed son Jaddoo Maun, born in a Sansee camp, brought up in intimate acquaintance with the tribe, and feeling a predilection for their mode of life, generally resided among these people and often accompanied them on their predatory excursions. In one of these he was killed, about the year 1515, leaving behind him an only son named Galeb or Gauleb, afterwards nick-named Munnoo, from the large droves of cattle which he used to drive away as his booty from the banks of the Jhelum and Chinaub across the Ravee towards Lahore and the Manjha country, where he generally disposed of his plunder. This Gauleb, though probably a Veraich by caste, thus headed a gang of plundering Sansees, until about the year 1549, when he died at Sund, or Sceende, of wounds received in one of his predatory excursions.

He left a son named Kiddoh, who being a man of quiet and steady habits and a peaceable disposition, removed from Sceende with some cattle, the only property left him by his father, first to the village of Keallee, and afterwards, about the year 1555, to Sukerchuck, then a very small village, one and a half coss south of the present Gujerawalla. Here by perseverance and industry, he, after some time, obtained possession of several small plots of ground, by the cultivation of which he maintained himself and his family. This is supposed to be the person who is called by the people of the country and by the Sansees, Ramthull, i. e. a person devoted to God, otherwise a good and peaceable man. Kiddoh died about the year 1578, leaving two sons, Rajadah and Prenoo. Rajadah having learned to read and write, Goormuckka or Loondee, not only pursued the labours of the field but kept a small shop in Sukerchuck; and is said even to have travelled about the neighbouring country selling salt, tobacco, &c. &c. This Rajadah died about 1620, leaving three sons, Thelloo, Thuckt, (otherwise Thuckt Mull,) and Neeloo. Thelloo and Neeloo were killed together in a fray near their own village while yet but lads. Thuckt Mull, however, lived to extend the small estate left by his father, and likewise scraped together a small fortune by shop-keeping and money-lending. He also purchased the leases of many small plots of ground about Sukerchuck and Keallee, and must thus have become a man of some influence and importance in the neighbourhood. He died about 1653, leaving two sons, Boloo and Bara, afterwards called from his fanatical disposition Bii Bara. Boloo at the age of nine or ten left his home, and joining a camp of wandering predatory Sansees, was killed at the age of eighteen in a night attack upon a village. Bii Bara, though assuming the character of a religious fanatic, had the tact and policy to advance his own worldly interests, and became sole possessor of nearly half the lands in Sukerchuck, or about two wells. He obtained the designation of Bii on becoming the chelah or disciple of a Sing or Seik in Gujerawalla, who taught him to read the Grunth or Holy Book of Baba Nanuk; and about the age of twenty-five he set out for Umritsir to receive the Pahul and become a Seik. But some accident having happened to him on the road he returned without effecting his purpose. He is, however, known to have kept his head unshaved, and to have gone about the villages of Keallee and Sukerchuck proclaiming the precepts of Baba Nanuk. He kept no shop like his father; but his sole occupations were telling his beads and reading the Grunth. On his death, which happened about 1679, he enjoined on his son Buddah the duty of reading the Holy Book and of going to Umritsir to take the Pahul and become a Seik. Buddah on the death of his father was a boy of only nine years old, but on growing up and finding himself in the possession of the little money left him by his father he seemed well disposed to follow the paternal example and lead a quiet and religious life. It happened, however, that he became acquainted with some plundering Seiks, and by communication with them his ideas and views underwent a change. He now, however, as it suited his purpose, remembered his father's injuction to become a Seik, and accordingly went with some of his new friends to Umritsir, where about the year 1692 he took the Pahul and thus became the first Seik of the family. On this occasion his name was changed from Buddah to Boodh Sing.

On his return from Umritsir, Boodh Sing built himself a large house in Sukerchuck, which was his head-quarters, and where he continued to win the respect of the people both of Sukerchuck and Keallee, and so became one of their chowdries or head-men. But he not only looked after his interests in the villages, but, connecting himself with the gangs of predatory Seiks and Sansees, won himself the reputation of the boldest and most successful freebooter in the country. He generally however confined his achievements to the carrying off of cattle from far-away districts of the south; and the herds which he carried off were either appropriated to his own estate, or sold about Lahore and Umritsir. He rode a piebald mare, which became as famous as himself in the country, and was called by the people Desee, whence her rider obtained the nickname of Desoo. Boodh Sing was distinguished for the most intrepid courage; for his sagacity and shrewdness, which bore him successfully through all his schemes, and for his ready wit and good humour. He was also famed for his regard to the rights and property of the poor. As an instance of this it is told that having once carried away above a hundred head of cattle from about Nunkhona, in the south, he some days afterwards met a poor widow, who, ignorant of whom she was speaking to, told him that she had come a long way to petition Desoo for the return of five head of cattle belonging to her and her fatherless children which had been stolen. Boodh Sing told her that it would be useless to go to Desoo, as he was a hard-hearted inexorable man; he said however that he in consideration of her poverty and her loss he would give her twenty head of cattle. He kept his word, the story says, and actually sent the cattle by some of his own people, further promising to afford her and her property protection ever after. Boodh Sing, according to tradition, swam the Jhelum, the Chinaub, and the Ravee, fifty times on his piebald mare. He had twenty-seven sword cuts and nine matchlock wounds in different parts of his body. He lived however through all the brunts incident to his vocation and died of apoplexy in 1716. On the day of his death his wife through grief stabbed herself to the heart and they were both burnt together. They left two sons, Nodh Sing and Chund Baun Sing, who was head of the Scindawalla branch of the family.

A short time after his father's death, Nodh Sing began to neglect the cultivation of his lands, and sought wealth and fame in plundering expeditions. But he soon made many acquaintances who turned his thoughts from what they described as the low and unprofitable plunder of cattle, to the more respectable and gainful business of a Tharvee, or highway robber. This new line of depredation he accordingly adopted, and soon became notorious throughout the country, from Rawul Pindee to the banks of the Sutlej.

He now became acquainted with many of the newly made Seik Sirdars, and in 1730, contracted a marriage with the daughter of one of them, Golaub Sing, the son of Beesoo, a Sansee Jat of Majeetia. This Golaub Sing and his brother Ameer Sing, on becoming Seiks became also Tharvees, and were so active and fortunate, that in a short time they had amassed considerable wealth, and were considered as the Sirdars or Chiefs of Majeetia.*

About the year 1721, Nodh Sing with a few select friends and relatives of himself and his wife united under his leadership as a Bratheree or Brotherhood, joined the Missall or Camp of Koopur Sing Gujerattia, commonly called the Fyzolpooria Missall. In this association, which existed about the time of the first Affghan invasion, Nodh Sing and his brethren amassed considerable wealth, by the plunder of the baggage and stragglers of the invading army. The spoils they won were carefully stored by the fraternity in the neighbourhood of Sukerchuck and Keealee, &c. After a long and successful career of plunder, Nodh Sing was in 1747 compelled to retire from the active practice of his vocation, by a matchlock ball received in an affray with some Affghans; and after lingering for five years he died of the effects of the wound. His death occurred in 1742, and he left behind him four sons, Churut Sing,- born in 1721, Dhull Sing, born in 1724, Jeet Sing, born in 1727, and Nanoo Sing, born in 1732. Of the last it is only necessary to say, that, from his religious habits he was invariably called Bii Nanjo Sing, and that he died without issue. Churut Sing, the eldest son, after his father's death was only nominally connected

* This was the origin of the Majeetia family, the principal representative of which at the present day, is the well known Lena Sing.

with the Fyzolpooria Missall, as he kept aloof from that body, leaving his younger brothers to act in his stead. Even these he soon called away from the camp, having other views of aggrandizement for himself and his family. In 1752, or the beginning of the following year, he, with a few of his relatives and followers, joined by a number of Mujbees, Sansees, and other roving plunderers, formed a separate body of robbers, and they soon became notorious throughout the land for the audacity and success with which they executed their schemes of plunder and rapine. So great was the dread which their acts inspired, and so strong the confidence of the people in the prowess of the Seiks in general, that one Mahomed Yar, a Sansee, and Chowdree or Chief of Keeallee, tendered to Churut Sing his right and title to that village, on condition that he would protect it against other robbers of his class. He also joined the band with some fifteen mounted followers, and thus added to its strength. About the same time Milika Sing, another robber, took by force the village of Mereliawalla near Gujerawalla, and being a friend of Churut Sing, he also joined his camp with about twenty horsemen. In this way, the originally small band soon mustered above one hundred and fifty active and daring plunderers. Being now irresistible, Churut Sing took forcible possession of all the villages around Gujerawalla, and also the Serai of Kutchee, in which he intended to establish his head-quarters.

About the year 1773 Churut Sing appears to have been usually guided in his enterprises by the counsel and advice of one Ameer Sing of Gujerawalla, whose grand-father was a Sansee of the name of Sunnuth, residing in the vicinity of Gujerawalla, and who was said to have been a hundred years old when he took the Pahul and became a Seik. This Ameer Sing originally belonged to the Fyzolpooria Missall, but subsequently robbed on his own account, and became well known on the roads, even from the banks of the Jhelum to the walls of

Delhi. He thus amassed considerable substance, and, becoming the proprietor of some large farms about Gujerawalla, was looked upon as the chief man of the district. He had three sons, Dhull Sing, Ameer Sing, and Jode Sing. He had also two daughters, to the eldest of whom, about the year 1756, Churut Sing was married. From this time the wealth and power of the two families were united; and the allied chiefs, Ameer Sing and Churut Sing, now raised a banner and formed a Missall of their own. The first chiefs of the new clan were Churut Sing, with his two brothers and his three brothers-in-law; but until Ameer Sing's death he was considered and respected as its head and chief adviser, although from age and infirmity, unable to take an active part in its proceedings. After the death of Ameer Sing, the new tribe became known as the Sukerchuckia Missall. About the year 1777 Ameer Sing counselled his followers to build themselves a fort better adapted to their present wants and purposes than was Kutchee-ko-serai. On this work the Missall began, but the walls were not advanced beyond the first stage, when the chiefs of Lahore, Bahadoor Khan, Afzul Khan, and Koja Sei, jealous of the power of their neighbours, moved out with a force to disperse the band and destroy its stronghold. Churut Sing, now the chief of the Missall, received timely notice of their design, and with about a thousand men of his band was ready to receive them. When the Mahomedan chiefs left Lahore on this enterprise, they were joined by about fifteen hundred or two thousand volunteers, Seiks, Sansees, Mujbees, &c. many of them in actual but secret league with Churut Sing and his Missall. Thus reinforced the Lahore chiefs encamped about a mile and a half east of Gujerawalla, to prepare for the contemplated attack. However, on the second night of their stay in this place, they were surprised and furiously attacked by Churut Sing, and their treacherous allies turning against them, their rout was complete. Their forces sought for safety in an immediate and precipitate flight, and the chiefs themselves narrowly escaped with their lives, leaving their camp and all its stores to become a spoil to the victorious Missall. By this feat Churut Sing extended his fame and established his power as head of the Sukerchuckia Missall.

In 1762, when Ahmed Shah Abdallie with his Affghans made his appearance in the Punjaub, Churut Sing, too prudent to come in contact with the main body of the invaders, secreted his family and property in the hills about Jummoo, while he with his band prowled about the skirts of the Affghan host, harassing their march, cutting off stragglers, and plundering their baggage. The only satisfaction the invaders obtained was in the destruction of the fort of Gujerawalla which they levelled to the ground.

It was at this time that Churut Sing, whose family had been removed for safety to the hills, became acquainted with the Jummoo family. Chiefly, it is supposed, at his instigation Bejerei Dehu, the son of the Rajah of Jummoo, rebelled against his father, Runjeet Dehu. It is certain, at least, that in 1774, he, with other Seiks, went to assist the son against the father; and it was in the winter of the same year that he met his death from the bursting of a matchlock in the hands of one of his own followers, during a skirmish at Thillo ke Tallao, a tank lying about one and a half, or two coss, to the south-west of Jummoo.

Churut Sing left a son named Maha Sing, born about the end of 1759 or the beginning of 1760; and who consequently at the time of his father's death was about fourteen years of age. Too young to take any part in the government of the Missall, this task fell to the lot of his mother, the widow of Churut Sing. She, aided by the counsels of her paramour, a Brahmin named Jey Ram Misser, rebuilt the fort of Gujerawalla destroyed by Ahmed Shah's army, and which now began to be known after the name of the young chief as Maha Sing ka

Ghurree, in like manner as it had previously been called after his grandfather and father. Ameer Sing and Churut Sing. In the year 1775 the mother of Maha Sing conspiring with Jey Sing, the Chief of the Kunnia Missall, procured the assassination of Jodh Sing Bhaungee. Towards the latter end of the same year Maha Sing married the daughter of Jugputh Sing of Jheend, who was commonly called Mai Malwine or the Malwa Mother. Shortly after this he gained great celebrity by the capture and plunder of the fort and town of Russoolnuggur, subsequently called Ramnuggur, and by his victory over the strong tribe of Mahommedans called Chettas, the original occupants of Russoolnuggur and the district surrounding it. Golam Mahomed Chetta held out against him for some years, but was at length defeated and slain in a pitched battle. His son was taken prisoner and by order of the victor blown from a gun. After this Godjar Gola, the brother of Golam Mahomed, surrendered with his four sons, and received a small jaghire for his maintenance. In his war with the Chettas, Maha Sing had an army of 6,000 men.

About ten months after the marriage of his parents, and in the the winter of 1776, Runjeet Sing the son of Maha Sing and the Mai Malwine was born. In 1778 many Chiefs and Sirdars from various other tribes joined the Sukerchuckia Missal now under the sole and personal command of Maha Sing, who was still considerably influenced by the counsels of his mother and her favourites. In the winter of 1778, however Maha Sing put his mother to death with his own hands. He had long suspected one Hakeekuth Sing, of carrying on a criminal intercourse with her, but had never interfered to put a stop to it or taken any serious notice of the matter. It happened however that one Khodadad Khan, the son of Ramneth Khan, a man of some note at Jelalpore near Gujerat, and who after his father's death had killed his mother for merely attempting to engage in a criminal intrigue fled from his home and joined the Sukerchuckia Missall, with some fifteen or twenty horsemen. Maha Sing received him and his band and treated him with great respect. It chanced however, that two years afterwards, the chief of the Missall at an entertainment, and when his Sirdars and principal followers were present, jocosely questioned Khodadad Khan about the death of his mother. This annoyed the matricide, and he tauntingly replied that his mother met her death at the hands of her own son, for only intending to do what his, Maha Sing's, mother was daily committing with the knowledge and almost in the presence of an insensate, shameless, cold-blooded son. This sharp rebuke confounded Maha Sing, who however said nothing further at the time. But thenceforward he seemed more thoughtful and appeared to be revolving some painful matter in his mind. More than a month passed without any thing happening to change the face of affairs. But at the end of that time Maha Sing having had occasion to leave his home, and returning suddenly a few days after, found his mother carousing with Hakeekuth Sing and others. This scene revived, in all their force, the feelings with which the taunt of Khodadad Khan had inspired him, and he determined to wash out the disgrace in his mother's blood. Having on some pretext sent Hakeekuth Sing aud the other revellers from the house, he entered his mother's apartment and shot her dead with his own matchlock. He then, restraining his followers who would have assisted him, cut off her hand with his sword. After this he summoned Khodadad Khan and showing him the body of his mother and his own bloody sword, said he hoped that he and the world would acknowledge that he had at length redeemed his character and avenged the honour of his family stained by his mother's conduct. As to Hakeektuh Sing he declared that having no proof of his guilt he could not slay him then, but would watch his opportunity to revenge upon him the injury which the honour of his family had, as he strongly suspected, suffered at his hands. His true reason for sparing Hakeekuth Sing, however, was supposed to be that he knew that his death would be the signal for his own destruction by the Kunnia Missall, which was then very powerful. On hearing of the murder of his supposed mistress, however, Hakeekuth Sing, though attended by some three hundred followers, immediately fled to his jaghire near Wazeerabad. After all, it was by those best informed on the subject, asserted that the principal paramour of the Mai Wuzeerabadia, as the mother of Maha Sing was called, was Joy Ram Misser, the Gooroo or religious preceptor of the family. This man, on hearing of the murder, fled to Peshawar to avoid a similar fate.

In 1780 or 1781, Maha Sing exchanged turbans, in token of brotherhood, with Bejerei Dehu, now become Rajah of Jummoo, and shortly after found means to attack and plunder Jummoo and its district. In 1782, joined by Jessa Sing Ramgharria and Rajah Sansar Chund of Teera, he fought and slew Goorbux Sing the son of Jey Sing and chief of the Bhaungee Missall. In 1787 he besieged Gujerat, then ruled by Sobh Sing son of Gujer Sing, who was married to Purthaubee or Purthaub Kour, his, Maha Sing's, own sister. During this siege however he became dangerously ill from the effects of drinking and other irregularities of living, and early in 1780 was brought home to his fort of Gujerawalla where in a few months afterwards he died. It is commonly reported that remorse for the murder of his mother drove Maha Sing to drinking as a means of drowning all disagreeable thoughts, and that he was often heard to declare that liquor alone could make him forget his guilt. He had also another cause of disquiet in his jealousy of his wife whose fidelity he suspected even from the day of their marriage. He was, it is said, more than once heard to express strong doubts as to the paternity of Runjeet his reputed son; and he regarded one Luckpath Rao, formerly his father's dewan and minister, and still a young man of good person and engaging address, as his favoured rival in the affections of the Mai Malwine.

EARLY HISTORY

OF

RUNJEET SING.

At the time of his father's death, Runjeet Sing, who now became chief of the Sukerchuckia Missall, was a mere child, and his mother and mother-in-law—he had been already married to Mehtab Kour, daughter of Goorbux Sing and Suda Kour—ruled the tribe in his name. These two women, both of them of evil repute, were chiefly aided and influenced by their paramours. In 1793, however, Runjeet being now about seventeen years of age, followed the example of his father by putting his mother to death. For several months before this tragical event the young chief had formed many plans and schemes for convincing himself of the innocence or guilt of his mother whom he had strong reason to suspect of being engaged in criminal intrigues with one Laik Misser. In pursuance of these schemes, Runjeet one morning before day-break quietly entered the chamber of his mother, and finding that Laik Misser was actually there, he passed on silently to another apartment where he summoned two or three of his followers and provided himself with a sword. He then returned to his mother's chamber in the full determination to slay both her and her paramour. Laik Misser, however, hearing some noise and immediately suspecting the cause, had made his escape. Runjeet entered the room and found that he had fled, and his rage at being thus thwarted was redoubled on finding the fugitive's shoes, and a portion of his dress in the apartment. He however, placed a restraint on his wrath or rather dissembled it, and speaking quietly to his mother, promised her pardon on condition that she would confess her crime and produce her accomplice. She however, replied only by abuse and invective, upbraiding her son with having cast an undeserved slur upon her character, which she asserted was as pure as he or any one could expect. This contention betwixt them continued for some time, when at length stung to madness by her reproaches, Runjeet drew his sword and made a blow at her as she was sitting up on her bed half naked and with dishevelled hair. On this with joined hands she implored mercy, but it was now too late, she was cut down and slain by the sword of her son. Having dispatched his mother, Runjeet hastened with his followers in pursuit of Laik Misser, and promised a reward of five hundred rupees to any one who should take him alive, and thus give him the pleasure of putting the criminal to death with his own hand. The man escaped, however, for the time, and Runjeet returning from the pursuit performed the funeral obsequies of his mother with all proper ceremony and all outward tokens of respect and regret. Yet he never showed anything like remorse for what he had done, only remarking whenever the death of his mother was mentioned, that it was the just punishment of her crimes, and that it was better that she should have died early than live a long life of guilt and shame.

It is said by some that Laik Misser having fled for protection to Suda Kour, the mother-in-law of Runjeet, was by her delivered up to the vengeance of the young chief who put him to a cruel death. The most authentic accounts however say that he first escaped to Umritsir, and that he subsequently as a Brahmin threw himself on the protection of Suda Kour, who in spite of both the entreaties and threats of her son-in-law refused to give him up. Finding, however, that Runjeet was determined, no matter by what means, to get his intended victim into his hands, she sent him, it is said, under a strong escort across the Sutlej, and even as some assert as far as the Ganges. All however that is certainly known is that Laik Misser was never more heard of in the Punjaub.

Not long after these events had occurred, Runjeet committed another act of cruelty in procuring the assassination of Dewan Lekoo, formerly the manager of his father's affairs, and who had incurred his wrath by refusing him in his minority more than five rupees a day for his expenses, and by otherwise treating him in what the fiery youth considered a disrespectful manner. Not long after the murder of his mother, Runjeet sent ten or twelve of his men-at-arms to Kodrabad, where the dewan was collecting the revenues of the district, with strict injunctions to put him to death. These orders were strictly obeyed, and the soldiers speedily returned to their chief to report the execution of their dreadful task. For many years after this, Runjeet continued to be guided by the counsels of his mother-in-law Suda Kour, who ultimately, however, died in prison in 1827 having been placed in confinement by him for refusing to give up the fort of Dhinee, on the left bank of the Sutlej.

For some years after the assumption of power by Runjeet Sing, the history of the Sukerchuckia Missal exhibits no event of particular importance. All was peace and quiet, and the young chief went every year with the whole of his tribe to Umritsir to bathe in the holy tank, and to be present at the Goormatta or yearly council of chiefs. Thus smoothly the time passed until the year 1798, when an event occurred which, as it formed the first step of the ladder by which Runjeet mounted to power, requires to be particularly described.

By original agreement among the Seiks, Lahore was portioned out under the rule of three Sirdars, namely Gujer Sing, Seedoo, of Gujerut, Lena Sing, Koloo, of Lahore, and Soba Sing, Kunnia. These chiefs were now dead but their sons were living. The son of Gujer Sing was Sobh Sing, who generally resided at Gujerut; the son of Lena Sing was Chete Sing who usually dwelt at Lahore; and the sons of Soba Sing were Mohur Sing and Mean Sing. Two Mussulmans of the name of Meea Ashuk and Meer Mokun-ood-deen were however considered the principal Varseedaurs or Chowdries of Lahore. They were opulent and influential; and without their interference or sanction, few matters could be settled in the city or its neighbourhood. The daughter of Meea Ashuk was married to another Chowdrie whose name was Meer Buddur-ood-deen and who happened to be on unfriendly terms with certain Kotrees and Brahmins of the city. These men, in order to be revenged on Buddur-ood-deen, went in a body to Sirdar Chete Sing who resided in the Summun Boorj or fort of Lahore, and told him a long story of the treachery of their enemy, who they alleged was in constant communication with Zeman Shah the sovereign of Affghanistan. They even brought forward false papers, bearing a forgery of Buddur-ood-deen's signature, for the purpose of corroborating their statement, and by these means they convinced Chete Sing of its truth. He accordingly, in a great rage, sent forth and had Buddur-ood-deen seized, and without allowing him to make his defence, or even to have an interview with him, ordered that he should be heavily ironed and cast into a dungeon. On hearing of this, Meea Ashuk the father in law of the unfortunate man, with Meer Mokun-oo-deen, Chowdrie Kukka, Abruth Khan, and many other chief men and inhabitants of Lahore went in a body to Chete Sing to convince him of the innocence of Buddur-ood-deen and the malice of his enemies, hoping thereupon to procure the immediate release of their friend. Chete Sing however, refused to listen to them, and in an angry and haughty manner ordered them from his presence. On this, Meea Ashuk Meer Mokun-oo-deen and their companions returned home much enraged and disappointed, and swearing vengeance upon the Kotrees and Bramins, as also on Sirdar Chete Sing. They however persevered in their attempts to procure the release of Buddur-oodeen for nearly a month, when finding their representations and entreaties of no effect they determined to resort to other means. They deputed one of their number to wait upon Runjeet Sing, the young chief of the Sukerchuckia Missall, who then was at Russoolnuggur, otherwise Ramnuggur, on the Chinaub, for the purpose of inviting him to come and occupy Lahore, assuring him that all that they required was his presence there, as they themselves would do all that was necessary for securing their object. They also sent a similar message to his mother-in-law, the widow Suda Kour, inviting her to aid and join the enterprise. Nothing could have pleased Runjeet better than the project thus proposed to him, as his ambition was already boundless. He therefore immediately got together such a force of horse and foot as he could muster on an emergency; and being joined by numbers of straggling Seiks, Akalees, and Mujbees, he at once set out for Umritsir, on the pretence of going there as usual to bathe and perform his devotions at the holy shrine. His real object, however, was to obtain the counsel and aid of his mother-in-law, who being fully as ambitious as himself, willingly gave him both encouragement and assistance, and even the sanction of her own presence and company. Thus re-inforced, Runjeet at the head of about five thousand men, most of whom, however, were but stragglers, proceeded at one march from Umritsir to the Shalimar Gardens near Lahore. Here he was met by Meea Ashuk and Meer Mokun-ood-deen, who informed him that they had provided all that was necessary to secure his easy entrance into and capture of the city. They told him further that for this purpose they had made a large breach in the wall betwixt the Kidderee and Yakkee Gates. But Runjeet, either suspicious of treachery or disdaining to enter the city in such a manner, determined not to pass through the breach which had been made for his convenience. It was therefore resolved that he should advance at eight o'clock the same morning towards the Shalmee and Loharee Gates, which Meer Mokun-oo-deen and Meea Ashuk promised to have open for his admission. Acting on this plan Runjeet made a rapid march from the Shalimar Gardens to the place appointed; and before Sirdar Chete Sing was aware of his presence or design, he had entered by the Loharee gate with about a thousand of his best men, while another body of about three or four thousand under the command of Dhul Sing, Baug Sing, and others, had entered by the Shalmee and Laharee Gates and taken possession of them and the ramparts on either side.

When at length Chete Sing became aware of the proceedings of Runjeet, it was only by being purposely misinformed as to his whereabout. He was told that the besiegers were outside the Yakkee and Delhi Gates, which were shut against them; and that the men in charge of these gateways were ready to fight for the chiefs of the city. On hearing this Chete Sing took four or five hundred men and leaving the fort by the eastern gateway he went towards the Delhi Gate, intending to aid and encourage the guards in their resistance. However before he had proceeded far, he was met by a confidential retainer, who coming to him in haste begged of him instantly to return to the fort if he would save his life, for that by treachery the enemy, five thousand strong, had been admitted into the city, and that also by treachery he, Chete Sing, had been misled into the belief that he would find them outside the Delhi gate, the object of this manœuvre being to enable Runjeet Sing quietly to occupy the fort, while the chief was seeking him elsewhere. On receiving this intelligence, Chete Sing returned to the fort, barely in time to shut the Hazaree Baug gate against Runjeet's cavalry, led by himself in person. A moment later and Runjeet's horsemen would have entered the fort along with its defenders. As it was they gallopped up just in time to shoot two or three of the gate-keepers as they were closing the gate. Thus disappointed Runjeet returned to a little distance and opened a desultory fire of matchlocks on the place from all quarters. This firing, which was promptly answered by Chete Sing with his five hundred men inside, was kept up for about twenty-four hours. However on the next morning Chete Sing finding treachery on every side, surrendered on condition that his life and the lives of his followers should be spared, and that he should have a jaghire sufficient for the maintenance of his family. These terms Runjeet granted, and gave to the fallen chief, whom he treated with much respect, the village of Vennia* and its appurtenances worth about seven thousand rupees a year.

The story of the subsequent career of Runjeet Sing has been too often told to warrant its transcription here. His gradual rise from being the chief of a tribe of roving plunderers to the sovereingty of a nation is a subject of history. Having once tasted the sweets of conquest in the capture of Lahore as related above, he, like the young tiger who has lapped blood for the first time, was eager for further prey. His ambition having once been gratified grew with what it fed upon and nothing less than the mastery of all around would content it. Thus prompted the chief of the Sukerchuckia Missal, and now the Lord of Lahore, began a career of conquest and subjugation that ceased not until it had brought him to a wall of impenetrable mountains on the one hand, and on the other in contact with a foreign power whose frontier was to him as impassable as the Himalayas themselves.

In 1805 Runjeet was recalled from a career of victory in the west by intelligence that a body of fugitive Mahrattas, closely pursued by a British army, was approaching his eastern frontier. This was unwelcome news, as he had no desire to see the

---

* The village of Vennia is about 24 miles from Lahore, and was lately in the hands of Multanee Sing.

Punjaub a battle field for two foreign armies. He, however, hastened to Lahore and there received Jeswunt Rao the chief of the Mahrattas, but gave him so little encouragement to hope for aid, that instead of continuing his flight through the country the fugitive chief was content to make terms with his pursuers, and thus the evil which Runjeet dreaded was averted.

In 1808, the British Indian Government desiring to engage Runjeet Sing, now one of the acknowledged princes of India, in a grand combination against the ambitious designs of Napoleon who meditated an invasion of the country, sent one of its servants, Mr. (afterwards Lord) Metcalfe on a mission to the Seik Chief. The British envoy found Runjeet engaged in the subjugation of the various independent states betwixt the Sutlej and the Jumna. As the British claimed the sovereignty of all the territory up to the Sutlej they protested against these proceedings of the Seik Chief; and being ready to back their protest with an armed force, Runjeet deemed it prudent to listen to their remonstrance. Negotiations ensued, and the result was that he was allowed to retain possession of the states he had already won, while those which had not yet submitted to him were taken under British protection. He was by the treaty now executed, confined in a great measure to the right bank of the Sutlej, not being allowed to maintain more troops to the south of that river than were absolutely necessary for the internal duties of the small states then belonging to him. The Sutlej thus became the proper boundary of his dominions to the south and east, and so it continued until his dying day.

It was while Mr. Metcalfe was at Umritsir carrying on negotiations with the Maharajh of the Seiks, as Runjeet now called himself, that an event occurred which, though trivial in itself not only inspired the latter with a profound respect for the power of his British neighbours, but made him anxious to possess himself of similar means of securing respect.

Among the followers of Runjeet, and the principal agents of his successes, were the Akalees, a body of fanatic Seiks somewhat analogous to the Gazees among the Mussulmans, and whose head-quarters were at the holy tank of Umritsir. These men, whose designation signifies "Immortal" were in the habit of rushing forward furiously upon the enemy in the beginning of a battle and throwing him into confusion, thereby often doing good service to their chief, who knew their value, and gave them every encouragement. They were led by one Phoola Sing, a desperado of a most fierce and sanguinary character and who figures prominently in the history of Runjeet's early career. There is reason, however, to suppose, that these fiery bigots served the Maharajh rather out of hate to the Mussulmans than out of regard for him, for this same Phoola Sing their leader came to Mr. Moorcroft when he was in the Punjaub and offered his and their services to the British Government.

It happened that while Mr. Metcalf was at Umritsir the Mohurum a period of particular solemnity among the Mussulmans occurred. The men of that faith in the suite and escort of the envoy accordingly prepared to celebrate it with the appropriate rites. This, which was looked upon as an insult to their sacred place, gave great umbrage to the Seiks in general and to the bigoted Akalees in particular; and while the Mahomedan procession in honour of Hassan and Hussain was in progress, the fanatics, led by Phoola Sing, opened a fire of matchlocks upon the Mussulmans. Though greatly overmatched in numbers the Moslems of the envoy's escort, which consisted only of two companies of infantry and a few troopers, were not disposed to submit to this treatment. They therefore broke up their procession for the moment, seized their arms, gave battle to their assailants, and having after a fierce struggle beaten them off, proceeded with their ceremonies as if nothing had occurred to interrupt them. Runjeet himself was a witness to the close of the contest and to the defeat of his

"Immortals," and complimented the envoy on the bravery of his small band of followers. He saw, however, in this incident enough to convince him that an army disciplined as these men were, was not to be assailed with any hope of success by his own wild troops, and he gave up for a time his cherished design of measuring his strength with that of his haughty neighbours. Having thus learned the value of discipline, he was seized with the desire to possess a disciplined army, and as is well known, was not content with idly desiring it, but using all means available for effecting his purpose, at length saw himself at the head of a force such as no eastern power had ever before possessed, and with which he hoped when the opportunity occurred to be able to battle with the British for the sovereignty of Hindostan.

In 1818 Run'eet Sing made himself master of Moultan and soon afterwa. s of Peshawar. In the following year he conquered Cashmere and annexed it to his already extensive dominions. The following account of the fate of the man who was the immediate agent of these and his other conquests will serve to illustrate some curious points in the character of the Maharajh.

While Runjeet was engaged in the conquest of the Hazareh, Chotah, and Gundeghur districts, he found Mahomed Khan, the chief of Goolzeree, a much more powerful and obstinate enemy than any other of the chiefs around him. For this reason he deputed Misser Dewan Chund, the commander of his troops, to visit the chief and endeavour to bring him to terms by making many fair promises. But the Misser when he went on this embassy was not aware that Runjeet's only object was to get Mahomed Khan into his power, when he could do whatever he pleased with him. He therefore exerted all his powers of persuasion to induce the Mussulman chief to accompany him to his master's camp near Rawul Pindee, and he finally succeeded in his purpose. Runjeet at first treated

Mahomed Khan with great respect, so that the suspicions of the chief being lulled to sleep, he was induced by specious promises, and on Misser Dewan Chund becoming security for his safety and for the fulfilment of the promises made, to accompany the Maharajh to Lahore. Scarcely, however, had they reached Lahore, before Runjeet, forgetting all his oaths and promises, threw Mahomed Khan into prison and otherwise so ill treated him that his life was despaired of. Misser Dewan Chund, ashamed and indignant at such conduct to a man for whose safety and well-being he had become security, daily remonstrated with his master on the subject. But the only effect of his upbraidings was to induce Runjeet to remove his victim to another and more distant prison—the fort of Kangra—and this was done so secretly that the Misser did not know of the removal. One day he went before Runjeet in open durbar, resolved on making a grand effort to obtain the release of a chief whose reliance on his word and on the promises he had made had alone brought him into the power of his enemy. On this occasion he spoke so boldly and expressed his opinion so freely that Runjeet became enraged, and even went so far as to threaten the Dewan himself, telling him that instead of concerning himself so much about the safety of Mahomed Khan, he would soon have occasion to look to his own. On receiving this reply Dewan Chund quietly left the durbar, and returned to his house greatly distressed. That same night he took poison, and within twenty-four hours thereafter was a corpse. Runjeet on hearing of the death of his faithful servant professed to be much afflicted, and immediately sent orders for the release of Mahomed Khan; but it was too late, the unfortunate chief was dead, having sunk under the treatment inflicted on him by order of the treacherous Seik. On learning this the Maharajh felt or seemed to feel so much remorse that for two days he would taste no food, and for several days after was not in a mood to be spoken to.

SECRET HISTORY

OF THE

LAHORE DURBAR.

Some years prior to Runjeet Sing's death, or rather from the date of Heera Sing's birth, Raja Dehan Sing, by means of the wiliest insinuation had so well worked himself into the old Lion's favor, that he may be said to have held the reins of government entirely in his own hands. Thus established as the only, or at all events the chief, favorite of the one-eyed monarch, he unremittingly employed every endeavor to get rid of the old Seik Sirdars, and so weakened their authority that there soon remained not one among them all who possessed either the power or the courage to oppose him in any of his wishes. So far even did his influence extend, that no Sirdar, however high in rank, even though he were the king's son, was allowed to enter the presence of the Sovereign without the minister's sanction being first received. Frequent instances have been known of Kurruck Sing and Shere Sing being obliged to wait for hours together, and to bribe the gate-keepers and court attendants to procure them permission to go and pay their respects to the old King. About this time he succeeded in forcing on Runjeet the opinion that his only son Kurruck Sing was not of sound or proper mind, and consequently unfit to govern, as he would be expected to do. In support of this assertion care was taken that by the insufficiency of means placed at his disposal, the greater part of the expeditions on which he was sent should either partially or entirely fail, and accordingly he was regarded as being incapable of command. But in fact it will readily be acknowledged by all who knew any thing of Kurruck Sing, that in the early part of his life he gave the promise of, or in reality possessed, all the abilities requisite for a sovereign of the Punjaub; with perhaps one exception, viz. that while not so crafty as the minister, he was more religiously and peacefully inclined, and far less ambitious. Yet though peaceful, he proved when roused to energy that he possessed no small share of personal bravery, activity, and determination. It must however be owned, that during the latter years of Runjeet's life, when through the intrigues of the wily minister, Kurruck Sing was treated even by his own father as imbecile and unworthy either of power or confidence, and when all hopes of returning favor were destroyed, his mind gradually assumed a dark and gloomy aspect. This was instantly regarded as a corroborating proof of his being dull and possessed of no abilities; spite of all however, he seemed to bear the whole with a religious meekness and silent acquiescence.

Shere Sing again, was from the first, or not long after his birth, disowned by the king as not being his lawful son, and was only treated nominally as such, being allowed certain jaghires and lands to live on, sometimes commanded to do duty, and to go on campaigns and expeditions with the same order and in the same manner as other Sirdars.

About this time too, Kurruck Sing and Shere Sing, but more particularly the former, were but seldom allowed to remain at or near the Court, being generally sent away and kept at a distance on the frontiers, on some foolish or trifling excuse. And while the heir to the throne was being thus treated, Rajah Heera Sing, the minister's eldest son was by the instrumentality of female intrigue and Dehan Sing's craft, so brought up and cherished as to be considered the favorite and adopted child. The king's mind was so worked on that he could neither sleep nor rest without having him at his side.—It was he and he alone that could lull the old chief to sleep. An airing could not be taken in the Royal Palkee without his being seated in it too. In short when he was absent Runjeet became uneasy, peevish, and vexed, and only seemed anxious for his return. Five hundred rupees, and sometimes more, were nightly laid beneath his pillow by the old king's hand, to be distributed to the poor by the young prince on the following morning. Of this it is no exaggeration to say that ten rupees daily was never known to be distributed in the way of alms, or for the purpose originally contemplated. It might also be mentioned here that at this period, by the express orders of Runjeet and of Dehan Sing, Pundit Jellah acted as the tutor and guardian of the young Rajah—his mother having died in 1832.

Rajah Dehan Sing had at all times full permission to enter Runjeet's Zenankhana, and hence it was that the majority of his intrigues and schemes succeeded; the women there obeyed him, for they dreaded him far more than they did even their own lord. Heera Sing was (it might be said) a continual resident here—and though young was well tutored how to act in any case or circumstance. Through him all the secrets of Runjeet Sing became known to the minister and his party. They were thus privy to every thing in and out of Court; nor could any thing be done even in the most secret recesses of the King's private chamber without their knowledge. Thus things went on working in favor of the Dogra party, until the old king was on his death bed. Then and only then was Kurruck Sing, his son, called for into the presence of the dying monarch, who, placing his hand in that of Dehan Sing, gave over the charge of his son and heir, to his much esteemed favorite and minister. He now enjoined Rajah Dehan Sing to place Kurruck Sing on the throne, to act as his guardian and protector, to treat him in every way as the only son and heir of his old master; and he told him that the only return he expected for his past favors was, that he would act towards Kurruck Sing the part of a good, loyal, and faithful minister and servant. Thus the old king died and Kurruck Sing was placed on the guddee.*

The new sovereign was well aware how his late father had been duped in every way by the minister; and accordingly one of his first orders was, that though the Rajah Dehan Sing should be treated in every respect as a good councillor and minister, the former custom and privilege of his own and his son's free admission into the King's Zenankhana should no longer be allowed; adding that as there was no further occasion for such admission, he politely entreated that Dehan Sing would not require it again. In a private and confidential interview with the Rajah, Kurruck Sing in the mildest manner assured him that by this act he did not intend to lessen his power, or that his interest as minister, should suffer or be in the least prejudiced. Dehan Sing however replied, that without this permission he could not act as he wished, nor as he formerly did. Thus first began the breach between Kurruck Sing and his minister;—the latter of whom harboured from this time a settled hatred to the monarch, his advisers, and his old servants.

This order of the king's procured for him many admirers, who regarded it as promising to ensure the best results to his regal career. Among others, there was one more prominent than the rest. This was Cheyt Sing, who suggested, that, as Rajah Dehan Sing publicly gave out that he would not allow any one to sit on the Lahore guddee who did not grant him all the powers and privileges which he possessed in the time of the old king, if he would not act

* At Runjeet's incremation Rajah Dehan not only hypocritically shed tears, but twice or thrice affected to force himself forward to become as good a suttee as the best and dearest of the old king's wives.

as a minister ought, there were others who could be found to occupy the place, who were even more loyal and trustworthy than he. The minister soon felt, that, for his own interest, some step must speedily be taken; and his wily and crafty disposition was not long in devising a deep scheme. It was given out that Kurruck Sing, with Cheyt Sing and his other admirers, had leagued with the British, and was ready to acknowledge their power, to place himself under their protection, to pay six annas in every rupee of revenue for the expenses incurred by this act, and that all the Seik troops should then be disbanded and the Sirdars done away with. These, and similar stories, he contrived to have so rumoured about, that nothing else was talked of;—and every body, even the common soldiers, reprobated and reviled Kurruck Sing and the advisers of a plan for thus bringing a foreign enemy into the country and giving up all power into their hands. Affairs stood thus, when, by Rajah Dehan Sing's order, Koonwur No Nehal Sing, was hastily recalled from Peshawur, where he was at the time of his father's accession to the throne.*

Rajah Goolaub Sing accompanied the prince, and had so tutored him both in Peshawur and on his way to Lahore, that he entered the latter city the avowed enemy of his father. The minister, his brother, and their party, pleaded their cause and played their part so well with Koonwur No Nehal Sing and his mother, that they obtained their permission, along with that of other Sirdars to assassinate Cheyt Sing and to imprison the Maharajh or use other means to deprive him of power. They revived the story of intrigue with the British, and produced forged letters bearing the signatures of Kurruck Sing and

* He arrived from Peshawur on this occasion in six days, and would certainly—(according to the private orders sent by Rajah Dehan Sing to his brother Rajah Goolaub Sing) have left that city many days earlier than he did, but for Goolaub Sing's being detained by the then Captain Wade who was encamped at the time at the mouth of the Khyber.

Cheyt Sing in proof of their charge. The minister and his brother upheld that this step was the only one to be taken by which to secure the country from the power of the Feringhees. Every thing was agreed to, and even No Nehal Sing's mother was so worked on by her fears of the Feringhees, that she consented to the dethronement and imprisonment of her husband; and thus the whole of this conspiracy was carried on with the utmost secrecy until the time was ripe for action. Then it was that the minister, with his two brothers, Rajahs Goolaub and Suchet Sing—accompanied by the Sirdars and most of the Scindawallas went into the fort (two hours of the night still remaining) and entered the sleeping room of Kurruck Sing. On their way there they were met by two Biias, whom they cut down, and further on they met a Gudwaii or water carrier who had a few minutes before been with Kurruck Sing. This man was now returning to the king who had just gone into his sleeping room (as was his custom at that hour) to pray. Immediately on perceiving the conspirators, the Gudwaii, who was a little in advance, ran forward to give the alarm to Kurruck Sing. At this moment Rajah Dehan Sing, who carried a short English rifle and was a good shot, fired and the Gudwaii instantly fell. Goolaub Sing immediately remonstrated with, and even sharply reprimanded, his brother for this act of indiscretion; and at the same he time gave strict orders to the whole party to make as little noise as possible, as whatever was to be done, could only be accomplished in silence and by the sword. The party now advanced to the king's bedroom; but on their approaching it, Cheyt Sing, being alarmed by the noise, and fearing some unseen danger, quietly slipped out and concealed himself in a long and dark chamber named the Kaubgãã close to and in rear of the monarch's apartments. The conspirators on approaching these, were challenged by the guards and two companies under arms, who at first seemed inclined to make some opposition. This however was a mere feint; for when Rajah Dehan Sing advanced *alone* towards their commanding officer—and holding up his *six* fingered hand—pointed to the Prince, without a word being exchanged the whole of the two companies silently grounded their arms, and sat or lay down as regularly and simultaneously, as though they had been previously well trained to it. After this, they were even more silent than the other party, who were now so awed by Rajah Goolaub Sing's looks, as to be afraid even to whisper to one another. Kurruck Sing was soon surprized and bound. He imagined in his terror that he was about to be killed, and in all probability he would have been put to death —the minister and his brother being only anxious for an opportunity to destroy him—but for the presence of his son No Nehal Sing, and the injunctions of his wife Chund Kour, both of whom had joined in the plot on the condition that no bodily injury should be offered to Kurruck Sing. Cheyt Sing was now searched for, and was soon found in the dark chamber before mentioned, where, in a corner, with a drawn sword held in both hands, but trembling with fear, and without the power of using it, he stood and cried like a child for mercy. Immediately on his being discovered, he was dragged to the door way, into the presence of the minister, who, as soon as he identified him, with his own hand drove a long knife twice though his body. Falling wounded to the ground, the unfortunate Cheyt Sing was literally hacked to pieces by the infuriated assassins. Two hours after this Kurruck Sing was confined in the fort; and the party having returned, Koonwur No Nehal Sing was proclaimed king; the old sovereign being put down as an enemy to the state, and one incapable of holding the reins of government.

Blinded by the promises made to him by the minister,

No Nehal Sing soon became elated with the success he had attained. Brahmins, fakeers, &c. were brought forward to prophecy the endurance of his rule and the success of his arms, which they declared would shortly conquer Delhi and extend even as far as Benares itself. To flatter his credulity and to humour his ambition some of these Brahmins requested and absolutely got from him promissory bills of the right and title to large sums of money and presents of jaghires and land, about Benares, Delhi, &c.—all to come into force when his empire extended so far. Thus governed by the craft and wily machinations of his tutors he sincerely believed in all; and his ambition soon led him to consent to the imprisonment of his father. By this low yet deep policy a most rancorous enmity was established between the father and the son. Of the former king, No Nehal Sing never spoke but in terms of contumely and reproach. He would see him but seldom, and when he did it was only to abuse him for his supposed unmanly conduct and pusillanimity.

Thus was Kurruck Sing's spirit and constitution broken down. Shortly afterwards he was reported to be sick, and by the help of his doctors, who had their part appointed them, was in a very short time beyond all hopes of recovery. His son however was taught to believe that he was only feigning to be ill, with the hope of being able to effect his escape and make his way over to the British.* For this reason Kurruck Sing was but little noticed by his son during his illness; in fact he never saw him but once, and then but a short time before his death,—on which occasion the father was treated by his only son in a manner revolting, even to the natives around. There is nothing at all astonishing in this when we remember the shameful proceedings adopted

* To give this the semblance of probability and truth strong guards were placed over the person of the deposed monarch.

by the minister to keep alive and feed the flame of bitterness and enmity in the mind of each. During all this time No Nehal Sing never once imagined—even when his father was proclaimed as being beyond recovery—but that he was dying from natural causes, brought on perhaps by taking too much unwholesome medicine in support of his feigned illness. It has already been stated that Kurruck Sing saw his son but once during his illness, though he often implored and begged that he would visit him. Dehan Sing in the meanwhile kept up the outward appearance of peace maker, as though he were sincerely desirous of producing a reconciliation between the two parties—or, as he expressed it, to bring them to a proper sense of their duty as father and son. But still he took care by sinister means to instil the rancorous poison of enmity so deeply into the minds of both, that all his outward endeavors for an amicable settlement and meeting must necessarily fail. Thus, he was seen more than once with tears in his eyes imploring No Nehal Sing to see his father—as it became a son to do—in kindness, friendship, and love. Failing in this he would proceed to the father and represent to him the manner in which he had acted for the benefit of both—but that unfortunately, and he grieved to say it—he had not sufficient power, to destroy the inimical feeling that existed in the breast of No Nehal Sing towards his father.* In fact the old king was frequently told that he must now begin to be aware that his son's object was simply to gain a convenient opportunity to assassinate him. At length Kurruck Sing died; and it neither must nor can be made a secret, that he died from the slow effects of small doses of "Sapheda Kaskaree," *(white lead or the acetate of lead)* and "Rus

* Several of the secret enemies of the Rajah assisted privately or connived at all this,—being well aware that the fate of him and his family was inevitably sealed the moment Koonwur No Nehal Sing should enter into the full possession of the throne.

Camphoor," (*Corrosive Sublimate,* or *the native muriate of mercury.*)*

No Nehal Sing was not present at the death-bed of his father, whose continual cry in his dying agonies (agonies caused by the cold spasmodic affections of the limbs and bowels) was, that he might yet have the pleasure of seeing his son in order to pardon the parricide. From this it would appear, that Kurruck Sing was aware that he had been poisoned—though he considered his son to have been the principal agent in the deed. The language employed by him on his death bed was, however, declared by the minister to be the ravings of a dying man—and he pretended (as did the doctors also) that his viction was at the time insane. Notwithstanding this it was still thought that the cries of the unfortunate father might weigh on the mind of his son; and consequently the latter was purposely kept out of the way, and informed that his father was cursing him, and only giving vent by means of execrations, even in this his last hour, to his hatred and enmity. Thus was No Nehal Sing induced to allow his father to fall a victim to his enemies without even visiting him; while the father on his part, with his last breath, kept calling for his "dear and only son." When the death of Kurruck Sing was announced to his son,† instead of being affected by it, he seemed to think that now the day of his rejoicing and happiness had arrived, and calmly gave orders for the incremation of the corpse.‡

* Bii Goormuck Sing was acquainted with the whole of the particulars of the conspiracy, and not only hinted them to Kurruck Sing, but also warned him of his danger; and at the same time strongly remonstrated with the parties employed in this treacherous and murderous affair.

† When the news first reached the prince, he was on a party of pleasure, hunting near Shahbelore. He did not, however, give up the sports of the field for two hours afterward.

‡ One of the late king's wives—a young and most beautiful lady of about twenty years of age—the sister of Sirdar Mungul Sing,—was, by the contrivance of Dehan

This ceremony was performed in an open space opposite the mausoleum of Runjeet Sing, and near the Hazooree Bagh, within the precincts of the palace; and while the body of the late sovereign was being burnt, the new Maharajh, No Nehal Sing, stood by the blazing pile of his father. Rajah Dehan Sing was at his side. Ere the corpse was consumed, however, the prince felt desirous to leave the spot, and to perform the ceremony of ablution in a nullah at a short distance. On this the minister politely represented to him that it would be contrary to rule and etiquette for him to leave the place before the body was consumed, and even went so far as to appeal to his sense of duty to the memory of a dear and lost father! No Nehal was thus persuaded to stay a little longer; but presently, on the plea of sickness—it is said that he really was sick—he left the spot. He then proceeded on foot towards the bathing place which was at the distance of only about one hundred and twenty yards. While on his way the minister again brought him to a stand, for a moment, to remonstrate with him on his indecorous haste; the prince, however, was not to be detained, and he went on towards the stream. He was attended by the whole court, and followed by five elephants; but as it would have been considered irreverent for him to ride past the funeral pile on his return, the elephants were sent back to wait at a little distance. Having washed, the prince set forth on his return. He had to pass first through a gateway, then across a court yard, and lastly through a deep arch-way leading from this court-yard to the spot on which the corpse had been burnt, and near which the elephants were now in waiting. Just before he entered this archway the prince took the hand of Meean Oottum Sing, the eldest son of Goolaub Sing and

Sing—who for some occult reason procured it—shamefully treated and forced to become one of the victims at the suttee on this occasion.

nephew of Dehan Sing, and the two proceeded through the gateway together. As they emerged from the passage, the young Maharajh made a momentary halt while he addressed some jocular remark to his companion, and the next instant a crash was heard,—the beams, stones, and tiles fell from above and the two young men were struck to the ground.*

The largest of the stones fell on the Meean and killed him on the spot. The young prince too fell senseless, but after a moment struggled to rise. No one, however, could tell at the time whether the blow was mortal or not. Dehan Sing immediately took up the prince in his arms, and placing him in a palkee, which, as it would seem, was in readiness for the purpose, had him conveyed to the fort, and there locked him up in an inner apartment. Lena Sing Majeeteea, attempted to follow the palkee; but Dehan Sing, as soon as he saw the Sirdar's object, instantly pushed him away. In vain did some others of the chief Sirdars entreat admittance—in vain did the mother of No Nehal in a paroxysm of rage and anxiety come and beat the fort gates with her own hands—admittance even into the fort there was none, still less into the prince's apartment. None of the female inmates, not even his wives were suffered to see him. Every thing was kept locked up

* Captain Gardner says, "I myself was present at the commencement of the ceremony of cremation, that is, when the torch was applied, standing close to Rajah Dehan Sing, being by his special orders, in attendance on him. Before the prince had left the spot, however, I was directed by the Rajah to go and bring forty of my artillerymen in their fatigue dresses, whom he said he wanted there immediately. When I returned with these men the catastrophe had just occurred, and No Nehal Sing was being carried in a palanquin into the Hazooree Bagh. I then received an order from the Rajah to send my men to their camp, as their services were no longer required. What services it was intended or expected that they should render, I have never been able to ascertain. While on the spot, however, I learnt all the particulars of the affair, and have since verified them by the evidence of a most respectable merchant of Lahore, the state jeweller to the Durbar, who, before several British officers, corroborated what I have said of the events which preceded the death of No Nehal Sing."

for a while—the palkee bearers were sent to their homes*—and the minister with but two of his followers and chief hillmen remained with the prince.

The numerous Sirdars and others, who were assembled outside the gates were ordered quietly to retire, being informed at the same time that the prince was in a likely way to do well—that he was but wounded, and for the time insensible—and that notwithstanding the severity of the contusion, he had already given evident signs of life, and that there were strong hopes of a speedy recovery. In about two hours afterwards the minister, committing his charge to his two hillmen, left the fort, and proceeding first to the mother of the prince, had with her a private conference. He now informed her of her son's death—but under strict injunctions to keep the matter secret—telling her that all her hopes of reigning or even of retaining her present station depended entirely on this point. He protested further, that when he first placed the prince in the palkee, though not then entirely insensible, he was mortally wounded; and that about half an hour after he was removed into the fort—during which time, he said, he had done all he could to preserve the prince's life—he had breathed his last, there having, as he asserted, been a contusion of the brain. He did not leave the mother, until he had persuaded her to believe all he wished, and then departing to his own

---

* Captain Gardner says, "They were servants in my own camp of Artillery, and were five in number. Two were afterwards privately put to death—two escaped to Hindostan, the fate of the fifth is unknown. One of the palkee bearers afterwards affirmed, that when the prince was put into the palkee, and when he was assisting to place him there, he saw that above the right ear there was a wound which bled so slightly as only to cause a blotch of blood of about the size of a rupee, on the pillow or cloth on which his head rested while he was in the palkee. He added, that the blood neither flowed nor trickled in any quantity, before his being taken out. Now, it is a curious fact, that when the room was opened, in which his corpse was first exposed by the Rajah, blood in great quantity, both in fluid and coagulated pools, was found around the head on the cloth on which the body lay."

house, he convened an assembly of the principal Sirdars, (those chiefly whom he feared most) and went over the self-same arguments with them also. Thus, though revealing the whole to a few, he still kept the matter a secret from the public! He had promised Chund Kour, during his interview with her, that she should reign in the place of her son, but his great object was to ensure her silence until the arrival of Shere Sing, to whom he had privately written, reminding him of his promise, and telling him, that now was the moment—that he should ride post by night and day, and arrive quickly. Shere Sing arrived, and as soon as he had presented himself, the death of the prince was publicly made known, and preparations for his funeral obsequies were made accordingly.

Dehan Sing, well aware that should Chund Kour become the sovereign of the Punjaub, it would not be long before the only party he now really dreaded, (the Scindawallas) would hurl both him and his family from the high position they then held, speedily endeavored to urge upon the Sirdars the necessity of placing Shere Sing on the guddee. With the utmost wiliness he pleaded that the turbulent Seiks neither would nor could be ruled by a woman; and that he felt it would be utterly impossible for him to act with or consult a woman on affairs of importance. Some were for this, others again against it; however Shere Sing was by the minister installed in state and proclaimed the reigning monarch. Although Chund Kour and her party strenuously opposed this movement, still for the time the minister had his way; and with his usual tact, he was soon enabled to win the army over to his side. The Scindawalla family and Rajah Goolaub Sing espoused, in appearance at least, the cause of Chund Kour:—for it is a well known fact that in all important intrigues, it was the policy of the two brothers, by appearing to divide, to side with and lead the two opposing parties. Goolaub Sing came from Jummoo to head the party of Chund Kour, who, as it had been promised by both the brothers that she should be placed on the guddee at the death of her son, considered her right and title as just; and though the minister had broken faith with her, she placed such entire trust in Rajah Goolaub and his promises, that she held full and confident hopes of ultimate success.

Thus now the Court was divided into two parties, each breathing destruction against the other, when all of a sudden the minister, *apparently* seeing that he alone could not stand out against all the Sirdars, requested Shere Sing to desist for a while from his purpose, and sending him back to his jaghire, bid him wait until (as he said) he should be able to bring over all the troops to his side, and thus place him upon the guddee without opposition. Shere Sing, accordingly, accompanied only by a small body of his own troops, was induced to leave Lahore, while the minister on his part left for Jummoo, but not until he had made arrangements for engaging the army and its officers to side with him. The real object of this movement, evidently, was that Dehan Sing and Goolaub Sing might the better concert their plans, and with the greater probability of ensuring success.

For about thirty days Dehan Sing remained at Jummoo, during which time the emissaries he had left at Lahore secretly to ply the Seik soldiery, had so well played their part as to have received promises from the different corps that as soon as the minister and Shere Sing should present themselves at Lahore, they would place the latter upon the throne. These promises were given on consideration that the army should receive an increase of pay, together with large presents—terms which only were afterwards partially fulfilled.

At length, when the soldiery were considered as ripe for the purpose, letters were forwarded to Rajah Dehan, informing him that he might now safely advance and bring Shere Sing along with him to Lahore. Jewalla Sing (Shere Sing's mooktear) was in the meantime intriguing with the soldiery, in order that they might place his master on the throne without the aid of the Dogra faction. His object in pursuing this line of policy was the hope that by this means he himself might attain to the Wuzeership. Shere Sing himself considered this to be the best and most feasible plan for attaining his purpose; but yet he stood in too great a dread of the Rajah's interest and power, not to flatter him by the most solemn protestations that he considered the object in view could only be attained through his instrumentality. Thus while on the one hand he was assuring the minister of his reliance upon him alone— he had on the other hand actually given Jewalla Sing a written promise, that in case the Khalsa troops agreed to and succeeded in the capture of Lahore and the ejection of Chund Kour and her party, without the aid of Rajah Dehan Sing, he (Jewalla Sing) should be appointed Wuzeer. While matters were thus progressing, Dehan Sing sent a notice to Shere Sing that every thing had now been so far settled with the army as to warrant his at once proceeding to Lahore, at the same time advising him to approach the city by the Shalimar Gardens, at which place the minister agreed to meet him. This step however he deemed it prudent not to take, certainly not until he knew how the Seik army was disposed towards Shere Sing on his approach to the city.

Not suspecting the Rajah's intentions, Shere Sing, with about three hundred of his followers, left Koonoowan (his usual sporting residence) and marched for the city. On his arrival at the Shalimar Gardens, he felt at first somewhat disappointed and astonished to learn that Rajah Dehan Sing had (up to that moment) not even left Jummoo. This suspicious conduct of the Rajah's was immediately regarded by Jewalla Sing and his friends as furnishing a good opportunity for Shere Sing to induce the Khalsa troops to march against the city without loss of time. The plan was supported by the argument that Shere Sing could now, by a quick movement and a vigorous attack so surprize the city as to make it an easy conquest, while Chund Kour and her adherents, panic struck by the revolt of the army, would be glad to give up the keys of the fortress even before Dehan Sing could possibly arrive. Shere Sing accordingly sent emissaries to the army then encamped at Meean Meer to acquaint them with his arrival and immediate intentions. On this the troops sent him word to come the next day, and publicly to encamp at Buddhoo-ka-ava—an old brick kiln, on the top of which General Avitabile has erected a Bara Deree or house surrounded by a defensive wall. This house had for some time been considered and employed as the rendezvous of the Punches* of the army in general, whenever any assembly was convened for the purposes of business. This spot was now considered the most fit for Shere Sing to encamp on, as he would there be in the midst of the troops, and his right and title to the guddee could be fearlessly proclaimed, and if necessary, means be taken to enforce his immediate enthronement. There was, however, a party in the army who desired the presence of Rajah Dehan, he having in a measure become the security for the fulfilment of all the promises made to the troops—and being known as a man of wealth and interest—qualities which Shere Sing did not possess at all. Jewalla Sing soon managed, however, to satisfy, or at all events silence, this party, and accordingly on the next morning Shere Sing took up his position at Baddhoo-ka-ava—where the whole of the Punches and a large number of the officers of the Khalsa army came and paid their respects to him, and then publicly proclaimed him as the sovereign of the country. To insure his

* These Punches or deputies of the troops were men who by superior ability or cunning had secured an influence over their comrades, and who were encouraged to undertake the office as much by the expectation of the numerous presents which fell to their share, as by the importance which it gave them in the eyes of others. Their anger being dreaded by all, their favour, individually and collectively, was courted by high and low alike.

safety four battalions of infantry and two of cavalry with several pieces of artillery were quickly stationed around the mound, while a heavy discharge of cannon as a salute proclaimed to the startled citizens of Lahore—now roused to a sense of their danger—the intention of the army to support Shere Sing.

Rajah Goolaub Sing, who ever since the death of No Nehal Sing, had in a manner publicly avowed his intentions to favour the claims of Chund Kour, was considered the head and main spring of her cause. Rajah Heera Sing, the eldest son of Dehan Sing, was likewise of her party, and while he remained in Lahore made it appear that he had joined his uncle against his father—a deep-laid scheme to save appearances, a trick which the wily brothers of Jummoo had often played before. The intent of this manœuvre was, that by ostensibly becoming enemies to each other, and by the appearance of opposition in their political views, they were enabled to become the leaders and controllers of the contending parties, whereby their object was secured whichever side was successful, and they were enabled by their private agreement to direct the current of affairs more entirely to suit their own intentions and advantage. However, from this it may be inferred that Rajah Dehan Sing did not leave his brothers at Lahore without a proper arrangement with them as to the part each had to play in the tragic drama that was about to be performed. Rajah Goolaub was well aware of the moment when Shere Sing was to leave Koonoowan for Lahore, as well as of the real disposition of the Khalsa towards him. But it was only on the day on which Shere Sing arrived at Shalimar that Goolaub seemed to have the slightest notion of his approach or of the intentions of the army.

CHAPTER II.

THE SIEGE OF LAHORE BY SHERE SING.

ON hearing that Shere Sing had arrived at Shalimar, Goolaub Sing consulted with Chund Kour and the chiefs who supported her cause, namely, Jemadar Khoosheeal Sing, Sirdar Teja Sing, and the several members of the Scindawalla family, most of whom he had probably himself gained and enlisted on her side, that they might be caught in the snare which was laid for their destruction. After this consultation he sent orders for all his own household troops, then encamped at Shahdera, to cross the river immediately and to encamp on the parade ground adjacent to and to the north of the Soomun Boorj of the fort. These troops had scarcely reached the spot appointed, when they received further orders to march to the attack of Shere Sing and his partizans in their position at Shalimar. The force sent on this service was composed chiefly of Rajah Dehan Sing's own troops! It consisted of two small battalions, with ten Horse Artillery guns, belonging to that chief, one battalion belonging to his brother and avowed confederate Rajah Suchet Sing, and one belonging to his other brother and concealed ally Rajah Goolaub Sing, in all about two thousand men and ten guns! This Dogra force had not proceeded half a mile towards Shalimar, when Goolaub himself, attended by about a hundred horse, galloped up to them, ordered them instantly to countermarch, and returning with them at a rapid pace, hurried the whole into the Hazooree Bagh or palace garden, and with this force immediately occupied the whole fort, stating as his reason for the measure that the whole Khalsa army had declared in favour of Shere Sing, and that it would be madness to proceed with so small a force against that prince, supported as he was by at least sixty thousand men.

Although Goolaub Sing up to the moment when the struggle actually commenced, believed that Shere Sing was too much under the influence of Rajah Dehan to venture on any thing like open hostility during his absence and without his concurrence, he was aware that the prince, strongly supported by the whole Khalsa, might be induced to make a vigorous effort to gain his point by private negotiations, and without the aid of his principal but still absent supporter Dehan Sing. Goolaub was too old a pupil in Runjeet's school not to be able to see through the schemes of Jewalla Sing and the duplicity of Shere Sing. He was likewise well aware that his brother in his letters to the prince merely advised him to proceed towards Lahore and to encamp at Shalimar, where the whole or most of the troops would go out to him, and where he might strengthen himself and act according to circumstances, but on no account to commence open hostilities until his, Dehan Sing's, arrival from Jummoo. He promised on these conditions to endeavour by means of his influence with his brother Goolaub Sing to obtain for Shere Sing by negotiation the object of his wishes, and to give him possession of the throne and the capital without a shot being fired. However, contrary to the wish and expectations of Rajah Goolaub Sing, Shere Sing early on the following morning took up a position at Bhoodhoo ka Ava, and thereby convinced the Dogra chief of his determination at once to attack the city and fort in the absence and without the concurrence of Dehan Sing. Goolaub saw clearly that his success in this enterprise, independent of the aid of his party, would be a deathblow to the hopes of himself, his family, and friends. He therefore determined to oppose to the last any attack made by the prince, and not to listen to any terms till the arrival of his brother Dehan Sing on the scene of action. He would then, as previously arranged, after some show of negotiation, yield to the influence of Dehan Sing, so as to make it appear to Shere Sing that he entirely owed his elevation to that chief and his party.

Having thus taken up a threatening position at Bhoodhoo ka Ava, Shere Sing and the Khalsa troops busied themselves in preparation, for an immediate and vigorous attack on Lahore. This day's work, however, cost the prince nearly all the money he had brought with him, together with all that he could borrow, and which he had to bestow upon the troops in gifts ere he could bring them into train for the approaching conflict. On the other side Goolaub Sing the same morning convened a large assemblage of the friends and supporters of Chund Kour in the Soomun Boorj, to whom he depicted in the most lively colours the greatness of the coming danger, and exhorted them to be faithful and courageous in the cause of the princess, confirming the allegiance of waverers by administering an oath of constancy. After this a private consultation was held by Rajah Goolaub Sing, Jemadar Khoosheeal Sing, Sirdar Teja Sing, and the heads of the Scindawalla family. Here Goolaub Sing earnestly enjoined the chiefs to enter the fort immediately with their troops and to put the place in a posture of defence, as it was quite uncertain when the attack might be made. The Scindawalla chiefs answered that they had already done what the Rajah now advised, while Jemadar Khoosheeal Sing, Sirdar Teja Sing and others declared their readiness to act on his suggestion at a moment's notice.

On the evening of this day Goolaub Sing, mounted on an elephant, went amongst and reviewed and inspected the troops, and saw that every gateway and bastion round the city was properly secured and provided for defence. He took with him on this visit many large bags of money, which he liberally distributed in handfuls to the soldiers at the different posts, receiving in return strong assurances that at whatever point Shere Sing might make the assault he should be vigorously opposed and repelled. The Rajah on returning from this tour again entered the fort, and sending for the officers and men of the different divisions of artillery then in the city, himself in person administered an oath to each one individually,—the Mahomedans on the Koran, and the Hindoos on the water of the Ganges—that they would to the last resist any attack made by Shere Sing on the fort or the city. After this ceremony had been performed each officer and man received, and with at least seeming thankfulness, four months' pay, as a gratuity from Chund Kour; this with promises of further favours being considered sufficient to bind the whole to the cause of the princess. When this business was completed, which was at a late hour of the night, every man repaired to his post, and soon the fort and city of Lahore were to all appearance buried in slumber, too soon to awake to scenes of tumult and bloodshed.

About an hour and a half or two hours before day break the Dogra sentinels stationed along the ramparts of that part of the fort which faces the city, reported that large bodies of horse with lighted matches had passed along the road leading towards the artillery barracks of Sultan Mahomed and Meva Sing, or towards the Badshahi Musjid, and that they seemed to have entered the city by the Yakkee and Delhi gates. The sentries thought, moreover, from the conversation which they had overheard that Shere Sing must then have entered the city. This was soon ascertained to be the fact, with the only difference that the prince had by previous arrangements entered at a wicket gate which then existed in Meva Sing's barracks and close to and west of the Badshahi Musjid, while the large bodies of cavalry which supported him, entered, first by the Yakkee and Delhi gates, and afterwards by the Tunksallee and other gates. It then appeared that the guards and keepers of the gates all round the city, after having on the previous evening accepted large sums as presents from Goolaub Sing, and sworn to be faithful to Chund Kour, had, on the receipt of somewhat more valuable gifts from the other side, transferred their service and allegiance to Shere Sing, to whom, in virtue of this agreement, the gates were quietly opened at the time appointed.

Thus before daylight Shere Sing was not only in possession of four or five of the principal gateways of the city, but had actually entered the place in person with about two thousand infantry, while about five thousand cavalry had gone in by the gates, and all assembled quietly and privately in the open space now included in Meva Sing's artillery barracks. Shere Sing himself took up his quarters for the time in Meva Sing's own house, which was close to the wicket by which he had entered the city. Thus proceeding as silently and quietly as possible, the prince before day was, by means of further bribes, in possession of both the gateways leading into the Hazooree Bagh, as also of the Badshahi Musjid and the large magazine which was then in that edifice.

While matters were thus proceeding outside, Rajah Goolaub Sing concentrated his Dogra troops in the upper fort and made all requisite preparations for whatever might occur. He also sent directions to Jemadar Khoosheeal Sing and Sirdar Teja Sing to repair to the fort with such men as they could command, but for reasons best known to themselves, these chiefs on various pretences and excuses declined to comply with the Rajah's request. There were about twelve hundred Seiks on duty in the fort before the Dogra force entered; they were the two battalions in charge of the treasury called the Mootee Mundur, and were under the command of Boodh Sing Maun. These Seiks perceiving the course which affairs were taking, showed some inclination to become mutinous, and even went so far as to threaten the Dogra intruders with destruction. Indeed it is probable that they would have attempted to carry their threats into execution had not there been just light enough for them to see four guns heavily loaded with grape, and with matches lighted, ready to open upon them. This spectacle induced them to remaim quiet and to become more civil to their unwelcome visitors; and their only thought now was how to get safe out of the fort. They asked Rajah Goolaub for leave to withdraw, and he for obvious reasons readily granted it. But it was too late for them to retreat, the fierce strife for which so many secret and silent preparations had been made, was about to begin.

As day dawned upon Lahore the watchers on the ramparts of the fort heard the tramp and murmur of the advancing Khalsa army as it marched in at the several gates of the city. The increasing light then showed a cloud of dust raised by the tread of the advancing thousands, and which threw a lurid and ominous gloom on all around. Presently the fierce cries of some seventy thousand wild infantry, and perhaps fifty thousand still more savage followers attracted by the scent of plunder, rent the air in loud acclamations. Above all was heard the Seik war cry—*Wah Gooroo jee ko Futteh! Wah Gooroo jee ko Khalsajee!* as the host, disdaining further attempts at secrecy, advanced to the assault. The small and silent band on the walls of the fort calmly beheld the approach of the dense columns of infantry, the squadrons of cavalry, and more fearful than all, the enormous train of the Khalsa artillery. The entire circuit of the fort now presented a closely wedged mass of men, forming close up to the very walls. Presently the artillery was drawn into position, and coolly unlimbered ready to open its terrible fire on the devoted place. The number of guns was so great that they formed as it were one entire and connected battery round the fort; and yet others, for want of room in the first rank, had to take up positions in the rear, or to fire from wherever space could be found to work them. Calmly and silently the besieged viewed these formidable preparations for the assault. They had merely closed the two gates, the one leading into the Hazooree Bagh and the other towards the eastern verge of the city; but inside each of these gates they had placed two guns loaded with grape. They also manned the walls as well as their numbers would allow with the men of the Dogra or Phirman battalion, who lay concealed, ready to deal out destruction on the dense masses below. At this time the Hazooree Bagh was thronged with a motley multitude of Gorchars, or troopers, Akalees, Infantry, Cavalry, and Artillery. Shere Sing himself took up his position in a marble summer house in the middle of the garden, and by his personal and repeated orders a space in front of the gateway of the fort was cleared with much difficulty, and twelve guns were placed so as to bear on the wooden portals, at a distance of not more than thirty-five or forty yards in front of them.

The scene at this moment was of a strange and fearful character,—the dense mass of fierce men heaving to and fro almost up to the walls of the fort like an angry sea beating against a rock. The tumult of their wild music and still wilder cries as the host clamoured to be led to the attack was stunning. Soon however, the horror took another form. The entire circle of guns—about two hundred and thirty pieces of artillery—simultaneously opened a fire of blank cartridge. This was done probably in the expectation of terrifying the defenders of the fort, but if so about fifty rounds from each gun were thrown away to no purpose. The effect, however, of this firing was awful, stunning all, besieged as well as besiegers, and shaking the fort even to the old foundatious laid by the Emperor Akbar. At length the firing ceased suddenly, and then ensued a calm and silence so profound that the stillness was not less awful than the previous uproar. Not a sound, not a whisper was heard on either side as the besiegers waited to ascertain the effect of this singular assault. Then the twelve guns pointed at the Hazooree Bagh gate were quietly loaded,—ball cartridge with a canister of grape driven home over it. The matches were lit and ready to hurl destruction on the feeble portals. Loud and savage voices were heard, fiercely demanding the opening of the gate. But the call was unheeded :—immediately then the twelve guns were fired at once, and the old wooden gate, with thirty-seven out of thirty-nine men placed inside to defend it, fell before the terrible discharge. The two guns loaded with grape were now all that opposed the entrance of the beseigers, and there was left but one out of sixteen artillerymen to fire them. The besieged were panic struck for a moment by the fatal effect of the enemy's fire. At this instant a band of two or three hundred Akalees rushed forward over the ruins of the gate and the bodies of its fallen defenders. One of them had advanced so far that he was able to thrust his sword into the muzzle of one of the guns, by way of taking possession of it, when the sole remaining artillery man, with a little khalassie who attended on him, fired the two guns at once, and nearly a hundred corpses fell out of the mass of men that was rushing forward. The assailants recoiled for a moment before this close and withering fire, and the defenders of the gate were enabled to load and fire their guns again with as destructive an effect as before. Thus the twelve guns drawn up before the gate were almost unmanned, and the greater number of their horses were killed. This first gleam of success for the besieged was heightened by the promptitude with which the Dogra men, without awaiting orders from Rajah Goolaub Sing, poured their fire of musketry from the walls upon the confused mass below. The effect was that in about ten minutes the Hazooree Bagh was cleared of the besiegers, who left behind them about three hundred killed, one hundred wounded, and about fifty prisoners taken by a sally of the Dogras sword in hand. During the confusion Shere Sing escaped from the garden back to his former quarters in the barracks of Meva Sing, and he thought it prudent to keep himself out of harms-way during the remainder of the siege.

While all this was passing in the Hazooree Bagh, the eastern gateway was attacked in a similar manner, but by only six guns instead of twelve. The first fire beat down the gate and killed eleven men inside, but the return fire of the two guns within and the musketry of the Dogras on the ramparts above, quickly silenced the assailing battery, killing all the men and horses attached to it. The guns were thus left, as in the Hazooree Bagh, under the fire of the garrison.

Thus repulsed in their first attempts, the Khalsa opened a heavy and general fire from their artillery all round the place, at a distance of not more than sixty or a hundred yards. This fire was continued with such vigour and rapidity that it threatened the destruction of the old walls, which seemed likely to crumble away before it. But the artillery-men being within the range of small arms, and quite unsheltered, fell so fast under the well-directed fire of the garrison on the walls, that in about an hour the whole of the formidable line was silenced and deserted. The Dogras on the ramparts could now count no less than one hundred and forty-six guns with none but dead and wounded men, horses, and bullocks around them, and so completely commanded by their fire that none dared to approach them. This sight had the effect of inspiriting and encouraging the besieged; and the besiegers retired to a more respectful distance, sheltering themselves behind and in the houses of the city. Thirty-six guns of large calibre belonging to the division of Sultan Mahomed were the last to be silenced by the fire from the fort, the artillery-men having hit upon an ingenious but barbarous method of protecting themselves. They had seized and taken by force many women of the city, courtezans and others, and compelling them to stand in front of and around their guns, some of them actually bound to the wheels, the Dogras in their gallantry to the sex or their pity for the individuals, averted their fire, and thus the Seiks by this cruel stratagem were enabled to continue their's in perfect safety. But at length the Dogras found that the fire of these guns, thus strangely protected, was not only making sad havoc in their ranks, but was likely to bring down a portion of their defences; they therefore reluctantly set to work to silence these as they had done the others by a vigorous return. Even now, however, greatly to the credit of their gallantry and humanity be it said, they took all possible care to avoid injuring the wretched women, aiming with their best skill to strike their enemies without hitting their involuntary protectors. The best proof, not only of their kind feeling but of their skill as marksmen, is the fact that of a thousand or twelve hundred women who were thus barbarously exposed, only nineteen lost their lives, while not less than one hundred and eighty-six of the artillerymen were shot down at their guns.

The rest of that day was passed in comparative quiet, which afforded to the little garrison an opportunity, of which they were not slow to avail themselves, for repairing as well as they could the damage done, and for strengthening their defences in anticipation of a renewed attack. They were, however, exposed throughout the day to a desultory and almost harmless fire from the Seiks, who had taken up secure positions in and behind the houses of the city; and some of the guns which had from the commencement of the fray been blocked up in narrow passages and lying unemployed, were now, under cover of houses and walls, dragged off to a distance and brought to bear upon the defences of the fort. By favour of the darkness the Seiks managed also to haul up their deserted artillery, but not without considerable loss from the watchful garrison. The guns were placed in houses and behind walls, and pointed on the place through embrasures made for the occasion; and thus the Seiks awaited for the day to renew the assault.

About four in the morning a tremendous cannonade was opened from the concealed batteries. The garrison were unable to return this fire with any effect, from the fact that the fort had no embrasures through which they could point their guns. The place, built originally by the Emperor Akbar merely as a temporary residence for himself and his family, was never furnished with the means of defence by the aid of artillery, and possessed nothing more than loop-holes for musketry. The garrison now, however, endeavoured to overcome this defect by breaking out embrasures in the ramparts; but they soon found that this was impracticable, and the attempt dangerous from the frail nature of the masonry, which, old and decayed, came down in masses from the shock of their own guns. In two instances not only were guns thus buried under heaps of ruins, but some lives were lost. They then resorted to the expedient of erecting batteries of wood and earth within the fort, and knocking down the wall in front of them—a process in which they were much aided by the fire of the besiegers; and thus they were enabled to return the fire of the Seiks with considerable effect.

All this time four guns and a part of the garrison was employed in the indispensible task of keeping quiet the twelve hundred Seik troops that had been found in the fort, and who, had they not been thus overawed, would have glady created a diversion in favour of their friends and comrades outside by falling on the strangers within. But they were kept from doing injury, and confined to the area of the building called the Thuckt or Throne, where they sat silent and sad like so many prisoners of war.

Thus for three successive days and nights was a heavy and incessant cannonade kept up by the Seiks upon the place, and returned by the garrison to the best of their power. Several large breaches were formed, and so perfect were they that many of the Dogras of the garrison, during the night, found easy egress and ingress through them, when they sallied forth upon the besiegers or made their arragements to repulse sudden assaults.

But though the Seik artillery told ruinously on the walls and ramparts, it was not nearly so annoying to the garrison as the fire of five or six matchlock-men posted on each minar of the Badshahi Musjid, and who were thus able to command every corner of the place with their destructive weapons. These men were Mochees by caste and hunters by profession and remarkable for the certainty of their deadly aim. They were in all about forty in number, and were employed by Shere Sing on this occasion, receiving a pay of from ten to twenty rupees a day each man. The light artillery of the fort was unable to make any sensible impression on the towers upon which these death-dealing marksmen were perched, and could do nothing more than now and than dislodge a few stones from the top. One of the guns of the place however on one occasion tumbled three of these men from their exalted and seemingly secure position, just as they had exposed themselves to full view while in the act of placing a block of stone to serve as a defence from the fire of the Dogra musketeers, who were almost as expert in the use of their arms as those wild huntsmen themselves, and who engaged heartily in a hot rivalry with them at that murderous game. In proof of the skill of the hill-men, it may be mentioned, that they killed five and wounded eleven of the Mochees thus favourably posted, by sending balls through their shoulders and arms, while they were in the act of using their ramrods, when alone those parts of their bodies and only those were visible to their keen-eyed enemies below.

On the evening of the third day the garrison received information that the large drains and water-courses leading from the fort into the ditch had been charged with powder and were to be exploded as mines at night-fall. They thereupon opened a heavy fire on the suspected points, while parties of Dogras went in and abstracted all the powder, filling the mouths of the drains with earth, &c. On the same night, by an accidental circumstance it was discovered that a considerable part of the fort was undermined on the side next the Hazooree Bagh and near what is called the Goolab Khana. Beneath the walls in that direction several old caves and hollow places existed, and the besiegers entering these places under cover of night had formed extensive mines under the fort. In carrying on these operations the miners broke into a low subterraneous room in the fort, in which a party of Sultan Mahomed's artillery were ensconced; this caused an alarm and a discovery, and the besiegers were not without some trouble expelled, losing forty-seven workmen and about fifty soldiers, most of whom were killed by the bursting of shells thrown by hand into these vaults and passages.

On the following morning intelligence was given to the garrison that Shere Sing in person had taken up his position in the Badshahi Musjid. They thereupon formed a scheme for blowing him and the building into the air, and made their preparations accordingly. It was well known to them that the Musjid contained a large magazine of powder stored in wooden boxes, skins, &c. This they wished to explode, if possible, by means of shells and red hot shot; but just as they were about to commence operations, they received information which induced them to desist, being told that though there were at least five thousand maunds of powder in the Musjid, there were certain subterranean passages communicating between that edifice and the fort, which were also filled with powder, and terminated in other vaults or magazines of powder beneath the fort itself.

Towards evening on the fifth day of the siege, intelligence was received of the approach of Rajah Dehan Sing, who had arrived from Jummoo. This induced Shere Sing to order that the fire on the place should cease, while he endeavoured to negotiate with Rajah Goolaub Sing. That chief, however, on overtures being made, refused to treat, alleging, that he could not think of negotiating until his brother made his appearance and consented to become a mediator in the affair. This determined answer, together with the great loss which the besiegers had sustained without any success to counterbalance it, induced Shere Sing to send a deputation to Dehan Sing, who was coolly amusing himself hunting the wild boar, some three or four miles from Shahdera. The messengers were instructed to tender a sort of apology for what had occurred, to make excuses on behalf of Shere Sing for the part which he had played in the tragedy, and to endeavour to persuade Dehan, that the untoward events which had occurred originated only in the rashness and obstinate disobedience of the Seik troops, who were described as in a state of mutiny and resolutely bent or avenging their slaughtered comrades. Dehan Sing and his younger brother Suchet Sing, however, were not to be thus pacified. They publicly taxed Shere Sing with falsehood and duplicity, and declared that he might now take the fort, if he could, for himself,—that he might go on freely expending the Khalsa troops and his own money for another month if he liked, with little hope of eventual success; but that they could no longer consent to be security for him to the army, or assure him against the consequences when he should no longer be able to satisfy the demands of the soldiers for money, as they found that during the past few days between four and five lakhs of rupees had been expended in vain attempts to satisfy the mob of armed men. By these representations Shere Sing was brought to consider the matter more seriously than he had hitherto done. During this evening and in the night he repeatedly ordered a total cessation of hostilities; but the Seiks would not now listen to him, declaring that they could never desist until the fort was razed to the ground, and all the garrison slain in revenge for the death of so many of their comrades. But Dehan Sing's agents persuaded Shere Sing that this was but the pretext of the Seik troops, whose real object was to take the fort by assault, and to indulge their long-cherished desire to plunder the treasury which it contained. These and similar persuasions and advices induced Shere Sing to take the affair into his serious consideration; and during the night he sent five hundred of his best and most faithful Gorechars, or cavalry, to Dehan Sing, accompanied by several chiefs, who in the most humble manner and on behalf of Shere Sing, craved pardon for what had been done amiss, and entreated Dehan Sing to accompany them to the city, where Shere Sing was waiting his appearance in the greatest anxiety and suspense. On receiving this humble message, both the Dogra brothers, Dehan Sing and Suchet Sing, with about five hundred of their own adherents, who had accompanied them from Jummoo, and the body of cavalry sent by Shere Sing, appoached Lahore on the sixth day of the siege. As they came near the walls, Shere Sing with a strong escort and numerous retinue went out in person to meet them and to conduct them into the city, assigning as his reason for guarding their persons so carefully, that the troops just now entertained hostile feelings against every one who bore the designation of a Dogra. On meeting Dehan Sing, Shere Sing actually humbled himself so far as with bare feet and joined hands to entreat forgiveness for what was past, which he declared again was not through any fault of his. Dehan Sing, knowing well how to treat the prince, at first affected a cold and haughty demeanour; and in a severe tone he told Shere Sing that he, the prince, had more need to fear the Khalsa troops than himself had. He remarked further that as Shere Sing acknowledged that he could not manage the soldiery, he would show him what he himself could do in that way. He then galloped off, attended by only ten or twelve horsemen into the midst of the Seik multitude then collected outside the Tanksallee gateway to witness his entry into the city. The soldiers received him with loud acclamation, and while Shere Sing followed at some distance, Dehan Sing entered Lahore among a crowd of Seik troops, who saw in his arrival the hope of further bribes and presents. The Rajah flattered and pleased the soldiers around him by expressing his sorrow at their loss, and the small return they were likely to obtain, assuring them that had his advice been taken not a drop of blood would have been spilt, while their object would have been obtained in one short day. He said, however, that if they would not be too hasty now, he had the strongest hopes of being able to put every thing to rights yet, and of seeing every man of them well rewarded for his loyalty and devotion. By these arts, Dehan Sing, before two hours had elapsed from the time of his arrival had worked himself into the confidence of the Seiks so far that a cessation of hostilities ensued, and every one looked upon him as the man by whose friendly mediation alone peace could be restored. Negotiations began that same evening, and in the morning of the seventh day since the commencement of the siege the Seiks found, as they had not done before, time and opportunity to collect and burn or bury their dead, and to clear the city and the Hazooree Bagh of the carcases of cattle and horses with which they were strewn. The return showed that on the side of the besiegers 4786 men, 610 horses, and 320 bullocks had been killed; while the loss of the garrison did not in killed and wounded exceed 130 men. During these seven days, the Dogras of the garrison had received from Goolaub Sing as presents from himself, and Chund Kour, various sums amounting in the aggregate to about one hundred rupees for each private soldier, the officers being rewarded still more liberally.

One or two other incidents which occurred during this short and vigorous siege may be here mentioned. The Seiks, under the pretence of procuring wood for the erection of batteries, or out-works for the protection of their guns, dismantled nearly half the houses in the city, and committed excesses almost incredible and perfectly indescribable. Even had Shere Sing interfered to prevent these atrocities, he had not the power to enforce his command. The people thronged in crowds to witness the operations of the siege, and might be seen daily in numbers seated, in seeming unconsciousness of danger, on the walls and roofs of houses and in other places within the range of muskets from the fort. But as the garrison knew by their appearance that they were not of the enemy, they never received any molestation.

On the seventh and eighth days, when the Seiks were engaged in burning their dead who were consumed in large heaps, they were seen to throw upon the pile some who were merely wounded and still alive. These poor wretches implored their mercy but in vain, their cries and entreaties were answered with jeering inquiries, if they were afraid to go to heaven—"Biia cherjou, cherjou,—kee kofe ounda?"—"Mount, brother, mount, what are you afraid of?" The object of the soldiers in committing these barbarities was merely to secure the little property they found on the persons of their murdered comrades,—for this petty incitement they were ready to commit atrocities so horrible!

When negotiations began on the seventh day of the seige, Rajah Heera Sing and the Scindawallah chiefs came out of the Soomun Boorj, where they had remained with a few followers, for the purpose, as they said, of affording protection to the princess Chund Kour. Rajah Goolaub now found little difficulty in inducing this lady to agree in the views and designs of himself and his brother. She implored him to become the protector of her person and rights, formally nominating him as her mooktear or agent, and committing all her interests into his hands. He thus procured from Shere Sing and the army terms for her and her supporters more favourable than they could otherwise have obtained; in this, however, as might be expected, he sought his own advantage and that of his family and faction much more than that of his client. The conditions on which it was agreed that the fort of Lahore should be given up and Chund Kour resign her claims to the guddee, were, first, a jaghire of nine lakhs for the princess —Kuddee Kuddeealee was the place named, adjoining the Jummoo states—and Goolaub Sing was to have the management of it for her;—second, that as it was the Ranee's wish to live as the faithful widow of Kurruck Sing, Shere Sing should never make any pretensions to her hand;—third, that the Dogra garrison of the fort should be allowed to march out unmolested and with flying colours;—and fourth, that security should be given for the due fulfilment of these conditions.

In obtaining a jaghire of nine lakhs of rupees per annum in the part of the country adjoining his own dominions, under pretence of holding it for Chund Kour, the chief of Jummoo secured an object of no small consideration with him; while by the lady being allowed to continue in a state of widowhood he was secured in quiet possession of the advantages thus obtained. Eventually, however, the Rajah secured to himself not only this jaghire but almost all the lady's money and valuables, which under the pretence of safely keeping for her, he carried off to Jummoo.

Matters being satisfactorily arranged, it was settled that the Dogra garrison should leave the fort on the evening of the eighth day. In preparation for this movement, Goolaub Sing employed himself in filling his tumbrils and waggons, sixteen in number, with silver money, allowing only thirty rounds of ammunition for each gun, to be used is case of emergency. Furthermore, a bag of gold mohurs was entrusted to the care of each of five hundred of his most faithful adherents; and again, a quantity of jewellery and valuable trinkets was delivered to the charge of his own orderly

Gorchars or mounted body guard. Then taking with him twelve of the best horses that had been in Runjeet Sing's stud, and many valuable articles of pushmeena, &c., Goolaub Sing at the head of his men marched quietly out of the fort after dark on the evening of the eighth day. The clause in the capitulation which allowed the garrison to depart with all the honors of war was not taken advantage of, Goolaub fearing, and with but too much show of reason, that the Seiks, instigated by their own revengeful feelings, or the machinations of Jewalla Sing, might fall upon the little band when it was unable to protect itself and plunder and perhaps murder them all. As it was, however, the Dogra force without molestation reached the bank of the Ravee opposite Shahderah and there encamped for two days. During this time Goolaub Sing went to pay his respects to the new Maharajah, Shere Sing, to whom with his own hand he delivered as a token of homage and as a propitiatory gift, the great diamond called Koh-i-noor, which he had contrived to secure. On the occasion of this interview he endeavoured to impress on Shere Sing a sense of his own loyalty and patriotism, declaring that he now had at much risk and trouble to himself secured for the new Maharajh, the treasures of the state which but for his exertions would have been plundered by the Seik soldiery and the rabble. To this he added, that being a Rajpoot and an old servant of Runjeet Sing, his gallantry and loyalty alike engaged him to protect the person and reputation of Chund Kour, the virtuous widow of Kurruck Sing, and daughter-in-law to the great Maharajh himself. Thus he made the best use of some four or five hours which passed during his interview with Shere Sing, and next day crossing the Ravee to Shahdera, with the whole of his force he took up as strong a position as he could find, and sent to Jummoo for a re-inforcement of two thousand of his best troops. He took these precautions because he found that the Khalsa troops were becoming utterly uncontrollable by the power of Shere Sing, and he had reason to apprehend that at the instigation of Jewalla Sing they would even yet attack him. He found, too, that at the instigation of the same chief, Shere Sing had enticed many of his troops to desert, and on his learning this fact he obtained leave of absence, through the interest of his brother Dehan Sing, the Wuzeer, and marched to Jummoo with his whole force.

The deep policy of the Jummoo brothers was now beginning to develope itself. They had got rid of the unfortunate Kurruck Sing, and of his active and ambitious son, No Nehal Sing; the .Ranee Chund Kour had been set aside, and Shere Sing was placed on the throne simply that he might be the more completely in the power of these his worst enemies. It now only remained to dispose of the new Maharajh, to replace whom Dehan Sing had in his hands a young child, the reputed though not the real son, of Runjeet Sing;* and then, with the Khalsa troops entirely at his command, Rajah Dehan Sing, aided by his brothers, would be supreme.

* The present Maharajh, Dulleep Sing, of whose birth and parentage more hereafter.

CHAPTER III.

GOOLAUB SING AND AFFGHANISTAN.

GOOLAUB SING did not remain long at Jummoo, whither he went after the surrender of Lahore. He was ordered off to Cashmere to quell a mutiny among the troops, and he did this effectually, by cutting to pieces and almost annihilating two battalions who had killed their Governor, Meean Sing. From Cashmere he went to the Hazareh country, where he overcame Paindah Khan, Nawab of Trinoul, who was continually causing disturbances in that quarter. While in Hazareh the news of the insurrections against the British at Cabul reached him. It may here be mentioned, that when the old King, Zeman Shah, passed through the Punjaub, on his return to Cabul, he was escorted by Goolaub Sing's troops under a confidential officer, and from that time a close communication was carried on betwixt Zeman Shah and the Dogra chief. There is, moreover, reason to suspect, that during Zeman Shah's march through the Punjaub, the seeds were sown which shortly produced the rebellion in Affghanistan, and the fearful disasters of the British army in that country. Certain it is, that Goolaub Sing expected and foretold such an outbreak, full two months before it occurred. Another suspicious circumstance is well known,—that both Goolaub and his brother Dehan Sing were in constant and secret communication with most, both of the Barukzye and Suddoozye chiefs at Cabul, for at least six months before the insurrection broke out; their dealings with either party being a profound secret to the other. It may likewise be inferred that both parties were acting in the affair which ensued as the instruments of, or strongly instigated by, their friends in the Punjaub. The communication with the Barukzyes was kept up through the sirdars of Peshawur, then continual residents at the Court of Lahore, and who acted a prominent part thoughout the whole affair.

Rajah Goolaub Sing was in the Hazareh districts when Brigadier Wild arrived on the Attock, and it was through his sinister proceedings that so much difficulty and delay was experienced in crossing that river. In accordance with engagement and in order to keep up appearances, the Mahomedan Brigade in the Seik service was ordered to march with and assist the British troops in the passage through the Khyber Pass, and if necessary to Jullalabad. Now though orders to this effect were publicly issued, and the Mahomedan Brigade had already marched, it is an indubitable fact, and one that might easily be proved, that these troops were privately instructed and had received orders to act in a contrary manner. These orders went from the Hazareh country, where Rajah Goolaub Sing was then encamped and they were conveyed to Peshawar by the hands of one Mirza Mahomed Yar, better known as Mirza Firmar. The manner in which the Seik contingent acted at that time is well known. When the British troops had advanced to the pass, their Punjaub allies becoming, *to all appearance*, mutinous and insubordinate, returned at the most critical juncture, leaving the British force to its fate. Thus the Seik contingent, in a disorderly manner, marched back to the Attock, where it encamped on the western bank of the river, Rajah Goolaub Sing being encamped on the eastern one. The meaning of this conduct was that it was intended to cause delay and discomfiture to the British in their advance into Affghanistan; and it certainly had its expected effect for a time. The disasters that Wild's brigade met with were owing to this cause; had it not been for this, it would have reached Jullalabad much earlier, and mnch evil and bloodshed might thereby have been saved. The news of this brigade having reached Jullalabad would have had a great effect in deterring the Affghan chiefs and people from acting against the British force then in the country; and it would have inspirited the latter to behave with greater vigour and resolution in repelling the attacks made upon them. It is probable that had this brigade reached Jullalabad, the army would never have left Cabul, or if it did so, would have done so under a treaty that would have been held sacred by the Affghans, a strong British force being at hand to punish its infraction.

Soon after this defection of the Seik contingent, General Pollock arrived at Peshawar, and in a few days afterwards Goolaub Sing made his appearance, after a very leisurely and evidently reluctant march from Hazareh. Though a British political agent was in his camp, urging him day and night to expedition, it took him forty-two days to march from Hazareh to Peshawar, a distance of but little more than the same number of miles. While Pollock was encamped at Peshawar, every effort was made to delay his advance, and to frighten the native troops and thereby to prevent their entering the much dreaded Khyber Pass. The means used for this purpose caused some desertion, but had they succeeded to the full, mutiny in its worst aspect and at the most critical moment would have been the result. General Pollock, however, happily overcame all difficulties and escaped all dangers—more, perhaps, than he is aware of even to this day. He acted with promptitude and determination, and his efforts being nobly supported by his troops, he safely reached Jullalabad, and thus not only relieved Sale's division, but formed by the junction a force capable of carrying all before it even to the walls, and even within the gates of Cabul. Rajah Goolaub Sing thus disappointed, put the best face on the matter, declared he had done what he could for the assistance of the British, and seeing no further need for his *services* marched back for Jummoo.

CHAPTER IV.

MURDER OF JEWALLA SING AND OF RANEE CHUND KOUR.

IT has been seen how Jewalla Sing, the Mooktear or agent of Shere Sing, under promise of being made Wuzeer, exerted himself to obtain for his master possession of the throne and capital, without the aid and influence of the Dogra family. In the interval between Shere Sing's first appearance at Shalimar, and his return from Konoowar to Lahore, and while Dehan Sing was at Jummoo, Jewalla Sing had strenuously exerted himself to bring over the troops to his master's interest, and it was chiefly by his bribes and promises that their services were secured on behalf of Shere Sing. Elated with his success in this matter, the Mooktear fancied that with the aid of the troops he had won over he could take the fort by force of arms, and advised his master not to allow Rajah Dehan Sing on his arrival to interfere in an affair, which he, Jewalla Sing, could settle without his assistance. It was he who instigated the Khalsa troops to attack the fort during Dehan Sing's absence, and it was only by the energy and resolution of the Dogra garrison that his object was defeated. Even when Dehan Sing arrived, and when Shere Sing, repenting of his attempt to take the fort without his aid and advice, ordered a cessation of the fire upon the place, Jewalla Sing, unwilling to be baulked in his ambitious designs, persuaded the troops to continue the attack, and thus for twelve hours the orders of Shere Sing were of no avail;

and indeed they would have continued inoperative, had he not, attended by Dehan Sing and many officers, personally gone among the troops, and by gifts and persuasions induced them to desist. Again, when the Dogra garrison marched out of the fort at night, and proceeded to encamp at Shahdera, they would have been attacked by the Seik troops at Jewalla Sing's instigation, had it not been that Shere Sing and Dehan Sing learning their intention, were personally on the alert to prevent its being carried into effect. All these things were well known to the Dogra Chiefs, and the knowledge served to enrage them against the ambitious Mooktear, and led them to determine on a murderous revenge. Having determined on the destruction of their enemy, their first step was to rob him of the confidence and favour of his master. Their plans for this purpose were so well devised and skilfully executed, that it was not long ere Shere Sing regarded his too zealous servant as a secret, deep, and crafty foe. With this suspicion in his heart, the Maharajh commanded Jewalla Sing into his presence to account for his conduct; but the Mooktear, then encamped at Shalimar with a body of six thousand cavalry, who were in his interest, apprehensive of the intentions of his master, refused to obey the summons. In this contumacy he was encouraged and countenanced by his troops, who declared that they would either excuse him to the Maharajh, or, if necessary, protect him against the anger of his master. This conduct of Jewalla Sing, of course enraged the Maharajh still more, while it served to confirm the suspicions which he had already entertained of Jewalla Sing's treachery. After waiting, therefore, for about twenty-four hours to give time for his revolted servant to return to his duty, if so disposed, he put himself at the head of all the troops in and about Lahore, and attended by Rajah Dehan Sing and a numerous train of Sirdars, went forth against the contumacious Mooktear. He found Jewalla Sing at Shalimar, with his six thousand Gorechars drawn out as if for resistance; but on the Maharajh making his appearance in person, the Mooktear gave up all thought of resistance, and went forward to meet his angry master. He was then prevailed on to accompany the Maharajh and his attendants to Lahore, and on his arrival there, he was immediately heavily fettered and thrown into a deep dungeon, without being allowed an interview with the Maharajh or an opportunity of exculpating himself. Shere Sing relenting, would have given his old servant a hearing, but Rajah Dehan Sing took care to prevent this, and to widen the breach between them. Thus the unfortunate Jewalla Sing was kept fettered in his dungeon, the only food he was allowed being a daily ration of half a seer of flour, kneaded with on equal quantity of salt! He was likewise whipped every day, and had hot irons applied to the soles of his feet. To this cruel usage he was subjected for a month, but as he did not sink under it in that time, Dehán Sing obtained an order for his removal to the fort of Shaikoopur for a period of six months, as the minister said, by way of punishment. Hither he was accordingly sent, without having an interview with his master, and in about ten days after his arrival he died under the barbarous treatment which he experienced at the hands of his jailors, the tools of Rajah Dehan Sing. Some time afterwards Shere Sing was informed that he had died a natural death, and so no more was said or thought of the hapless Jewalla Sing.

When the fort of Lahore fell into the hands of Shere Sing, Rajah Goolaub Sing made it one of the conditions of surrender, that the person and property of the Ranee Chund Kour should be respected, and that to maintain her in suitable dignity, a jaghire of nine lakhs of rupees should be allowed to her. To these terms Shere Sing, at the persuasion of his minister, Dehan Sing, gave his consent, and as already mentioned, the jaghire assigned to Chund Kour was that of

Kuddee Kuddeeallee, a tract at the foot of the hills, reaching from Bhimber to the river Jhelum and adjacent to the districts held by Goolaub Sing. This chief had so far ingratiated himself with the Ranee that she had made him her Mooktear or confidential agent, and hence the management of all her property, including this jaghire, came into his hands, and as may be supposed, he turned the trust to the best advantage for himself. Chund Kour never got more out of this jaghire that was settled upon her, or out of the other property, than served her for a bare maintenance. She left the palace and the fort at Lahore, and went to reside in the house in the city formerly belonging to her late son, No Nehal Sing. She might have remained in the palace, as Shere Sing wished her to do, and have accepted of his offer to make her one of his wives by the process of *Chudur dalna*, or throwing the sheet over her, but for the intrigues of Golaub Sing, who well knew that if this came to pass, her jaghire and property would be taken out of his hands. He feared also that should she become the wife of Shere Sing, that prince would soon induce her to disclose secrets respecting the money and jewels which she herself had entrusted to Goolaub Sing to carry out of the fort on the occasion of its surrender, as well as regarding the treasure and valuables which he had carried away on his own account. He had but a frail and confiding woman to deal with, one whose only thought, unhappily, was how she might satisfy her thirst for pleasure; as, therefore, he promised her full scope in this matter and as much money as she might require on condition that she should not listen to the overtures of Shere Sing, who he said only wanted to lead her to her destruction, she readily consented to remove into the city, where she was assured of the protection of Goolaub Sing, and of his brother the Minister, who bound themselves by oath to be faithful to her interests.

Thus things went on for some months, Chund Kour implicitly relying on Goolaub's promises and acting on his advice. Shere Sing, meanwhile, was burning with rage on finding that Chund Kour not only refused his hand and protection, but that, as he was craftily persuaded by Dehan Sing, she scoffed at and scorned his pretensions. He was told that she had declared that he was either a fool or a madman to suppose that she, the daughter of the great Jeymull Sing, and of the famous house of the Kunnias, would ever think of allying herself with Shere Sing, the son of a washerman! Shere Sing, however, hindered her from living constantly in the city, and she was therefore compelled to divide her time betwixt the city and the fort, occasionally residing in the former, in the house of her late son. Thus matters stood when Shere Sing, with his whole Durbar, proceeded towards Wuzeerabad, on which occasion he left secret but strict orders with the slave-girls of Chund Kour to put her to death in his absence. To four of these slaves he promised jaghires of five thousand rupees each, in case of their fulfilling his commands; and these women were thereby induced to destroy their mistress by dashing out her brains with a heavy stone while they were engaged in dressing her hair. After committing this treacherous and cruel deed, the four slave-girls were made prisoners by some hill-men in the service of Dehan Sing, and Meean Sing, Shere Sing's thanadar in the fort, and on Dehan Sing's return he ordered that the hands of two of them should be cut off, one escaping through the aid of a faqueer, and the fourth being released in consideration of her giving a large sum as the ransom of her life. The murder was perpetrated in her house in the town, built by No Nihal Sing. By the death of the unfortunate princess, Shere Sing considered himself released from apprehension of future claim on his throne, but the event served the interests of Goolaub Sing still more than those of him who had directly brought it about, inasmuch as it gave him undisturbed possession of all the property of the deceased Chund Kour.

CHAPTER V.

THE ASSASSINATION OF SHERE SING AND DEHAN SING.

RAJAH GOOLAUB SING had but just arrived at Jummoo when his brother Dehan Sing, the Wuzeer, wrote to him, informing him of his differences with the Maharajh Shere Sing, and requesting him to repair to Lahore to consult on the policy to be adopted under the circumstances. He accordingly hastened to the capital, and after a very short stay, returned home again. In that brief visit, however, the line of conduct to be pursued was determined on by the brothers in consultation; and it will soon be seen what it was and how it was carried out.

Lena Sing, a chief of the Scindawalla family, had been imprisoned by Shere Sing for the part which he had taken against him on his accession. Uttur Sing and his nephew Ajeet Sing had taken refuge in the Company's territory at Tanaisur, from which place the latter went to Calcutta. They now, through female influence, and on the intercession of Bii Ram Sing,* were recalled from exile, and Lena Sing was released from confinement. On receiving

* This Bii Ram Sing, now for the first time appeared on the stage of political life. He never was a friend of Bii Goormuck Sing, whom he considered his rival in the favour of Shere Sing, and these two *religieux* understood each other so well that they cherished beneath their robes of sanctity an enmity too deep to meet the vulgar eye. Bii Goormuck Sing and Misser Belee Ram were united in policy, fate, and fortune; and Misser Belee Ram and his family were the deadly foes of Rajah Lall Sing and his family. Bii Ram Sing, on the other hand, was a staunch supporter of Lall Sing; perhaps, for the good reason that he was a protégé of the Dogra family, and they had a strong arm to uphold and assist him. Thus Bii Goormuck Sing and Misser Belee Ram were enemies of the Dogras, and Bii Ram Sing, through his alliance with Rajah Lall Sing, was their staunch friend. Be-

the order for their recall, accompanied by private assurances of safety from Bii Ram Sing, Ajeet Sing and Lena Sing returned to Lahore, but Uttur Sing went at once to his jaghire. On the arrival of the Scindawallas at Lahore, Bii Ram Sing became the medium of private communication betwixt them and Rajah Dehan Sing. The Minister endeavoured, successfully, to impress upon them a belief, that it was by his means and influence they were recalled and restored to the possession of their former jaghires and lands. He showed them the utmost confidence and consideration, and acted his part so well with them that they became the staunchest friends of him and his party, and ready to become, as he intended they should be, the tools and instruments of his plan. Further, he represented to them, in glowing colours, the baseness of Shere Sing, who, he said, however kind he might outwardly appear to them, was at heart their implacable enemy, and would, were it not for his, Dehan Sing's, presence and influence, exhibit his hatred towards them in ill usage. Thus were the Scindawallas prepared to execute the Minister's purpose. These private intrigues were carried on for some time, and the Scindawallas were enabled plainly to see into the real state of affairs, and to perceive the rancorous enmity that existed betwixt Shere Sing and his Minister, and the danger to which the Maharajh was exposed.

It was shortly after Goolaub Sing's hasty visit to Lahore, and the consultation betwixt the brothers, that Dehan Sing appeared to become aware that there was in existence a reputed

---

sides this, as has been before said, Bii Ram Sing envied and hated Bii Goormuck Sing as a successful rival in the favour of the sovereign, and had thus a purely personal motive to join in any plan that might lead to his downfal. He likewise indulged a deep hate against the Maharajh for exhibiting a preference for his rival; and this was a direct reason for his allying himself with Shere Sing's enemies. He, then, at the instigation of the Dogras, in his character of a holy man. prevailed on the favourite women of Shere Sing to beg an order for the recall of the Scindawallas.

son of Runjeet Sing, a child of five or six years of age, whom it now suited his purpose to consider the rightful heir to the throne, and whose cause he determined to espouse. This child was now frequently sent for by the Minister, who fondled and caressed it, and made a great shew of respect for it. In this conduct Shere Sing saw evidence that he had nothing more to expect from his *quondam* friend and upholder. He, therefore, strove in many ways to get rid of him; but the Rajah was not so to be shaken off. The Maharajh was no match for the subtle enemy who was now planning his ruin. Thus matters proceeded until the Scindawallas, seeing how affairs stood, thought that the opportunity presented itself of doing something for their own aggrandisement, at the expense of both the sovereign and his Minister. They well knew that they were regarded with suspicion by Shere Sing, whom they considered as an upstart and an usurper; and they were fully aware that the Minister admitted them to his friendship solely for the purpose of making them his tools and would afterwards cast them off, perhaps even cause their ruin and death, without scruple.

Having concocted their plans, the Scindawalla brothers first waited on Shere Sing, and in a private conference told him, with apparent candour, that as his loyal subjects, and as his brethren in caste, religion, and family, they could not refrain from putting him on his guard against the machinations and designs of his Minister. Then, having prevailed on the Maharajh to take an oath of secrecy, they assured him that they were actually commissioned by the Minister to assassinate him, Shere Sing; and that for this business they had been promised a jaghire of sixty lakhs, that they should be the guardians of Dulleep Sing, the child whom it was proposed to place on the *guddee*, and that while Dehan Sing was ostensible minister, they should be the actual regents during the minority of the new Maharajh. This declaration, made with such confidence, had no other effect on Shere Sing, a brave and intrepid man and a good soldier, than to excite his indignation against his treacherous Minister.—"Here," said he, drawing his sword, and offering it to the Scindawalla Sirdars, Lena Sing and Ajeet Sing,—"here, if you have orders to slay me, and are willing to commit such an act, here is my own sword! But, remember one thing,—not many days will pass before you will be treated in the same manner by the men who now make you their tools." At these words the Scindawallas appeared affected and astonished, and asked the Maharajh if he really believed they could act in such a manner;—they said that they had come, not to destroy, but to save him. They assured him of their devotion to him, and proposed that as the just punishment of the Minister's evil and treacherous intentions they should put him to death immediately. This alone, they assured the Maharajh, would ensure his safety, for that if the Minister were allowed to live any longer, he would certainly find means to execute his murderous designs on his master. Shere Sing with seeming reluctance agreed to their proposal, and they took care to obtain a writing under his signature, exonerating them from all the guilt of an act which was represented as necessary for the safety of the state.

Having made these arrangements the Scindawallas explained to Shere Sing that they would now retire for awhile to a place called Rajah Sansee, near Umritsir, there to prepare themselves and a party of their chosen soldiers for the enterprise which they had in hand, and that thence they would return to him shortly, under the pretence of performing their *hazaree*, or a strict inspection of their troops, which the Maharajh was to order. At this review they were all to appear in the best order they could assume, fully armed and accoutred, with matches lit, and to go through the matchlock exercise before the Maharajh, who was then to call on Dehan Sing to come forward and examine the troops. Then at a signal agreed upon, they would immediately surround both him and his son Heera Sing and shoot them to death. They told the Maharajh thus much, they said, that he might on their return from Rajah Sansee be ready and willing to meet them, and that no suspicions should prevent his acting the part assigned him.

Having thus settled matters with Shere Sing, the Scindawallas took their leave, proposing to start next morning for Rajah Sansee as had been agreed on. They went, however, straight to the house of the Minister, and in a private interview with him, and after some oaths of secrecy and other preliminaries, they exhibited to him his death warrant, signed by the Maharajh himself. Seeing the effect this produced on the mind of Dehan Sing, they proposed that they should put Shere Sing to death. To this the Minister readily and fully agreed, and made them great promises of reward and favour in case of their success. Now, therefore, they made with him arrangements precisely similar to those which they had settled with the Maharajh, or rather the same arrangement was adopted, the intended victim only being changed. They, however, went so much further as to instruct Dehan Sing by his influence with the army to cause the posting of such troops about the palace on the day appointed for the tragedy as should be no hindrance to the work in hand. The Scindawallas then took their leave of the Minister, and next morning as had been agreed on, marched for Rajah Sansee. Here they remained a few days, and then returned, attended by some five or six hundred cavalry, all chosen men, well armed and equipped. While they were absent, Rajah Dehan, under pretence of sickness, had secluded himself in his house in the city, while Shere Sing was residing at Shahbelore, three miles east of the city. The day on which the Scindawallas returned was the first of the month, and their approach to Shahbelore was announced early in the morning by the firing of the troops, as they went through a variety of exercises with their matchlocks—discharging them while at full speed, &c. On approaching the Maharajh's mansion at Shahbelore, the brothers, Ajeet Sing and Lena Sing, with a chosen party dismounted and entered the house, the Scindawallas having the privilege of doing so uninvited and unannounced. Being the first of the month there had been no durbar, and as they presented themselves with about fifty followers, who like themselves were armed and in armour, Shere Sing was just dismissing with presents some *athletes* who had been wrestling before him. They all made their obeisances to the Maharajh, who received them with a free and courteous air, being of course totally unconscious of any harm. Shere Sing quite unarmed, was reclining easily in his chair, when Ajeet Sing approached him and exhibiting a handsome double-barrelled fowling piece for his inspection, said in a loud and laughing manner, "See here! a piece which I bought for fourteen hundred rupees; I would not now take three thousand for it." On this the Maharajh stretched out his hand to receive the gun. It was loaded with two balls in each barrel, and both locks were at full cock. As Ajeet Sing handed it to Shere Sing, he, by an almost imperceptible and apparently unintentional movement, brought its muzzles to bear on the breast of the Maharajh, and fired—both barrels almost together. The unfortunate Shere Sing fell back in his chair, a corpse, the only words he uttered before he expired being—"*Ei ka dugga?*" "What treachery is this?" His head was immediately cut off, and such of his servants as made a shew of resistance were shot or cut down. The assassins then hastened to the garden, where the eldest son of the murdered king, a youth of thirteen or fourteen years old, was at his devotions. Lena Sing, with his sword drawn advanced towards the boy, who, alarmed at his ferocious and threatening looks, threw himself at his feet, and implored him as his uncle to spare his life. But the Sirdar, paying no more attention to his words than to reply to them scoffingly—"An uncle at such a time!" with one blow severed the lad's head from his body.

The party then quickly retired, and joining their comrades, who had waited outside while this bloody business was being transacted, about three hundred horse and two hundred and fifty foot, under the command of Ajeet Sing, went off at a smart pace towards Lahore; while Lena Sing with the rest, about two hundred cavalry, slowly followed. When about half way to Lahore the party under Ajeet Sing met the Minister with a few followers proceeding easily towards Shahbelore. Ajeet Sing saluting him told him that every thing was settled as he desired, that there was no occasion for his going any further, and requested him to turn back and accompany him to the fort, there to settle matters, to hold a council, to call the Sirdars, and make good all his promises. Suspicion seemed to flash across the Minister's mind, for he glanced at his escort as if to see how many men he had with him; and finding that he was greatly outnumbered, he had no option, but was obliged to agree to the Sirdar's proposal. He, therefore, concealed his suspicions as well as he was able, and with as frank and cheerful an air as he could assume, turned back with Ajeet Sing. Ere they had proceeded far the Scindawalla, knowing that every thing depended on his early arrival at the fort, proposed that they should quicken their pace, and, without waiting for Dehan Sing's assent, set off at a rapid rate. This soon brought them to the outer gate of the fort, which Ajeet Sing entered, accompanied by the Minister, and about five or six hundred soldiers. At the second gate in obedience to certain signs, most of the Minister's attendants were refused admittance, while all Ajeet Sing's entered. Dehan Sing's suspicions were now strongly excited, and he looked round to see how many of his men were with him. Ajeet Sing, however, attempted to divert his attention from what was going on, by keeping him in conversation on indifferent subjects. Still by his tone and manner the Minister knew that there was something wrong; but he was conscious that it would do no good to manifest anything like fear. He could not, however, refrain from asking Ajeet Sing who the men were whom he saw on the battlements of the fort; to which enquiry the Scindawalla replied that they were all friends, being his own followers. At this moment, while the Minister's attention was directed to these men on the walls of the fort, he received a shot from behind, discharged from a large rifle, and fired on a signal being given by Ajeet Sing with his finger. Immediately he received another shot from a blunderbuss, and then he was cut and hacked with swords. But he was a corpse at the first fire. A Mahomedan, one of the few attendants with the Minister, was the only one who made any resistance, and he was immediately cut down, and his body with that of his master thrown into the rubbish pit of the gun-foundry in the fort.

All this was just over when Lena Sing and his party arrived. On learning what had been done, Lena Sing reproved his brother for his hasty conduct. His own plan was to entice the son and brother of the Minister, Rajahs Heera Sing and Suchet Sing, into the fort, and then to destroy them all at once. Now he found that things would go against them, as Heera Sing and Suchet Sing were at large, and, taking the alarm, would raise the whole body of the troops for their defence, and to punish the murderers of the Maharajh and his Wuzeer. The Scindawallas, however, were not disheartened, and they resolved to do what they could to complete the business which they had begun. They therefore sent an express to Buddhoo ko ava, where the Rajahs were with the troops, informing them that the Minister and the Scindawallas were in the fort in close consultation on state affairs, and politely requesting their attendance. This message was first sent in the

Minister's name, but the Rajahs and their advisers, the principal of whom was Rae Kisseree Sing, who afterwards fell gallantly fighting by the side of Rajah Śuchet Sing, were too cunning to be easily deceived. They therefore sent answer that they would be very happy to obey the summons, but that it should come in the Minister's own hand-writing or bearing his signature. Thus failing to entrap them by subtlety, the Scindawallas sent five hundred horsemen to bring them by force. This measure, however, and the absence of the required written summons from Dehan Sing, had only the effect of confirming the suspicions of the Rajahs, that evil was intended; and therefore collecting around them as many of the troops as they could, they presented such a threatening front to the cavalry sent by the Scindawallas, that these latter deemed it prudent to return to the fort as they went.

In another hour the death of the Maharajh and his Minister became publicly known by means of some of those who had escaped and spread the news. On the receipt of this intelligence, Rajah Heera Sing and the Pundit Jella displayed the most contemptible pusillanimity, the former in particular; he threw himself on the ground in despair, crying like a child, until he was brought to a sense of propriety by the upbraidings of the brave Kisseree Sing. A consultation was now held as to the course to be pursued, and the result was that the chiefs present separated, and went among the troops to excite them to take vengeance on the murderers of their sovereign and his Wuzeer. So well did they play their parts on this emergency, that they speedily induced the whole Khalsa force to side with them. As a specimen of the manner in which this was done, the conduct of Rajah Heera Sing may be described. Assembling the troops he placed himself in their front, and unbuckling his sword and shield addressed them thus:—"I was brought up from my infancy by the great Maharajh Runjeet Sing, as his adopted son, and I am now about to be slain as my father has this day been by the Scindawallas, who have murdered your King, and his Minister, my dear father. And now listen, soldiers, they have done all this only because while they were in Hindostan, they made traitorous alliances with the British. They then agreed to do all this that has this day been done,—to call in the British and to deliver the country into their hands. In pursuance of this purpose they have, since this morning, sent off ten or twelve expresses in the direction of Ferozepore and Loodiana to inform the British authorities of their success here; and now if some bold and energetic steps are not immediately taken by you, you will, before three days have passed, hear of forty or fifty thousand British troops having crossed the Sutlej. If the British come and obtain their purpose, they will disband the entire Khalsa army. Yes! you will be compelled to give up your arms, and to go every man to his home. Your invincible power, your great and glorious name, will be lost in oblivion, and disgrace will be your lot. You will moreover, be so impoverished that you will have to seek, and seek in vain, an ignoble maintenance from the plough!* Soldiers, if you would avert this humiliation listen to me. The old king's coffers are yet full, but, believe me, I have no occasion to resort to them; my own, my father's, and my uncle's wealth is sufficient to keep up an army of a hundred thousand good and loyal Seiks for a hundred years, and I here solemnly promise that it shall all to the last fraction be expended on you. It is all yours and for your use. Now I here solemnly promise, and if necessary will confirm my word by an oath, that henceforth your pay shall be encreased one-half—each foot soldier shall receive twelve rupees a month, and every horseman one rupee a day. Listen to me, follow my instructions, and

* This was a leaf from his father Dehan Sing's political pocket-book, by an opportune reference to which the minister had often turned the Khalsa to his purpose.

by one unanimous effort, we will not only secure our country from danger, and ourselves from disgrace, but will also punish the Scindawallas for their treason and cruelty—the traitors to their race, religion, and country—the murderers of their prince and of his Minister!"* This was enough, the impatient troops would listen to no more,—they asked to be led wherever he pleased—to death or victory. They bade Heera Sing return to his own camp at Buddhoo ko ava to prepare for his enterprise, while they would quickly make ready one and all to wreak their just vengeance on the treacherous Scindawallas. Heera Sing told them to be ready to march at a moment's warning, but not to move too hastily, or without orders, and that in due time he would lead them on. But so eager and impatient were the soldiers, that though one-half of the number were at that moment engaged in cooking and preparing their evening meal, they made the drummers, fifers, and trumpeters, sound to arms; and where any one was slow in falling into the ranks, he was struck by his comrades, and some who delayed too long over their cooking utensils were knocked down with the butt-ends of muskets. In such precipitate haste did the army assemble to execute the design which it had so suddenly formed, that the cooking apparatus was left scattered about on the plain and in the camp. Thus by incessant sounding to arms, by hurrying and threatening the dilatory as well as their own immediate officers, the troops, infantry, cavalry, and artillery, were in an incredibly short time formed in line and ready to march against the traitorous Scindawallas. About forty thousand men now awaited but the order of Rajah Heera Sing to do his bidding and to hurl destruction on his enemies and the murderers of his father. However, it suited his purpose to keep them awaiting till after sun-set.

* This was all put down to Rajah Heera Sing, but it must be remembered that Rae Kisseree Sing was his prompter and encourager, and the chief instrument in bringing over the troops.

CHAPTER VI.

PUNISHMENT OF THE MURDERERS.

WHILE Heera Sing was making arrangements for avenging his father's death the Scindawallas were using every effort, by bribes and presents, to win over to their side all the troops and artillery stationed in the city and round the fort. They remained however, unwisely and unfortunately as it afterwards appeared, shut up in the fort, sending for the chiefs and leaders of the troops to come to them, and to assist them in attempting to work upon the soldiery. Had they, as Heera Sing and his party did, and as it was known that they did, gone among the troops personally, there is little doubt that they would have effected their purpose. As it was they failed. From the officers, indeed, they received oaths and assurances of support in return for their presents and promises, but the hopes thus excited were very imperfectly realised.

If instead of this they had gone among the soldiers, and used their eloquence in persuading them of their loyalty to the crown and their patriotism to their country, and to have dissipated the suspicion that they were in league with the British, they might with the aid of some few promises have gained their object without the immediate expenditure of a rupee. For as being true Seiks, of kin to royalty, being well known as good soldiers, and having in the army many friends and even some relations, they had great advantages over the Dogras who were looked on with jealousy as foreigners and upstarts, and who only kept themselves in favour with the army by the promise or payment of large sums of money, and by the trick of keeping themselves always before the eyes of the troops as the inveterate enemies of the British and devoted patriots in the cause of their country.

In order to conceal the death of the Wuzeer, the Scindawallas had in the early part of the day caused it to be proclaimed through the city that Dulleep Sing was now king and Dehan Sing was Minister; but finding soon that the murder of the Rajah was no longer a secret, they boldly proclaimed Dulleep Sing as king, and Lena Sing Scindawalla as Wuzeer.

The Seiks were little moved by the death of Shere Sing, at which indeed they rather rejoiced, as he had by the crafty policy of his Minister been made for some time to appear to the troops in the light of a harsh and severe disciplinarian; the object of this misrepresentation being to render him odious to the troops, and to enable Dehan Sing, by exhibiting himself as their friend and advocate, to strengthen his claims on their favour.

About an hour after sunset Rajah Heera Sing, with the Khalsa troops, and about a hundred pieces of horse artillery approached the city. About the same time or a little earlier, the Scindawallas, seemingly in the hope of appeasing the rage of the Seiks, sent out the body of Rajah Dehan Sing, sprinkled with rose-water, well scented, and wrapped up in a handsome Cashmere shawl; and with it they sent their assurances that the Minister was killed accidentally by one of their soldiers and entirely without their orders. They further expressed a hope that his death would not be looked upon as the effect of enmity or malice on their part, as they had borne no ill will towards the Minister, and were sincerely and heartily sorry for the untoward occurrence that had caused his death. In support of this assertion they showed also the dead body of the soldier of their party who had been killed by the Mahomedan who resisted the attack on Dehan Sing, declaring that this was the corpse of the mad or mutinous soldier who had killed the Rajah, and who had been instantly cut down by their own hands. All this was well designed and skilfully executed, but it did not effect the object of mollifying the troops or turning them from their purpose. The main body of the army marched towards the city, and their appearance was announced by the noise and tumult which they caused as they entered the eastern gates, each corps actually struggling with those next it for the foremost position. The fierce war cry *Wah Gooroo jee ko Futteh!* resounded through the city. The old fort was again invested and encircled by the infuriated mob of armed men, and the artillery was quickly at work beating down the feeble and tottering walls. Within the fort no means appeared to have been used for annoying or repelling the besiegers, and their artillery was, as in the former siege, drawn up close to the place and quite uncovered and unprotected. The besieged, though only about a thousand or eleven hundred in number, might, like the Dogra garrison on the former occasion, have silenced the guns and driven the enemy from them, for they were almost entirely picked marksmen. But no effort was made to return or silence the fire of the besiegers, and in consequence, before the dawn of the following day, several practicable breaches had been made in the walls. Now, however, Rajah Heera Sing sent for all the artillery officers, and by promises and presents induced them to undertake to effect one large and perfect breach through which the assault might be made with ease and success. To other inducements he added an oath that he would neither eat nor drink until he had feasted his eyes with looking on the dead bodies of those who had murdered his father. This declaration, with the presents and promises which he had lavished on them, was enough to excite the artillery to use their utmost skill and diligence to effect the purpose that he had enjoined on them. But there was still another and a stronger incitement which urged them on to the work more effectually even than the bounties and entreaties of the Rajah. The great body of the Khalsa troops, though they had themselves plundered above half the city, and had been well plied with presents by Heera Sing, were promised also the plunder of the fort, when they should have brought to him the dead bodies of his enemies the Scindawallas. The result was that the troops by threats and persuasions urged the artillerymen to incessant and greater zeal and diligence in their work. Hence by the time that the day was two or three hours advanced, a large breach, declared practicable, had been made in and near the tower at the S. W. angle of the fort.

By this time the widow of the murdered Minister and her female slaves were preparing to mount the funeral pyre with his corpse. But Rajah Heera Sing craftily delayed the immolation of his step-mother and her women, keeping them waiting in the presence of the troops, whose fury against the murderers of Dehan Sing was increased tenfold by the scene. The Rajah had it also publicly proclaimed that not only would he not eat or drink till the assassins were slain, but that the widowed Ranee would not mount the pile till she had beheld the severed heads of her husband's murderers. On this the troops wildly and clamorously demanded orders to advance; but ere these were given they had rushed forward, forty or forty-five thousand men, infantry and dismounted cavalry,—and were soon clinging and clustering about the breach like bees at the entrance of their hive. They quickly effected a good footing in the fort, and doubtless concluded that as they had met with no opposition hitherto their prize was won. But now the little garrison seemed to have shaken of its lethargy, and a resistance so fierce was offered as for a time appalled the host of Seiks. But as the close and deadly struggle continued, the superior numbers of the besiegers secured them the advantage. The loss of a thousand men on their side would hardly have been felt; but when so many of the small band who defended the place had bit the dust, the garrison was almost annihilated. Thus in about an hour all was lost, and further resistance out of the question. Ajeet Sing Scindawalla, now attempted to escape by getting over the walls, but he was seen and recognised by some soldiers outside, who regardless of the lavish promises which he made to induce them to spare his life, slew him immediately, and cutting off his head ran with it to Heera Sing, who, in his savage joy, rewarded them with many valuable presents of money, jewels, and even jaghires. The head of Ajeet Sing was then laid at the feet of Dehan Sing's widow, who on beholding it exclaimed, "Now I am fully satisfied. Now I am ready to follow my lord and husband; and," said she, addressing Heera Sing, "I will tell your dear father that you have acted the part of a brave and dutiful son." Saying this, she, followed by her women, ascended the pile, talking at the same time with the most perfect composure, ordering her affairs, making presents and giving alms. Her last act was to place the *kulgee* or warrior's plume of her late husband in the turban of her step-son Heera Sing. This done, she placed herself in a reclining posture on the pile, with her women, thirteen in number, around her; then with a smiling and joyful face she took leave of all around, and lastly in a proud and lofty tone she commanded that the torch should be applied. Her command was obeyed, and soon nothing remained but an undistinguishable heap of glowing embers.

An affecting episode in this fearful scene may be here related. A female child of ten years old, a slave-girl from the hills, an attendant on the widowed Ranee, was pronounced by all, including her mistress, to be too young to perform the rite of suttee with the elder women. The Ranee, therefore, fondly caressing her, and ordering her a liberal provision, gave her in charge to her step-son, Heera Sing, with the strictest injunctions to take care of her. But the child would not live; three times she threw herself on the pile, imploring her mistress to let her share her fate. With an energy beyond her years, she loudly protested by the dead and murdered corpse before her, that if she was not allowed to die now, she would by some other means put an end to her life. On this the Ranee and all around seeing her resolutely bent on performing the suttee, and that to prevent her doing so would be to no purpose, reluctantly allowed her to share the fate of her mistress and her older companions. The Ranee took her and placed her at her feet, while the others reclined around their mistress, who lay with the head of her husband in her lap,—the torch was applied to the pile, and the living and the dead were alike reduced to ashes.

The fight being over in the fort, the plunder, which had continued some time, was stayed by order of Heera Sing, and a search was made for Lena Sing Scindawalla who had disappeared from the strife, and was not found among the dead. This chief was soon found hid in a dark and secret subterranean chamber or cell to which with a broken thigh he had retired the night before. He was attended by one faithful follower, who defended his master to the last, but all in vain. The name of this gallant man was Rah Sing, a strong and large-bodied Seik of abont fifty years old. On being recognised as he stood sword in hand at the entrance of his master's retreat, he was repeatedly entreated both by Lena Sing and his enemies to sheath his weapon and make his escape, while he might do so. But he disdainfully refused to avail himself of the forbearance of the enemy, requesting only that they should not fire at him, and the Seiks, knowing him, and honoring his bravery, actually complied with his request. They, however, rushed on him with their swords, and after killing thirteen of them he himself fell covered with wounds. His dying petition was only that they would not kill his wounded master, and to this request also they promised compliance. But some bad spirit among them shot Lena Sing from behind, exclaiming as he did so, "Are we going to lose ten thousand rupees!" but this man was immediately killed by his own comrades. They however, cut off the head of the fallen chief and sent it to Heera Sing, who doubtless gave them the stipulated reward. Four hours later the victorious troops returned to their lines, and the public acclamations pronounced Dulleep Sing, Maharajh, and Heera Sing, Wuzeer.

The next day all the officers of the army were assembled, and Heera Sing gave them a written agreement of one month's pay for the whole of the troops as a gratuity for their services, and he likewise assured them of an augmentation of pay as promised. On the fourth day a general council of the army was called, at which all the Seik officers with two men from each company as Punches* or deputies attended.

---

* The designation *Punches* is here used in compliment to general usage, but at Lahore it is *Painches*. It may be well here to describe the origin of the custom of appointing deputies by the soldiers, a practice which has on more than one occasion, including that of the late war with the British, led to the most momentous results. On Shere Sing's accession the soldiers clamorously demanded the fulfilment of those promises which he had made, and which Rajah Dehan Sing had made in his name. Now, therefore, the pay of each foot soldier was raised from eight rupees a month to nine, and a gratuity of one month's pay, after some demur accepted by the troops, who had in fact been promised four months' gratuity. In lieu, however, of three months' gratuity, which was withheld, they demanded leave to attack and plunder the camp of Goolaub Sing, who was then after his withdrawal from the fort lying at Shahdera. They even threatened, that if permission to do this was refused, they would do it without. But luckily for Goolaub Sing and his little army, they had on the day he left the fort been reinforced by the arrival of a strong body of men from Jummoo, and being now in all about five thousand, they were able to make such a show of resistance and even of aggression, that the Seiks, some sixty thousand in number, watched to attack them Thus cheated on the one hand and baffled on the other, the Khalsa was, as may be supposed, in no pleasant mood. To appease them, however, Shere Sing and Dehan Sing went among them, and told them, that if they would send to the Durbar, in the Soomun Boorj, two men from every company, troop, and gun, they, the Maha-

The officers and Punches of the army being assembled at the Hazooreebagh, Heera Sing told them that he had summoned them to decide on the best means of tranquilising and governing the country, and that they might choose and appoint a

---

rajah and his Minister, would consult with them as the representatives of the whole army. It was further proposed by Shere Sing and the Wuzeer, that all the officers of the army should be present at this conference, and orders were accordingly issued for their attendance; but the soldiery would not agree to this, and to secure the absence of their officers, they put them under a kind of arrest until the consultation was over and its results declared. The meeting of this council was, as the Seiks themselves express it, *the birth-day of the Painches*. The deputies set forth all the claims and demands of the army, and the Durbar proposed measures for their satisfaction; but nothing was definitively settled, as the Painches declared that they would do nothing without consulting their brethren. In two days, however, matters assumed a more pacific aspect, and Shere Sing once more ventured to present himself in the Seik camp. When he did so the soldiers gathered around him declaring, that though they were well satisfied with the arrangements that had been made, there remained one matter yet which required to be settled. They stated, that during the time of Runjeet Sing many of their officers, aided by the moonshees or writers, had treated them in such a manner by fraud and extortion, that they could no longer consent to be commanded by them. They, therefore, demanded that the officers indicated should be either posted to other corps willing to receive them, or be dismissed from the service altogether. Shere Sing, inconsiderately, it may be, gave them full permission to act as they thought fit in the matter, and to select or reject the officers as they pleased. On this great confusion ensued, arising out of the conflicting opinions of the Painches as to which officers should be kept and which dismissed. One corps refused to take these officers, and another refused to give up those which were demanded by a third; and so a fierce contention arose among them which went so far that the drums of some battalions beat to arms, and there seemed every likelihood of a fierce and bloody strife ensuing. Shere Sing, however, to restore order and to extricate himself from the dangerous position in which he found himself, after having with some difficulty obtained a hearing, requested them to convene an orderly and regular meeting of their Painches, and therein to settle the matter amicably and quietly. Having given this advice, which had the immediate effect of restoring order, for the moment at least, he took the opportunity of withrawing from among the unruly mob of soldiers, and as he departed, uttered the words, "*Kucha pucka samalo!*" "Good or bad settle the matter among yourselves." These words had the effect of preventing strife among the soldiers, but they were the death warrant of many an unfortunate officer and moonshee. Shere Sing had not reached the city ere the troops had murdered many of their officers and moonshees, shooting some, cutting down others, and even burning some of them alive, rolled up in scarfs! Others were bound, gagged, beaten, and thrown into prison. When once the fierce lust of vengeance was let loose, Shere Sing found it vain to attempt to check it either by threats or promises. Hence

Wuzeer to conduct the affairs of the state. For himself, he said, he was unwilling to undertake the office, assigning as his reason that the enemies of himself and his family would impede and obstruct his administration. Nothing but a solemn guarantee on the part of the troops of their zealous and constant attachment to him and obedience to his orders, would induce him, he said, to accept an office so dangerous and unenviable. This declaration had its desired and expected effect. The officers and the deputies at once and unanimously declared that he and he alone should be the Minister of their choice. Dulleep Sing, they said, was their lawful sovereign, and only Heera Sing should be his Wuzeer; and they then and there promised and declared that they would at his bidding destroy any one who might venture to oppose or thwart him in any way whatsoever. His

---

for days the soldiers were seen going about hunting for their victims who had concealed themselves from their murderous rage. With such deadly enmity did they pursue the moonshees in particular, that even in the streets of Lahore they were heard to declare that they would kill every man, woman, and child, who could either read or write Persian, the language in which the moonshees kept the pay accounts. Thus in the very city any man who had the misfortune to look like a moonshee, if he appeared abroad was almost certain of being either shot or cut down without inquiry as to who or what he was. In cases in which the pursuers were doubtful as to the calling of their victim, they would search and examine him, and if they found upon him writing implements, or if his hands were soft and silky and fingers long and tapering, his doom was sealed,—without further parley he was put to death. Nor did the families of the moonshees escape, their houses were sacked and burnt, and their inmates tortured and ill used, in a manner that it is fearful to think upon. This may serve to shew the state and condition of the Seik army at the time when the Painches established themselves as its representatives. It may be mentioned also, that only one of the two deputies from each company possessed, much power or influence; these were called the head Painches, while the others were styled Kurr Painches, and were looked on as mere assistants or tools of their principals, and their business was chiefly to go among the soldiery and to stir them up to any thing that their chiefs might desire. The head Painches soon got into their own hands the virtual command of the army, and consequently almost the entire power of the state; for as they had the means of causing the removal of obnoxious officers, the leaders of the army were entirely at their command. This power they turned to their own advantage on every opportunity, selling appointments to the highest bidder, and receiving bribes from opposing parties only to side with the strongest when the hour of trial came.

wishes should be theirs, and whatever line of policy he might adopt, he had only to mention it to them, and they were ready to support it; and that when force was required for the execution of any part of that policy, he had only to give them the word and his will should be wrought; and by way of testifying their sincerity, they then on the spot proposed the murder or imprisonment of certain sirdars who were suspected of being privy to the conspiracy of the Scindawallas. By this as well as by their oaths and promises, Heera Sing was convinced that his purpose was fully supported; and he now, but with apparent reluctance, agreed to accept the office of Wuzeer.

Since the death of Shere Sing and his Wuzeer Dehan Sing, money and valuable property had been profusely lavished among the soldiery, and the pay of most of the officers had been advanced threefold. Horses, elephants, carriages, costly jewellery, stored up by Runjeet Sing were now scattered abroad in the most reckless profusion. Instances were known even of officers having chosen for themselves the best horses and elephants in the old king's stables, positively refusing to accept any other. In short the most licentious wishes, the most avaricious desires of the Khalsa, men and officers, seemed now fulfilled, and nothing which they coveted was withheld from them. But to effect this the treasures of money and property that had been accumulated by Runjeet Sing for many years, were so far drained that if not quite emptied it would at least take as many years of a policy like Runjeet's to restore them to their former condition. During the first two months after Shere Sing's death, betwixt thirty-five and forty lakhs of rupees were, it is said, abstracted from the treasury. But though so much money and valuables were lavished on the soldiery, it is thought that it was not more than perhaps an eighth part of what Heera Sing took to himself.

CHAPTER VII.

BIRTH AND PARENTAGE OF DULLEEP SING.

THOUGH the unfortunate Kurruck Sing was, as is believed, the only true son of Runjeet Sing, there were several others whom he permitted to use that designation, though it was well known they were not his children. Thus, Shere Sing, who afterwards came to the Guddee, and who was a reputed son of the old Maharajh by Metaub Kour, was in reality the son of a dhobee, or washerman, who afterwards rose to be mooktear to the princess. Tara Sing, again, said to be a twin brother of Sheer Sing, was the son of a carpenter. Multana Sing was the son of a slave-woman in the service of Mai Nekeen, the wife of Runjeet and mother of Kurruck Sing, his father being a farash or attendant on the Zenana. Lahora Sing was also the child of a slave-woman, and as was supposed of Boodh Sing Scindawalla. These two were imposed upon Runjeet by Neet Kour, widow of Cheyt Sing, former chief of Lahore, whom Runjeet on her hushand's death had taken into his Zenana, but who, for her profligacy, he afterwards discarded. It was on this occasion that for the purpose of obtaining from him a better provision than she could otherwise have claimed, she brought forward these children as those of the Maharajh and herself. Peshora Sing and Cashmera Sing were also the sons of two slave-women in attendance on the widow of Sahib Sing, their fathers being Joy Ram, a buneah, and the other a munass, a caste of Rajpoot about Jummoo, and then were adopted by the youngest Ranee as her offspring, when Runjeet gave them Seealkote as a jageer.

Dulleep Sing, the last of the reputed children of the old monarch, had, as is well known, as little claim to such dignified paternity as any of them. A somewhat larger space must, however, be accorded to the history of his birth and parentage, which must also include that of his mother, the far-famed Ranee Chunda.

Munnoo Sing, a poor jat of the Oolak caste, and a native of Gujerawalla, or a small village in its vicinity, at an early age entered the service of Runjeet Sing as a dog-keeper; but, after about fifteen years' faithful service in this humble office, he was raised to the station of a door-keeper. He was, however, always regarded as a sort of buffoon, and in that character was privileged to exercise such wit as he possessed at the expense of the Maharajh and his chiefs even in public durbar. This man was constantly telling Runjeet that he had a daughter, the most beautiful creature in the world, whom he would give to the Maharajh as his wife, and that she would make the old monarch young again. After some time he produced the little girl, and for months carried her on his shoulders to the durbar, or wherever Runjeet went. The old chief is said to have been pestered day and night by Munnoo Sing and his importunities; but for some time he treated the matter as a joke and nothing more. Yet he was vain enough to be pleased with the idea that Munnoo and others should believe and call him a fine able *jewan* or young man; and he felt some pride in being the object of the facetious remarks of the court and town, on the occasion of his anticipated nuptials with a girl who might pass for his great-grand-child. At length, whether out of one of those whims, which were so characteristic of the old Lion, or out of consideration to poor Munnoo, who had taken so much trouble on his account, or to put an end to the buffoonery of which he was the object, he one day eased the shoulders of his would-be father-in-law by committing the girl to the care of one Jewahir Mull, a rich Hindoo merchant of Umritsir, once Governor of Cashmere, and then in attendance at the Maharajh's Court. This man received orders to take the young Chunda home with him, and to rear her up at his house in Umritsir. Munnoo was overjoyed at this happy result of his labours, and in his exultation ventured to tell the Maharajh that as the world had now recognized him, Munnoo, as his father-in-law, it mattered little whether *he* did so or not. On this Runjeet told him, as he had often done before, that he was nothing better than a downright Booroowah—*anglicé,* a pimp.

However, the young Chunda was sent to Umritsir, where she remained for four or five years in the house of Jewahir Mull. There she might have remained in quiet much longer, her guardian receiving for her maintenance forty-five rupees a month—but that she had even at so early an age won for herself a character for pertness, forwardness, and something even worse. So loose and immodest was her conduct that Jewahir Mull, fearing perhaps that the contagion of her vices might spread to the members of his own virtuous family, informed the Maharajh that he could not allow the young Chunda to remain in his house any longer. As a reason for praying to be released of his charge, he represented, that though the girl was then only thirteen or fourteen years of age, she was in criminal intercourse not only with one Jewahir Sing Bussthenee, whose house adjoined his own, but that she had more than one paramour in the very bazars of Umritsir. This Jewahir Sing Bussthenee, a young man and a servant of the Maharajh, when questioned on the matter, candidly confessed all, and that to Runjeet Sing himself. The old monarch was well pleased to have such disclosures made in the presence of the girl's father, Munnoo Sing, whose confusion he enjoyed. Moreover, anticipating considerable amusement from that pertness and forwardness which the girl was said to exhibit, and from her generally precocious character, Runjeet readily consented to relieve Jewahir Mull of his charge, and the young lady was brought to Lahore to enliven the night scenes in the palace. Here she enacted a character almost similar to that which her father had performed before her, that of a licensed buffoon, her business being to put to shame all, both men and women, who were in any degree less depraved or less shameless than herself.

Numerous were the amours in which she was now engaged, some *with*, others *without* the knowledge and consent of the Maharajh. To give a detail of these affairs and of scenes acted in the presence of the old Chief himself and at his instigation, would be an outrage on common decency; suffice it then to say, that Runjeet actually encouraged and forwarded the amours of this woman, who passed as his wife, with a person known as Gulloo Moskee—formerly a beestee of the palace, but latterly an indulged favourite of the Maharajh—and that in nine or ten months afterwards the present Maharajh Dulleep Sing was born.

Though every one well knew, and none better than Runjeet himself, the history of this child and its parentage, it is a curious fact that the Maharajh on this as on other similar occasions, felt a pleasure in being considered at his age the father of a new-born child. Nor did Gulloo, or the mother of the infant, with others, scruple to congratulate the old man on the occasion, as though he were really the father of the babe.

Such is the true history of Her Highness, Ranee Chunda, up to the time when she presented to the Punjaub its future sovereign, for whom at the time no such splendid destiny could have been anticipated. The records of her life since that period are a part of the chronicles of the country, and will be found intertwined with the memoirs of its great men, and the narration of the events which have kept it in a state of convulsion for the last seven years.*

---

* The above is the *true* history of the lady who has acted so distinguished a part in the exciting drama which has been lately played at Lahore. That given out as authentic and commonly accepted as the story of Her Highness's early career, differs from it considerably in many particulars, but chiefly in giving the lady a more exalted origin than fortune had in store for her. It is as follows:—In the year 1828, Runjeet Sing, while in the neighbourhood of Gujerawalla, was told of the beauty of the third and youngest daughter of one Munna Sing, a Jat Seik of the Oolak caste, a Gorechar and Chowdry of Char, a small village about three miles south-east of Gujerawalla. On this he sent for Jewalla Sing Puddana, who was married to the eldest daughter of Munna Sing, and from him made inquiries as to Munna Sing's family. The result of these inquiries was, that Runjeet not only sent proposals to Munna Sing for his daughter, but also deputed one Dii Kurmoo with peremptory orders to bring the young girl Chunda and place her in the Maharajh's Zenana. In consequence of these proceedings the girl was soon domiciled in the tents appropriated to the female part of Runjeet's train. When the old chief arrived at Umritsir, Chunda was for the first time ushered into his presence, and he seemed much disappointed and not a little angry on finding, that instead of being sixteen or seventeen years of age, as represented by Dii Kurmoo and others who had first spoken of her to him, she was only between nine and ten. As, however, she had some beauty and a promising look, he ordered that she should be retained in the Zenana on a stipend of two rupees per diem; but it is certain that Runjeet never took any notice of the girl.

In the year 1834, the Maharajh had a favourite in one of the common moskees or beesties attached to his person. This man's name was Gulloo, a young and forward Mahomedan, who was introduced to the notice of Runjeet by his uncle Topee Mookee, who had been placed by the Maharajh in charge of the young Rajah Heera Sing, and who, by means not to be mentioned, had insinuated himself into the old chief's favour. Gulloo, however, soon became the principal favourite, and got so far into the good graces of his master as to be the only person allowed to mount his favourite saddle horses and to ride close to and in front of him. He was, moreover, allowed free access to the Zenankhana at any time, day or night, that he might choose to enter. He thus became acquainted, perhaps too intimately, with various inmates of the Zenana, but in particular it was not long before he had established a familiarity and criminal intercourse with the girl Chunda, that was notorious, not only in the women's apartments, but throughout the palace and even in the public durbar. Runjeet himself was well aware

The infant boy Dulleep remained in the fort with his mother, who appears to have made a successful use of her wiles to work herself into the good graces of Rajah Dehan Sing and the Dogra party, who—but of course for their own purposes—promised that her child's interests should not be neglected, but that he should be considered by them, equal at least to Shere Sing, Cashmera Sing, Peshora Sing, &c. Thus the boy Dulleep remained with his mother until 1841, when the differences between Maharajh Shere Sing and Rajah Dehan Sing arrived at a crisis. At this period Dehan Sing with the consent of the mother, in whose mind he had raised suspicions of the intentions of Shere Sing towards herself and her child, privately conveyed the boy to Umritsir, and there kept him in such privacy, that not even his mother knew the place of his concealment, and few of those in the fort at Lahore were aware even of the fact of his removal. There can be no doubt that had Dehan Sing been successful in his deeply laid designs, he would after the murder of Shere Sing, so long determined on by him, have placed the young Dulleep on the Guddee, as a convenient puppet in the hands of the Dogras.

The object of this manœuvre was to secure all the power of the state to the Jammoo family during a long minority, and with

---

of the state of affairs, but as Gulloo was a favourite of his, he did no more than speak to him in a jocular manner on the subject, without taking any steps for putting an end to the intercourse. It was remarked, however, that from this period the Maharajh never visited the lady or allowed her to appear in his presence; and when in the winter of 1836 he was told that she was in an interesting condition, he replied merely by a grim look, without making any verbal remark on the occasion. He still seemed to regard Gulloo Moskee with all his former favour, but when in February, 1837, the birth of Dulleep Sing was announced to him, his equanimity gave way, and from that moment he withdrew the light of his countenance from the otherwise happy father. It is to be remarked, however, that Gulloo was then ill of a disease which carried him off within a few weeks of the birth of the child.

the almost certainty that before the minority terminated, Heera Sing, the hope of the party, would be proclaimed by the unanimous votes of the soldiery, sole chief of the whole country. The death of Rajah Dehan Sing himself, however, dissipated these ambitious schemes; but still when, after his murder, Heera Sing and the Pundit Jellah came into power, they found that their best policy would be to bring forward the boy Dulleep and proclaim him Maharajh. The child had already been brought to Lahore by Dehan Sing, to be ready for the moment when it should suit the schemes of that wily chief to place him on the throne, after Shere Sing had been disposed of. It is a curious fact, that only a few minutes before Dehan Sing was shot by one of Ajeet Sing's followers, this chief asked the Rajah whom he considered the fittest person to place on the Guddee? On which Dehan Sing replied, that Dulleep Sing was the only person eligible for the dignity. He remarked however, that Lena Sing, Ajeet Sing, and himself would govern in the name of the boy, until he arrived at a proper age to rule the country unaided. Ajeet, however, knew the character of the Dogra Rajah too well to put trust in his words, and a few moments after this conversation had passed between them, the shot was fired which at once ended the life of Dehan Sing, and shook to its foundation the vast fabric of ambitious schemes, which he had reared for the aggrandizement of his family.

CHAPTER VIII.

THE WUZEERUT OF HEERA SING.

HEERA SING immediately on being installed as Wuzeer sent to Jummoo requesting the presence of his uncle, Goolaub Sing, at the capital. But that wily chief prudently refused to trust himself at Lahore until he was fully satisfied that the troops were reduced to proper discipline and obedience, and firmly attached to the cause of his nephew, which was that of himself and all the Dogra faction. He had, moreover, a personal reason for this unwillingness to trust himself in the power of the Khalsa prematurely, in the hate which they bore him for his share in the slaughter of some thousands of their comrades. However, at the commencement of the cold season, Rajah Goolaub Sing arrived at Lahore, where he was well received by all. He found, on his arrival, that owing to petty dissentions and differences among some of the Sirdars, matters were not going on so smoothly as was desirable. Lena Sing Majeeteea, indeed, from his belief in Goolaub's superior power and interest, had been induced to agree to the measures of Heera Sing, and he was now by Goolaub's influence allied in seeming friendship with the Wuzeer, who before strongly suspected him, in common with others, of intriguing against him. Rajah Suchet Sing, however, the youngest of the Dogra brothers, could not thus readily submit to the rule of his nephew. A rancorous enmity of long standing existed betwixt him and the Pundit Jellah, the chief adviser and mooktear of Rajah Heera Sing. Suchet Sing was, from his early youth, remarkable for his debaucheries. Like his brother, Dehan, he had risen to favour and station in the court of Runjeet by the most infamous means. They had both attracted the eye of the old monarch by their beauty of person, and secured his patronage by the most criminal compliance with his desires. This intimacy with the sovereign procured them free admission to the Zenankhanah, or female apartments, a privilege, which they both turned to good account.

It was in some bed-chamber intrigue that Suchet Sing came into collision with the Pundit Jellah, who like himself had the run of the Zenana, and turned it to a similar purpose. Hence arose the hatred which these two eventually bore towards each other, and which now began to display itself openly. The immediate cause of the outbreak was this. Suchet Sing had been for years the favourite of several of the court ladies, including some of the widows of Runjeet Sing. But at this present time his regards seemed fixed only on the Ranee Chunda, the mother of the young Maharajh Dulleep Sing. She on her part returned his affections with equal fervour, and in proof of her good-will bade him aspire to the Wuzeerut, which she promised to bestow upon him. This *liaison*, and its probable consequences, added bitterness to the jealousy of the Pundit, who saw himself likely to be supplanted in power as he had been in love. This feeling was shared by the Rajah, Heera Sing, the present Wuzeer, whose tenure of office was endangered by the ambition of his uncle. However, Suchet Sing was favoured by the Ranee, and countenanced by her eldest brother, Jewahir Sing, as well as some of the other sirdars. Before, however, their arrangements were fully completed, Suchet Sing, impatient for his promised honours, prevailed on Jewahir Sing to take the young Maharajh on an elephant and to go among the troops complaining of the harsh treatment which the royal boy experienced at the hands of his minister, Rajah Heera Sing, and his party. It was expected that this measure, with the promises of a large increase of pay by which it was accompanied, would have induced the troops to depose Heera Sing and to install Suchet Sing or Jewahir Sing in his place. But it happened that it was late in the evening when Jewahir Sing took the prince to the army, and the battalions, ready to suspect something wrong, were confirmed in their suspicions by a rumour which soon got abroad, that Jewahir Sing was planning the removal of the Maharajh from the country, with a view of placing him in the hands of the British. They therefore, ordered him to alight from his elephant, and placing a strict watch over him and his young charge for the night, promised that in the morning they would give him an answer, the night being required for deliberation. Immediately the Punches were at work, and a council was held in each battalion. The result was that the friends of Heera Sing prevailed, and it was consequently determined to acquaint the minister with what had occurred, and to receive his instructions for their further guidance. A message was accordingly sent to Heera Sing, who immediately returned a gracious answer thereto, expressing his admiration of the wisdom and loyalty of the troops, who had thus defeated what he represented as Jewahir Sing's plan for removing their sovereign into the British territories, whereby they had saved many crores of rupees, and much trouble and bloodshed that must necessarily have ensued had the traitorous design succeeded. This message, with liberal rewards, and the minister's presence among the soldiers next morning, induced them to give up Jewahir Sing and his followers, whom the young king was instructed to deliver over to the tender mercies of his Wuzeer to do as he thought proper with them. But the troops recommended that Jewahir Sing should be leniently treated, as they attributed his share of the business entirely to the instigation of Rajah Suchet Sing. This recommendation probably saved the life of Jewahir Sing; but the minister thought that the least punishment that could be inflicted upon him was to put him in irons and place him in close confinement. As for Suchet Sing, the dread of his power and influence, and the mediation of his elder brother, Goolaub Sing, were sufficient to secure his exemption from all personal punishment. But, to mark his displeasure and distrust, the Wuzeer ordered that the two battalions of Suchet Sing with some other of his men, who were constantly quartered in the fort, should be expelled. Furthermore, as these troops did not immediately leave the place on being ordered out, they were overpowered, disarmed, and otherwise ignominiously treated, and turned out by force. At the same time orders were issued prohibiting the entrance of Rajah Suchet Sing, or any of his people, without permission from the Wuzeer. This ill-usage galled the haughty spirit of Suchet Sing exceedingly. Treated with ignominy in the very presence of his mistress, and by the order for his exclusion from the fort, cut off from all chance of seeing or consulting with her, his indignation knew no bounds. But his knowledge of Heera Sing's present power and influence, together with the cautions and persuasions of his more prudent brother, kept him quiet for the time, and in the meanwhile, Goolaub Sing was induced to march for Jummoo, apparently for the sole purpose of removing his brother from Lahore, and thus to free the court from the risk of further disturbance. Goolaub, had, however, reasons more selfish for his desire to return to his domain in the hills. He had contrived to obtain possession of most of the property which his nephew Heera Sing had abstracted from the treasury for himself, as well as of all that had belonged to his late brother Dehan Sing; and, indeed, he had now found an opportunity of clearing Lahore of all that appertained to himself and his family.

Having then given full instructions and counsel to Heera Sing and Pundit Jellah for the guidance of their future policy, Rajah

Goolaub Sing, accompanied by his brother Suchet Sing, and about two thousand of his troops marched for Jummoo. The procession resembled, however, rather that of a caravan of merchants richly laden with goods and treasure than that of a body of soldiers. On arriving at Jummoo, Goolaub's first care was to attend to all the wants and wishes of his brother, and having conciliated him by all possible kindness, he proposed, that Suchet Sing, being without issue, while he Goolaub Sing had three or four sons (three legitimate and one otherwise) should adopt one of his sons and make him his heir. To this proposition Suchet Sing agreed, and thence forward Meean Runbeer Sing, commonly called Meean Peenoo, Rajah Goolaub Sing's youngest son, was publicly acknowledged as the adopted son of Suchet Sing, and heir to all his lands, jaghires, and property.

Having secured this long cherished object, Goolaub Sing turned his attention to the furtherance of his party's interests at Lahore. He caused a forged letter to be exhibited in durbar there purporting to be from Cashmeera Sing and Peshora Sing, by which these two reputed sons of Runjeet Sing were represented as deeply implicated in the Scindawalla plot, and consequently as accessories to the death of the late king and his minister. The effect of this forgery was strengthened and seconded by the villainous conduct of Kupoor Sing, one of the oldest and most favoured of Cashmeera Sing's own retainers. He was then kardar or governor of Seealkote, which had been given as his patrimony by Runjeet Sing to Cashmeera Sing:—Gurriawalla, a small fort to the west of the Chenab, being at the same time given to Peshora Sing.* On the evidence of these forged letters, and the testimony of this faithless servant, Goolaub Sing received orders from Lahore to take both the brothers as prisoners and to confiscate their lands

* The united revenue of both jaghires did not amount to a lakh of rupees.

and property. He, therefore, sent bodies of troops to Seealkote and Gurriawalla, and seized all the property of the accused, who, however, with their families escaped to the protection of a Seik Baba or Gooroo in the neighbourhood.* Hence they wrote both to Rajah Goolaub Sing at Jummoo and to the Lahore Durbar, protesting their perfect innocence, denouncing the forgery, repelling the charge founded thereon, and offering to undergo any trial that might be deemed necessary. They gave reiterated assurances not only of their neutrality in all state disturbances and intrigues, but also of their attachment to the present government. All their efforts to prove their innocence and avert the threatened blow were useless. Another reason was now found for getting them out of the way, or at least of keeping them constantly in the power of those in authority;—it was remembered that they were the reputed and acknowledged if not the real sons of Runjeet Sing, and it was feared that they might, on an opportunity offering itself, cause trouble and disturbance to those who held the reins of government. However, they were now, by Goolaub Sing's crafty policy, invited to Jummoo as for the purpose of conferring and settling matters with him. On their arrival he placed guards over them, ostensibly for the security of their persons, but in reality as their jailors. He now demanded from them a sum of fifty lakhs, as a fine; but as the Khalsa troops showed strong symptoms of their unwillingness to allow of the sons of Runjeet being treated in this manner, the project was for the present abandoned, and they were released on payment of about twenty thousand rupees only, and reinstated in their lands and property—or rather as regards the latter, such of it as had not been carried off by Goolaub Sing.

The princes had been made to give security that they would

* Such was the haste and alarm of their flight, that Cashmeera Sing's wife miscarried of her first child in consequence.

not molest their servant, Kupoor Sing, who had aided in bringing on their misfortunes; and they now carried him with them on their return home. Many days, however, had not passed when the exposure of new acts of villainy and treachery on his part so enraged his immediate master, Cashmeera Sing, against him, that he beat him, or had him beaten to such a degree, that the man actually died under the punishment. This occurrence seemed to Rajah Goolaub Sing to present a favourable opportunity for resuming his deep designs against his intended victims. He, accordingly, with all haste sent intelligence of the *murder* of Kupoor Sing to Lahore, and the Gooroo, who had stood security for Cashmeera Sing's good conduct, was not only called to account but threatened with punishment if he did not either realise his security or have the two brothers punished for their crime. The Gooroo, on this, acknowledged their guilt and his own responsibility, and not only wrote to Lahore, but went thither himself to declare to the Khalsa troops, that these two brothers deserved and ought to receive punishment for their offences, not the least of which, as he now said, was that of breaking faith with him their spiritual father. The consequence of this was that Rajah Goolaub Sing was ordered to attack and seize both Seealkote and Gurriawalla, and gladly proceeded to fulfill instructions so acceptable. Gurriawalla quickly fell into his hands; but the body of troops, seven hundred in number, sent against Seealkote were routed and dispersed with great loss by Cashmeera Sing's own personal guard, a body of only about two hundred chosen men.

Offensive operations against these chiefs having thus again commenced, they saw that the only hope of safety for themselves and their families was in a vigorous resistance. They, therefore, determined to hold out in the strong fort of Seealkote to the last extremity. Exasperated at the defeat and slaughter of his troops, Goolaub Sing sent off large bodies of men, with artillery, to attack their stronghold. But notwithstanding their overwhelming numbers, their assault failed, and they were, after continued and severe loss, compelled to raise the siege and retreat to a distance of five or six miles from the place. The princes had now with them about three hundred horse and five hundred foot. But occasionally they would sally out with about a hundred and fifty horse, and suddenly attacking large bodies of the enemy would put them to flight in thousands, burn and destroy their camp, and carry off all that was worth removal. These feats were not performed only under cover of darkness, as might be supposed, but sometimes in broad daylight, and one or both of the brothers invariably conducted the enterprise personally. The chiefs themselves almost daily went out hunting, hawking, and foraging for miles around, attended sometimes by not more than thirty or forty horsemen, while from eight to nine thousand of Goolaub Sing's troops, including two thousand cavalry, had invested the place, and were doing their utmost for its reduction. In one of these excursions, the two brothers, with about eighty horse, were hawking at quails, &c. for two hours in the fields of green corn, not more than six hundred yards from an entrenched camp, in which lay two thousand of the enemy's horse with two guns. But they remained unmolested, not a man of the besiegers daring to pass the bulwarks which their fear had induced them to form. To such an extent did the audacious gallantry of the two brothers and their followers work upon the timid spirits of Goolaub Sing's men, that it became necessary to send to Lahore for fresh troops. The Khalsa at first refused to proceed against the reputed sons of the great Maharajh; but afterwards on its being stipulated that no bodily injury should be inflicted on the princes, they agreed to go. They were not sent, however, but in their stead were despatched one of the Majeeteea battalions and two Mahomedan battalions, with the Shere regiment of horse, mostly Dogras or hill men, in the pay of the Maharajh. They were accompanied by artillery, heavy and light. But all this was to no purpose. The troops who were sent, either from their own reluctance to engage in such work, or their dread of giving offence to the great body of the Khalsa, or from dread of the daring garrison, could not be prevailed on to exert themselves for the reduction of the place. A new relief of troops was thus found necessary; and now the two oldest battalions, formerly belonging to Dehan Sing, and subsequently to Heera Sing, with five hundred cavalry and six horse artillery guns, were immediately despatched from Lahore. On the morning of the third day they arrived before Seealkote in the midst of heavy rain. This however did not prevent them immediately commencing operations for the reduction of the place. About mid-day the weather clearing up, the fort and town were closely invested; and about three o'clock in the afternoon a general assault was made on the latter. It was successful, and an hour before sunset the town of Seealkote was fully in possession of the enemy. But it was not taken without a gallant resistance on the part of the garrison, evidenced by the loss of the besiegers, about two hundred and fifty killed and three hundred wounded. The fort yet remained to be taken, and throughout the night a heavy cannonade upon it was kept up, so that by morning two breaches were in a forward state. A mine had also been commenced and had made considerable progress. About noon, however, the besieged princes finding themselves unequal to the defence, and their families being much annoyed by the shot and shells of the besiegers, offered to give up the place on condition of their being allowed with all their troops and personal property to march out unmolested. This was agreed to by the besiegers, and after dark the fort was evacuated, and Rajah Goolaub Sing's troops took formal possession. A battalion of half-irregular matchlock men, who had mutinied for an increase of pay while at Peshawur, and thence marched to Lahore, and were sent back with promises of compliances with their demands, while on their return, on their arrival at the Chenaub, altered their intention and marching towards Seealkote joined their fortunes with those of Cashmeera Sing and his brother. This occurred a few days before any troops from Lahore arrived at Seealkote.

The brothers were encouraged and instigated to the line of conduct which they had adopted, by Suchet Sing, who had promised them ample assistance both in money and men, but who never aided them with any thing more substantial than promises. Disappointed in their expectations from this quarter, the brothers now, instead of repairing to Lahore to present themselves to the Durbar, went off to the Manjh country, as the district betwixt the Ravee and the Sutlej is called, and there wandered about among the gooroos and faqueers, endeavouring to secure their intercession and mediation with the Court on their behalf.

Now it should be mentioned, that when the battalions of Dehan Sing, with six guns and five hundred horse, were sent off from Lahore against Seealkote, the entire body of the Khalsa troops protested strongly against the measure, in the apprehension that these troops would not only take the fort but that they would probably put the two sons of Runjeet Sing to death. These and such like considerations induced the troops, immediately after the departure of this detachment from Lahore, to create disturbances, which they carried to such a degree that Rajah Heera Sing, the minister, was for three or four days surrounded by them, and virtually kept a prisoner in his house in the city. The Khalsa swore vengeance and extermination against the Rajah, his party, and all the Dogras, in case any harm should happen to the two princes. They seemed as if nothing would appease or assure them. The terms they offered to the minister as the conditions of their return to their duty were—1st. That Peshora Sing and Cashmeera Sing should be preserved harmless, and safely escorted to Lahore, and that the troops should be recalled from Seealkote; 2ndly. That Pundit Jellah should be given up to them, or at least that he should be expelled from the durbar; 3rdly. They required the recall to office of Misser Belee Ram, an old and faithful servant of Runjeet Sing, and his head treasurer for many years; 4thly. They required the recall of their *Bii Gruntheea*, Bii Goormuck Sing, the spiritual adviser of the old King; and 5thly. The immediate release of Jewahir Sing, the uncle of the young Maharajh Dulleep Sing.

To these terms Heera Sing acceded so far as, in the first place, to send off expresses to Seealkote to stay proceedings against the princes, and the messengers arriving while negotiations for a surrender were pending, the besiegers were induced to accept the terms offered by the garrison. In respect to Pundit Jellah, the minister declared that he was his own private servant, and that when he should be found guilty of any crime he should be punished accordingly. As yet however, he said, the Pundit was in no way a responsible accessory to any act or policy of his, and he promised that, he should not thenceforth be allowed to sit in the durbar, and should either be dismissed his, the minister's, service, or at all events prohibited from meddling with state affairs in future. As regarded Misser Belee Ram and Bii Goormuck Sing, the minister said they were long since dead, put to death as traitors with the counsel and consent of the army; and as this was the fact, the demands for the production and restoration of these men were withdrawn. The fifth and last condition was immediately fulfilled by the issue of orders for the release of Jewahir Sing, who received a present of two thousand rupees for his own personal use and of ten thousand rupees for distribution among the troops who had released him. Having thus as far as he was able fulfilled the conditions demanded of him by the troops, Rajah Heera Sing was enlarged from the virtual captivity in which he had for three days been held, and having distributed some presents among the troops he was again treated as their favourite and extolled as a liberal and popular minister.

The news of the misunderstanding betwixt Heera Sing and the army reached Jummoo and inspired Suchet Sing with a hope of being able to supplant his nephew in the favour of the troops, and as a consequence in the office of Wuzeer. Four or five battalions had, moreover, it seems, in their temporary pique with the minister, sent an invitation to Suchet Sing to come to Lahore without loss of time. He accordingly hastened to the capital; but on his arrival found that the storm which promised to blow good for him had passed over, and that the wind was again in his nephew's favour. He, however, nothing daunted, arrived at Ekrar ke puttun, a ferry on the Ravee, three or four koss from Lahore. It was in the evening that he reached this spot, attended by only about ten horsemen. He immediately sent a messenger to the battalions that had invited him, announcing his arrival, but not receiving an answer so soon as he expected, the impatient chief determined to cross the river and present himself to the troops, hoping that his presence and promises would effect for him all that he required. In this, however, he was mistaken;—the very men who had sent for him were now the first to tell him that he had better retrace his steps, as Rajah Heera Sing having but two days before complied with the terms of reconciliation offered by the Khalsa, they were again faithfully bound to him; and that were it otherwise, these four or five battalions only could not think of standing out against the decision of all the rest of the army. They therefore strongly advised Suchet Sing to return to Jummoo and wait for a better opportunity. But the gallant Dogra, rash as he was brave, had determined not to draw back from the enterprise which he had once begun; and as he would not leave the camp at their suggestion the troops afraid of incurring the displeasure of their comrades by keeping him among them, actually *ordered* him away in the middle of the night. Ashamed of himself for having thus been duped, and exasperated against those who had betrayed him, Suchet Sing determined to brave the worst that could befall him. For the remainder of that night he remained in an old mosque, where he rested, surrounded by his followers, now about two hundred horse and one hundred and fifty foot. Meantime the minister, having in the evening heard of his arrival, sent several messages to him, bidding him retrace his steps to the hills, and conveying various fierce threats of rough treatment in case of his non-compliance. But this was just the way to induce a man like Suchet Sing to determine on standing his ground to the last, and it had that effect on him. He scorned the thought of humbling himself in any manner, and as he knew his case was now hopeless, he resolved to die where he was, with the few followers who still remained faithful to him, all but about forty-five of his own chosen men, having deserted him during the night.

Rajah Heera Sing had made every preparation for the attack, and daylight found the devoted little band surrounded by fourteen or fifteen thousand infantry, three or four thousand horse, and fifty-six pieces of artillery, heavy and light! Such a force did Heera Sing deem necessary to ensure the destruction of his brave uncle and the knot of resolute spirits that clung to him to the last. While this overwhelming force was making its preparations for the assault, Suchet Sing and his followers remained composedly in the mosque, hearing some passages of their holy book read to them. They were thus engaged when a tremendous cannonade was opened on the building. Still amidst the continuous roar of the artillery the reader went on, and still his brave audience strove to catch the sacred words. But soon the walls of the mosque were beaten down by the fire, and no longer afforded protection to those within. And now the reader closed his book, and Suchet

Sing and his followers arose to meet their fate like good soldiers as they were. As they stood up, a cry was heard without, and they beheld the host of fifteen thousand men with fixed bayonets, rushing forward upon them on all sides. When the enemy was within a hundred yards, Suchet Sing put himself at the head of his men and was rushing forward to meet the foe. But he was pulled back by his Wuzeer Rai Kissera Sing, and placed in the centre of the little band, who dauntlessly advanced to meet the hostile ranks. As they set forward, Rajah Suchet Sing exclaimed in bitter irony, that the number of troops sent by the Wuzeer was somewhat too small for the occasion! The handful of heroes, sword in hand, now rushed upon the thickest mass of their destroyers and so furions and desperate was their onset, that they actually broke through or drove back four entire battalions, killing upwards of thirty of the foremost ranks. Rai Kissera Sing, a brave and powerful man, with his own hand cut down nine of the most forward of the enemy, and several men were killed by the bayonets of their comrades in their attempts to flee. But this desperate valour availed not the devoted band so fearfully overmatched; in a short time forty-two of the men were lying dead on the field, and four fell badly wounded, of whom only one survived. Rajah Suchet Sing, it is hardly needful to say, was among the slain. The entire loss of the assaulting force was seventy-eight killed on the spot, and fifty-nine wounded, of whom twenty-seven subsequently died. About thirty more fell upon the weapons of their comrades in the panic and confusion of the onset made by Suchet Sing and his band. The total loss of the Khalsa, on this occasion, was, in killed and wounded, about one hundred and sixty.

When all was over, the troops were ordered back to their lines, and Heera Sing went out to view the bodies of his uncle and others of his relatives who had fallen with Suchet

Sing. He first came upon that of Rai Kissera Sing, who was well known at court as one of the best soldiers in the country, and who had that day cut down about twenty of the foe ere he fell. Several times had this strong and valiant man been struck down, but as often had he risen to renew the slaughter which marked his progress. At length with two mortal stabs of the bayonet he went down for the last time, but not before he had killed the authors of his death wounds. When Rajah Heera Sing visited the scene of butchery, Rai Kissera was still alive, and on seeing the Wuzeer attempted to utter the Rajpoot salutation "*Jye deb*," after which he made signs for water, when Rajah Heera Sing brutally answered his mute request by telling him it would have been well had he remained in the hills, where there was plenty of clear cold water. Rai Kissera Sing died shortly after. At the sight of his uncle's body, Heera Sing seemed much affected, and actually shed tears. He ordered that the corpse should be carried from the field in his own palanquin; and the like honour was paid to the bodies of Rai Kissera Sing, and of Bheem Sein, the principal mooktear of Rajah Suchet Sing. The rest were disposed of according to their rank and condition. That same day Heera Sing was present at the funeral obsequies of his uncle, whose body was burnt near the mausoleum of Meean Oottum Sing, the eldest son of Goolaub Sing, who was killed with No Nehal Sing.

It is believed that had it not been for the presence and influence of the Pundit Jellah, this affair would not have had so fatal a termination. But Rajah Heera Sing believed the Pundit to be an infallible astrologer, and when this worthy assured him that should he spare his uncle, he himself would not be alive to see the sun set that evening, the credulous Wuzeer fancied that his uncle's life alone could redeem his own. He was persuaded by his counsellor that one of the two must die that day, and that the troops were marching and would in two hours go over to Suchet Sing if they were not in the meantime sent to destroy him.

While these things were passing at Lahore, the unfortunate brothers, Kashmeera Sing and Peshora Sing, were wandering about the Manjh, seeking rest and protection. At length they joined the camp of one Bii or Baba Beer Sing, a *chela* or disciple of the Gooroo Oona Saheb. This religious man had for years roved about the Manjh, levying alms and contributions to such an extent that he was now very rich. He had, however, for some time past been considered as a disaffected and dangerous character, and was accused of instilling revolutionary principles into the minds of the Seik people and soldiery. To strengthen the suspicion against him, he had managed to collect and was able to maintain a force of twelve hundred infantry, two or three hundred horse, and two guns,—a strange following for a man professedly and professionally holy! To crown all, he had of late afforded an asylum to certain Chiefs and Sirdars who had fallen into disgrace at court, and who with their retainers swelled the Baba's force to about three thousand men and three guns. Whether Baba Beer Sing had any treasonable object in view, or intended to interfere in state affairs, cannot now be said. It is certain, however, that Heera Sing and the Pundit saw enough in his conduct and position to induce them to plan the extermination of him and his whole camp. Had they openly avowed this design to the army it would have cost them their lives, for the soldiers held the Baba in high respect and reverence. They flocked to him daily with their alms and offerings, and he in return treated them liberally, keeping a free table, which was supplied with food for fifteen hundred every day. Heera Sing and his adviser well knew then that they must proceed with the utmost caution in carrying out their design. Nothing but the most subtle contrivance, the most delicate management, could give them a chance of success. As part of the plan, Heera Sing in his own name and that of the child Dulleep Sing, wrote to Baba Beer Sing in the most humble and respectful terms, requesting his prayers and good will, telling the holy man that the Maharajh and his Minister considered him as their father, &c. The letters were accompanied by presents of money and other valuables, and by a written promise of a suitable jaghire whenever the Baba desired it. The object of this scheme was to throw the Baba off his guard, and it had its desired effect. General Mathaub Sing Majeeteea was now treated with the utmost kindness and attention. Valuable presents were lavished upon him, and to all appearance he became the favourite and confidant of the Minister. Heera Sing told this General that he was greatly perplexed and distressed by information which he had received from Hindostan, to the purport that Sirdar Uttur Sing Scindawalla had formed alliances with the British, as well as with some of the Seik Chiefs beyond the Sutlej. The Minister professed to be greatly troubled by this news, and begged the General's advice and assistance on the emergency. Mathaub Sing expressed his perfect readiness to afford both his counsel and assistance, and the Wuzeer then suggested to him that he should march with his fourth battalion to Umritsir, and thence write in his own name and in that of others to Uttur Sing, with declarations of friendship and attachment from himself and all the troops. These letters were however, to be of such a tenor as might induce the Scindawalla to come across the river and join Baba Beer's camp, the Minister being ready through the mediation of that holy man to be reconciled to him. To this plan the General agreed, and having taken an oath of secrecy, marched for Umritsir with his troops. He was, however, before his departure further informed, that it was not alone for the reason mentioned that he was sent to Umritsir, but that his presence was there required because an outbreak of hostilities between the British and the court of Gwalior was daily expected, and it was the Minister's intention, should the former suffer any reverses, to cross the Sutlej with the whole army. There was one Goolaub Sing, commonly styled Calcutteea, from his having commanded the escort of Gujer Sing, brother of Lena Sing Majeeteea, when that chief was some years before sent on a friendly mission to the Governor-General at Calcutta. This Goolaub Sing Calcutteea was known, for some private reason, to hold the Scindawalla family in the greatest abhorrence. He was now treated much as General Mathaub Sing had been, and the same disclosures were made to him But as from his known hatred of the Scindawallas he could not pretend to write friendly letters to Uttur Sing in his own name, he was instructed to forge as many as he required for his purpose, which was to induce the chief to cross the river and to join Baba Beer Sing's camp with a view to a reconciliation betwixt him and the Minister. Thus this General, having taken an oath of secrecy, was induced to march for Kussoor with his troops, the same reasons having given him for this movement as in the case of Mathaub Sing. These preliminary arrangements being completed, numerous letters, bearing the forged signatures of various Sirdars, Chiefs, Generals, Colonels, and other officers, were addressed to Baba Beer Sing, the purport of all being the same, entreaties that the holy man would exercise his influence to induce Uttur Sing to cross the river and join his camp, when he was assured that the writers would join heart and hand to procure the Scindawalla's restoration to his former rank and power, perhaps to raise him above his former position. The credulous Bii was thus induced to open a private correspondence with Uttur Sing, and, to assure him of what was promised, sent some of these letters to him. The Scindawalla was duped as completely as the Baba, and unwisely determined once more to try his fortune across the Sutlej. All his movements and intentions were, however, well known to Heera Sing, and through the instrumentality of the Generals above named, all Uttur Sing's correspondence was daily sent to the Minister at Lahore.

Thus matters had advanced towards a crisis when the day appointed for Uttur Sing's return across the river became known to the Minister who prepared his schemes accordingly. Shaik Imam-ood-deen, son of the Governor of Cashmere, and himself Governor of the Jullundur Doab, a well known enemy of the Khalsa, was now taken into the Wuzeer's confidence, and instructed in the part he was to act. He was on some pretence and at a certain time to be ready with at least fifteen hundred Muckthas, or irregular troops, near the Baba's camp. Then when the Khalsa troops had by some pretext been induced to surround the camp, and in the confusion and tumult which must necessarily ensue, the Shaik was to find some means of bringing on a disturbance. In the general *melee* which would follow, he was to make sure of the different victims, of whose names a list was given to him. Being notoriously an inveterate enemy of the Seiks and their race, the Shaik who governed the district in which the scene was laid, was just the man for this purpose, and he entered into the scheme proposed with the greatest readiness. Jewahir Mull, the Dewan of the late Rajah Suchet Sing, and a younger brother of Heera Sing, was likewise made privy to the affair, and was with about two thousand five hundred Chariyaree Gorechars to support and assist the Shaik in the performence of his part of the plan. Their rule of action was to raise and keep up as much confusion and hostility as possible among the mixed mass that were to be assembled at the camp of Baba Beer Sing on a certain day. By this it was hoped that the Seik battalions might, by the means to be employed, be involved, they knew not how, in a general fight, which should have the appearance of being brought on by some mischance, as was very often the case with the Seik soldiery.

All being now arranged, Uttur Sing's entrance into the Punjaub was publicly made known; and thereupon, Rajah Heera Sing, seemingly in the greatest consternation, immediately called a general assembly of the Khalsa officers and Punches. The meeting was harangued by the Minister in language which he had learnt by rote from the frequent repetition of Pundit Jellah. The purport of his speech was briefly as follows:—That since the death of Shere Sing the state and country had never been in such danger as now;—that Uttur Sing Scindawalla, supported by twelve or fifteen thousand British troops, had actually crossed the Sutlej into the Punjaub, and that the British army was encamped on the bank of the river; that Uttur Sing had renewed his former engagement with the British of six annas in the rupee as their share of the revenue; that they had agreed to occupy the country and to put him at the head of affairs; that they would disband the whole Seik army, whose assistance was now, if ever it had been, most urgently required for the maintenance of the national honor and independance; that Uttur Sing, with three thousand of his own followers, was encamped with Baba Beer Sing, and that they had only to show a bold front to him to induce him either to recross the Sutlej into Hindostan, or to accept terms of reconciliation and come to Lahore, where he, Heera Sing, would endeavour, at any cost, to make him a friend of the state; and lastly they had only to hint to Baba Beer Sing, that he was too holy and good a man to harbour or countenance one like Uttur Sing Scindawalla, who, as was plain to all, had actually sold his country.

The Seiks, after much hesitation, agreed to comply with the Minister's propositions, still declaring however, that they would not stir from Lahore if they thought they should have to fight against or injure the Baba. But Heera Sing in the presence of the troops prostrated himself at the name of the Baba, and prayed to heaven that the holy man might, by some divine interposition, be induced to separate himself from Uttur Sing, or be by some other means kept out of the way of harm; and he solemnly and repeatedly assured the Seiks that not a man of them felt a greater reverence and regard for the Bii than he did. Thus assured the battalions marched from Lahore, and Generals Mathaub Sing Majeeteea and Goolaub Sing Calcutteea advanced with their divisions from Umritsir and Kussoor. Meean Lall Sing, a relative of the Minister, was sent in charge of the whole expedition and to direct the plan to the desired result. Every thing turned out exactly to the wishes of the Wuzeer, whose plans were so well devised and arranged that they could hardly fail of success. The Seik troops, advancing on all sides, closed round the camp of the Baba and his companions. They still believed, however, that a reconciliation would be quickly effected, and that Uttur Sing would return with them to Lahore as a friend. From this anticipated event, they, the soldiers, hoped to reap a harvest of presents and favours on their return to the capital.

But these peaceful anticipations were not destined to be realised. Meean Lall Sing sent Seiks of different grades backwards and forwards betwixt the Khalsa camp and that of Baba Beer Sing, ostensibly for the purpose of persuading the holy man to give up Uttur Sing, or to compel him to recross the river. This, as it was intended it should, created some confusion and contention among the troops, who began to close round the Baba's camp. Meean Lall Sing improved this tumult to his own purposes, by advising the Seiks to unlimber their artillery and to range it in front of Uttur Sing's force, in the hope of overawing them by this significant threat, and thereby inducing them to yield. This, of course, greatly increased the confusion and uproar, and led by various imperceptible steps to a general engagement. When the firing commenced, General Goolaub Sing was engaged in a conference with Uttur Sing, who immediately on seeing the turn that affairs were taking, and knowing the character of the man, concluded that he had been treacherous, and either shot him with his own hand or by that of one of his men. The General had with him a guard of about thirty soldiers, and the precipitate flight of these men to their own side was the signal for the Khalsa to join in the affray. Immediately on the cry of these fugitives being heard, it was drowned in the roar of artillery which was now unsparingly used on either side. One of the first victims was the holy Bii, one of whose legs was nearly knocked off by a cannon ball. Uttur Sing and Cashmeera Sing, with some other Sirdars, fell in the hand to hand conflict which ensued. Numbers of their people were drowned in the river in the attempt to escape. The Seiks lost all their former reverence for their Gooroo, the sight of the rich plunder which his camp afforded being a temptation too strong for their piety. Their only object, now, was to secure every man for himself as much of the booty as he could; but for this they had to fight hard.

When the struggle was over the Baba was found breathing his last in exclamations against those of his own caste and creed. He now produced many of the letters which he had received,—the forgeries before mentioned—to prove, as he supposed, the treachery and villainy of the Seik chiefs and officers, who, as he believed, to the last, had written these letters, instigating him to take the part of Uttur Sing. "When," said he to the Seiks, around him, "you and your chiefs and officers wrote these letters to me with the most solemn promises both to myself and Uttur Sing, I relied on your good faith and agreed to your proposals, in the hope of obtaining for Uttur Sing and his family the means of a quiet livelihood; but you, calling yourselves Seiks, are worse than Mahomedans, you have proved yourselves a vile, treacherous, and unfaithful race, without piety or religion. Still my dying prayer to heaven is, may even your wickedness be requited by good." He then gave directions that his body should be thrown into the river, that his bones might not be left on such a land of iniquity.

It is a fact that to the very last moment before the conflict, the Baba had no suspicion that the Seiks entertained any hostile intentions towards either himself or Uttur Sing Scindawalla, as was proved by his actually having victuals provided for ten thousand men, saying as he ordered the slaughter of five hundred goats for the feast, that the Seiks were coming as his visitors, and he must entertain them as such.

All being over the troops returned to their camp, and marched that night or early the next morning, encamping for want of water on the bank of the river opposite Ferozepore.

Peshora Sing, the day before this battle, had come to Lahore to make his submission and to entreat pardon from his brother. But before he had been there many hours now news arrived of Cashmeera Sing's fate, and there being no other alternative, the Minister installed him in his former jaghires, &c. He was immediately sent off with presents and money to Gurriwalla, when he declared his intention to live a quiet and retired life. The wives and mother of Cashmeera Sing, who were in the camp of Beer Sing, were captured by Meean Lall Sing, and privately sent off towards Lahore covered up in a cart. But a rumour of this and of their bad treatment—they were refused even water to drink—coming to the ears of the Khalsa, the whole army shewed a strong disposition to mutiny, and two or three hundred men immediately set off in pursuit of the escort, which they speedily overtook. They beat the guard, Mean Lall's men, who fled, and the unfortunate women were released and brought back to camp, the troops engaging that they would prevail on the Wuzeer to provide them with suitable and honorable maintenance.

The Khalsa now called to mind the death of the revered Gooroo. They laid all the blame of his murder on Jewahir Mull and Meean Lall Sing, and rushed tumultuously upon the camp of the latter, who however escaped to that of the Gorechars, some twenty-eight thousand men, who for the time protected him, but by whose advice he during the night quitted their camp, and with only seven horsemen went off towards the south. Thence having disguised themselves they turned towards Lahore, but lingered in the neighbourhood of that city for some days before they ventured to enter it.

Peace and quiet were now restored among the Khalsa troops, but they long remembered with remorse the death of their revered teacher; and the men of General Court's battalion as being more particularly concerned in his murder, were thenceforward termed *Gooroomars,* or slayers of the Gooroo, and it was some time before any of their comrades would eat or drink with them.

Soon after this event of the death of Baba Beer Sing, Cashmeera Sing, and Uttur Sing Scindawalla, a great show of enemity was made betwixt Rajah Heera Sing and his uncle Goolaub Sing. Those well informed on the subject believe that though some slight misunderstanding may have existed in respect to money matters,—Goolaub Sing claiming the property of Dehan Sing and Suchet Sing, his brothers, and even keeping his hold of some of that entrusted to his care by his nephew—the display of hostility originated in that crooked policy for which the Dogra chiefs were notorious, and was merely intended as a blind to the world at large. However Heera Sing now publicly announced that he had for many months past in vain tried peaceful measures to bring his uncle to a quiet and amicable settlement of their differences. He, therefore, summoned a General Council of the army and requested its advice as to what was to be done to bring his uncle to terms, and its aid in carrying the measures determined on into effect. What he required from Goolaub Sing was—1. An increase of one-fourth of the revenue from lands belonging to the Sirkar and held by Goolaub Sing. [This it is believed was designed to cover the introduction of a similar scale of rent throughout the Punjaub.] 2. The restoration of all the lands, jaghires, and other property of Rajah Suchet Sing. 3. The restoration of all the property of the late Rajah Dehan Sing; and 4. The presence of Rajah Goolaub Sing at Lahore. To enforce these demands, twenty battalions of infantry, with a due proportion of cavalry and artillery were despatched towards Jummoo. But so slowly were they sent that the Seiks soon saw that affairs were as yet very irresolutely carried on, and they soon began to harbour a suspicion that some foul play was intended. This belief was strengthened by a reflection on the fact that the troops were sent forward by different routes, and separated into small detachments; while news came in which told that Goolaub Sing with not less than thirty or thirty-five thousand men was strongly encamped and ready either to give or receive battle. Moreover it was known that he had the power to raise in rebellion all the people of the Baar, or low jungle country, and of all that to the westward of the Jhelum as far as Attock; and it was also known that he was in close communication with Sirdar Teja Sing, Governor of Peshawur, and with Dost Mahomed of Cabul. He had likewise about this time procured the liberation of Zubburdust Khan, a refractory chief, from prison in Cashmere, where his influence was notoriously greater than that of the Lahore Durbar. Affairs stood thus when, on account of the suspicions of the troops, it was deemed inadvisable to move any further in the matter. The Khalsa was therefore ordered to halt and remain stationary where they were, scattered over the country in small detachments and not very far from Lahore. At the same time Bii Ram Sing, Dewan Denanauth, Shaik Imam-ood-deen (son of the Governor of Cashmere) and others were sent to Jummoo to endeavour by negotiation to bring the misunderstanding to a peaceable termination. To this mission Rajah Goolaub gave for answer that he would not treat until Meean Jewahir Sing, the younger brother of Rajah Heera Sing, should arrive from Lahore, when he would be ready to agree to almost any terms proposed. In a few days, therefore, Meean Jewahir Sing arrived at Jummoo, and ere long the troops were recalled to Lahore, every thing being satisfactorily arranged. The mission also returned to Lahore, bringing with them Meean Sone Sing, the second and now the eldest son of Rajah Goolaub Sing.

Six battalions were now ordered to proceed towards Attock and Peshawar, where troops were likely to be required, the rebel chief Zubburdust Khan having fomented disturbances in the Hazareh, Trinoul, and Moozufferabad districts. Many days had not elapsed when news arrived that the Moolkeas (inhabitants) of Hazareh, Moozufferabad, Kukka Bumba &c. had collected to the number of twenty-five or thirty thousand, and were joined by the brother of Paindha Khan with his troops. It was believed, however, in Durbar that they were headed or at least directed by some of the sons of Dost Mahomed, that they had actually taken all the forts from Hazareh to Cashmere, killing upwards of fifteen hundred Seiks, and that they were now on the point of attacking Cashmere itself. A day or two later news arrived of the capture of Cashmere, that the Durbar troops, twelve hundred Rohillas, had joined the insurgents, and that the Governor, with some five hundred men, was shut up in the fort of Hurree Purvut, near the capital. After this no certain intelligence arrived, accounts coming in of the roads being impassable from snow, and rumours going abroad of the Governor's death. Matters stood thus, when Meean Jewahir Sing arrived in haste from Jummoo on some special and private business; he had a secret conference with the Minister and after a stay of only two days went off on his return. On this the six Seik battalions and other troops that were in the Hazareh country received urgent commands to march immediately for Cashmere by the Moozufferabad road, which because of the snow was at that season of the year utmost impassable even for a single cossid or hurkara. To add to the difficulties reported, it was said that betwixt Moozufferabad and Cashmere, there were a large fort and twenty smaller ones, all in the hands of the insurgents. Shaik Imam-ood-deen, the son of the Governor, was accordingly sent off with two Seik battalions and about a thousand or twelve hundred Ramgoles and new levies, in great haste and badly equipped, to make his way to Cashmere by the Bimber and Poonch road. After these details it is not to be wondered at that nothing was done, that the various divisions of the army stood fast on the route, and never reached Cashmere, while in the mean time the storm that had threatened blew over.

Soon after Meean Sone Sing arrived at Lahore, and when to all appearance, the friendship betwixt Goolaub Sing and his nephew the Wuzeer was perfectly re-established, a report was got up, that an entire battalion, of Goolaub's troops stationed at Gujerat, had been cut up, and a large convoy of treasure attacked and plundered by Peshora Sing. The truth of the story appears to be that Goolaub Sing during the time of his differences with his nephew frequently made offers of alliance to the Prince, and promised him supplies of men and money to prevail on him to join against Heera Sing. Peshora Sing was thus induced to raise some eighteen hundred or two thousand men, horse and foot, to assist the Dogra chief. When Goolaub had settled his differences with his nephew, he without ceremony discharged about twelve or fifteen thousand of his troops, paying them but a very small part of what was due to them, and even taking their arms and accoutrements from many of them. Just at this time the men whom Peshora Sing had raised, and who were encamped at Gurriawalla demanded their pay. Thereupon the Prince being without money himself, wrote to Goolaub Sing, requesting the fulfilment of his promises and the transmission of funds for the payment of these troops enlisted for his service. Goolaub, however, seeing the ease with which he had been able to get rid of his own surplus troops, told Peshora Sing to act with his two thousand as *he* had done with his larger body—to turn them adrift without ceremony. But the Prince on receiving this reply thought it better to read and explain it to his men than to act upon it at once. He told them that he could not himself pay them, and he therefore gave them liberty to disband themselves and go where they might choose. Ultimately most of these men were induced to go to Gujerat and its vicinity, under some hopes held out to them of being paid their arrears. But they received nothing but insult and ill-treatment from Goolaub Sing's sirdars, moonshees, and other officials, who presumed upon the support of a battalion of their master's troops then and there present. However this treatment so enraged the insulted and cheated soldiers of Peshora Sing, that it brought on a bloody conflict in which Goolaub's force was routed with great slaughter, and the city of Gujerat taken and plundered. It is asserted, however, that Peshora Sing was not personally present on this occasion nor had any thing whatever to do with the affair. But at Lahore the Khalsa Council was assembled, and the matter was described in quite a different light with a view to obtain the consent of the army to the measures which it was intended to adopt for the purpose of getting rid of the Prince. Rajah Goolaub Sing, also, was preparing to act against the obnoxious chief with all his power and cunning. But the day after the consultation at Lahore, news arrived that the Prince had absconded, and as nothing further was heard of him for some time, all the schemes against him were laid aside.

Another important character now comes upon the stage of the Lahore drama,—Sirdar Jewahir Sing, the brother of the

Maharajh's mother. This worthy had for some time back been living at Umritsir, apparently and according to common report absorbed in revelling and drunkenness. Rajah Heera Sing had several times ordered him to present himself at Lahore, but to no purpose, he continued at Umritsir seemingly given up to his debasing pleasures and careless of the affairs of state. It is however suspected that his devotion to pleasure and indifference to political matters were in a great measure assumed for the purpose of hiding the real designs of an ambitious man. It is thought that Jewahir Sing employed the opportunity afforded by his residence at Umritsir in successful efforts to sow the seeds of disaffection and revolution among the Seiks, Akalees, Biis, Gooroos, and other fanatics who dwelt at or resorted to the holy city, or who were scattered throughout the Manjh districts in the neighbourhood. In time his plans received the support and countenance of many of the Seik sirdars, most of whom had become tired of the Dogra ascendancy. He had also brought over to his party many of the regular Khalsa troops, their officers and deputies. He now, therefore, returned to Lahore to complete his plans and to carry them into effect.

Then ensued one of those ominous calms which to those well read in the signs of the times foretold a coming storm. The approach of some appalling event might always be pretty surely predicted from the perfect silence preserved alike by the army and the court on political matters. This portentous silence was styled by the Seiks a *burra choop*. During this *choop* neither sirdars, chiefs, officers, or soldiers seemed inclined to speak on matters which they were inwardly revolving. No visits were paid, every man keeping at home secretly preparing for the approaching convulsion. The chiefs, both of the court and the army, were privately engaged in drawing armed men around them and sending out spies in every direction. Each battalion of the army quietly made arrangements to ensure its own safety, and to join its fellows when the moment for the struggle arrived. Such was usually the state of affairs in and about Lahore when any great crisis was impending; and such was the case now when Jewahir Sing was in the capital planning the destruction of Heera Sing and his own elevation to the Wuzeerut.

On the first day of the month the Ranee Chunda, the mother of Maharajh Dulleep Sing, according to custom, distributed one hundred golden *budhees* as charity in the name of her son. On this occasion she was threatened and grossly abused by the Pundit Jellah, and she complained of this ill usage to her brother Jewahir Sing. It now also come out that both Heera Sing and the Pundit had been in the habit of sending for the Ranee at night, and by threats of ill treatment compelling her to allow of criminal intercourse with her. Other disclosures were also made of facts too gross to be repeated here. It is enough to say that the Pundit had made an attempt to poison the Ranee under the pretext of administering to her medicine for a loathsome disease with which she was afflicted.

When all these matters became known to Jewahir Sing and the sirdars and soldiers, their rage against the Minister and the Pundit knew no bounds; but still they continued quietly to arrange their plans of vengeance. Jewahir Sing's intention was the utter extermination of the Dogras, and in this he was joined by most of the sirdars, while the troops seemingly sought nothing further than the removal of the Pundit Jellah. Day after day secret consultations were held, but no determination was arrived at. At length the main body of the army, impatient of further delay made an attempt to enter the city during the night; but in this design they were thwarted by the vigilance of the guard which was in the interest of the court. On hearing of the attempt Heera Sing sent to enquire the object of their visit, and was told that the army understood that the Maharajh Dulleep Sing and his mother complained of being treated as prisoners and that they were not allowed to go in or out without the special permission of the Minister. On receiving this reply, Heera Sing promised to withdraw all restraint on the Maharajh and his mother; and seemingly satisfied with this, the troops quietly returned to their quarters.

On the following day the Wuzeer assembled the officers and deputies of the army and took counsel with them for a long time. The result was that the majority declared their readiness to acknowledge and obey him as Minister, but required that he should dismiss the Pundit Jellah from his court and counsels. They further demanded that he should allow the Maharajh and his mother perfect freedom of person and action, and set aside a suitable jaghire for their maintenance. On the Minister agreeing to these terms the officers and deputies promised that they would the next day meet again and use their best endeavours to effect a settlement of all differences betwixt him and the reigning family.

That same night the Wuzeer and the Pundit received intelligence which induced them to make an attempt to escape towards Jummoo. Their plan, however, was acted on with such irresolution that it was nearly day before the fugitives, attended by Meean Sone Sing, Meean Laub Sing, and others, with about three or four hundred horse and foot, left the city under the pretext of going to inspect the troops at Meean Meer. They had scarcely cleared the Tanksallee gate when they heard the music of the different regiments saluting Jewahir Sing. On this they quickened their pace towards the Ravee, and on arriving at its banks, they ordered their Seik attendants to halt, while they with the rest crossed the stream. They then proceeded to the Burradaree of Thara or Thurgar, which was near the ford, and there dismounting, Heera Sing and his friends ascended to the roof of the building and sat down in consultation. The Rajah was now persuaded by the Pundit that the army would shortly return to its allegiance, and come and carry him back to Lahore in joy and triumph; and so they continued for a short time awaiting this event. Soon they perceived horsemen coming from the city at full speed. On this they remounted and sent two horsemen forward to learn the business of those who were advancing upon them. But when the messengers came within range of the approaching cavalry, they were fired on, and so returned to the Rajah's company, reporting that the enemy—for such their actions showed them—were coming on in force, that from the city and elsewhere large bodies of cavalry were rapidly advancing upon them. On hearing this Heera Sing remarked, that if they were to be attacked, it would be best to make a stand there, and to attempt to capture two guns which they saw galloping towards them unprotected. But at the Pundit's persuasion, the Rajah and his party moved off quickly towards the camp of the Chareeyaras, the late Rajah Suchet Sing's Gorechars, which they saw at a little distance, and where they hoped to receive protection. But on their approach, the fugitives found that the troopers were already on the alert to repel and pursue them, and they were therefore obliged to move on in another direction. They now advanced towards the Serai of Mukberah near Shahderah, and sought the assistance of some Patans encamped there. But here again they were repulsed. Thence they hastened onward to and through the village of Shahderah, where Heera Sing suggested that they should take the river-side road towards Meerawal, there being no troops encamped in that direction. But as usual the counsel of the Pundit prevailed, and his advice was to proceed by the main road towards Shah Dowla ko Pool. But they had not advanced more than six hundred yards from the village of Shahderah, when they were overtaken by the Seik horsemen, with some of the sirdars at their head. These on approaching informed Heera Sing that no harm should happen to him or any of his followers, if they would only give up the Pundit Jellah. But as the Pundit, thinking only of his own personal safety, continued making signs to the Rajah to push on without listening to the call of the pursuing horsemen, the party still hurried forward. The Seiks, finding all their efforts to bring them to a stand without resorting violence useless, and considering themselves treated with indignity, they, under the command of Sirdar Sham Sing Attarrewallah, and General Meva Sing Majeeteea,* attacked the flying party in the rear and on either flank; and thus a running skirmish was kept up until they had proceeded somewhat more than two coss, when all the infantry of the fugitives was either killed or dispersed. About this point Sirdar Jewahir Sing came up with the pursuit at the head of a body of horse, part of Ventura's dragoons.† The two guns also which had followed the chase were now occasionally brought to bear upon the flying Dogras. Still a party of Patan horse

* Meva Sing Majeeteea displayed on this occasion a most rancorous feeling towards the Dogras, riding about among the Seiks and calling on them to slaughter the *soors*. His brother Mathaub Sing was a *thrun ko braa*, or own brother of Heera Sing, who lavished on him a lakh of rupees within a few days of his death. Yet were these two the first to turn against the Minister, Mathaub Sing sending his battalions and guns to join Jewahir Sing. Again while he and his brother Meva Sing personally, with about two hundred of their cavalry, went in pursuit of the fugitive Wuzeer, the infantry of the former at his command entered the city and fort to disarm, plunder, and imprision any of the Dogras they might find there.

† This body of cavalry was well affected towards Heera Sing and his party, but when the rumour went abroad that *tumaum Khalsa*, the whole Khalsa, was united against the Minister, they, in accordance with the principle of union among the troops, fell into the general stream. It was a maxim of the army that the Khalsa should ever be united, and that whoever sought to divide it against itself should perish. The murder of Rajah Suchet Sing is an illustration of this mode of proceeding;—the brave but unfortunate chief was first attacked by the very troops on whom, in exchange for their promises of support, he had the previous night lavished upwards of sixty thousand rupees.

under Meean Sone Sing by occasionally facing about brought the pursuers to a halt and enabled the Rajah and his suite to gain ground upon them. Thus they advanced for ten or twelve coss, until about mid-day, when the Pundit completely, exhausted by his exertions, fell from his horse and was instantly cut to pieces by the pursuing Seiks. A little further on the Dogras entered a small village of some twenty houses, and here Heera Sing dismounted to quench his thirst, but he could not obtain anything to drink, and the Seiks coming up surrounded the place and set it on fire. The Rajah and his followers then remounted and attempted to escape, but here or in this neighbourhood the whole party was cut down, with the exception of six private soldiers, who owed their lives to the swiftness of their horses.

The heads of the different chiefs as they were cut off were brought in triumph into the city, and were next morning hung up in public view inside the several gates. That of Heera Sing was exposed at the Loharee gateway, and that of Sone Sing at the Moree gateway. The body and head of Meean Laub Sing were, however, saved from this indignity by Meva Sing and some other Gorechars who had served under and been well treated by him. The head of Pundit Jellah was treated with the greatest indignity by the Akalees, who would not allow of its being hung up with the others, but carried it about the city for some days, from house to house and from shop to shop, exhibiting it to the people amidst all kinds of indecent and insulting language, and extorting money from those to whom they thus exposed it. The unpopularity of the murdered Pundit was strikingly exemplified in the fact, that even the women on seeing his head thus made a show broke out into the most bitter exclamations against him. At length when the head of the Pundit had been exhibited to the whole city, it was by order of Jewahir Sing given to the dogs. Those of Heera Sing and Sone Sing were taken down from the gates and thrown into the ditch outside, whence after a few days they were privately conveyed into one of the inner chambers of Rajah Dehan Sing's house. There they lay for many months, and in fact it is believed that they were only removed from the place when Rajah Goolaub Sing on the 15th or 16th February 1846, came to Lahore on his way to meet the Governor-General, then advancing on the Seik capital with a British army.

Sham Singh
Ajeet Singh
Lena Singh

CHAPTER IX.

THE EXPEDITION TO JUMMOO.

THUS for the time triumphant over the Dogras at Lahore, Jewahir Sing and his adherents set themselves to the task of reducing all those places which belonged to or were held for Heera Sing and Goolaub Sing. For this purpose troops were sent against Jesrowta, Samba, Ramnuggur, and other places, under Lall Sing, Sham Sing Attareewallah, Futteh Sing Maun, and Sultan Mahomed Khan. On the other side a force was sent by Goolaub Sing from Jummoo under Meean Jewahir Sing, brother of Heera Sing, to aid and defend Jesrowta. But on the approach of the durbar troops, six horse artillery guns formerly belonging to Rajah Dehan Sing, and then in charge of a Seik officer named Uttur Sing, left Jesrowta and joined the Khalsa force. Thence their commander took them quietly to Lahore, where he was well received by Sirdar Jewahir Sing. In a few days after many more troops deserted, so that at length Meean Jewahir Sing had not strength to make any resistance. He accordingly, with all tho treasure and property he could carry away, evacuated Jesrowta and retreated to Jummoo, while the Lahore troops took formal possession of the town which he had deserted, and soon after occupied Samba and the whole line of country along the base of the lower range of hills. And now the durbar became so elated with its success that orders were shortly sent from Lahore to march and take Jummoo itself. The Khalsa troops accordingly advanced upon the capital of the Dogras, and encouraged partly by the successful result of some skirmishes, and partly by the large desertions of the Dogra troops, approached the place.

Goolaub Sing now sent word that in case Sham Sing Attareewallah, General Meva Sing Majeeteea, Sultan Mahomed, Futteh Sing Maun and two or three other chiefs would come to Jummoo and guarantee his personal safety, he would accede to all the demands of the Lahore Government. None of the chiefs named, however, would risk his liberty and life by venturing among the Dogras, except Futteh Sing Maun,- a brave old chief of Runjeet's best days, who volunteered to beard the Lion in his den. Accompanied by Wuzeer Buggenoo and one Gunput, formerly a Moonshee of Heera Sing, with a small escort, the old soldier repaired to Jummoo, where he and his companions were well received and entertained for three days. At the end of that period, Goolaub Sing gave them permission to return to their camp at Bobliana, with his answer, which was to the effect, that he was but a poor man and could not afford to pay the three crores of rupees which the durbar demanded of him, but that he agreed to give up all the property which had belonged to Dehan Sing, Heera Sing, and Suchet Sing, and in earnest of his purpose he sent along with the messangers, in banghy baskets and on camels and elephants, the sum of about three lakhs as a nuzzur for the Lahore Government. The Rajah himself, mounted on the elephant which carried Futteh Sing Maun, accompanied that chief outside the town, followed by the Wuzeer and Moonshee on another elephant. On arriving near the river, or a little beyond the outer gateway, Goolaub took leave of his visitors and returned into Jummoo. Futteh Sing and his company had not proceeded more than a mile and a half from the town, when as they arrived at a barrier called Soorghur, from its being the entrance into some hunting grounds covered with thick jungle, they were suddenly assailed by about five hundred armed Dogras and

Rohillas, who with one volley killed the three ambassadors and seventeen of their small escort, only one foot soldier escaping to tell the news in the camp at Bobliana.

This treacherous murder of a favourite chief greatly incensed the Seik troops, and made them so inveterate that the next day they advanced, and breaking through all the outposts of the Dogras, reached the Thavee, the river that runs under the walls of Jummoo. Here, however, Goolaub Sing strove to appease their anger by professions of sorrow for the death of Futteh Sing Maun, in which he disclaimed all participations; and he actually threw into prison some men who he said were his worst enemies, and had effected the murder for the purpose of widening the unfortunate breach betwixt him and the Khalsa, so that Jummoo might be taken and sacked and himself and his family involved in vain. Still however the troops pressed him closely for two days longer and gained the advantage in several small skirmishes. They had crossed the Thavee in three divisions, thus investing the place on three sides; and by this time Runjoor Sing Majeeteea had advanced from the hills and taken up a position on the fourth side, so that now the town was completely surrounded. Thus straitened, and seeing that his men, whom he treated very ill, were daily deserting in numbers, Goolaub again tried the effect of negotiation. He now sent out Meean Jewahir Sing, his nephew, and who as the son of Dehan Sing, was a great favourite with the Khalsa. This young chief had a short interview with Sultan Mahomed and Sham Sing, but he addressed himself principally to the troops, who he knew were most accessible to the arguments which he was instructed to offer, and with whom, as he knew, rested the power to accept or reject his conditions. It is to be observed too, that from the time when hostilities commenced, Goolaub Sing had constantly a number of the Punches of the Khalsa with him in Jummoo, and that these men, who doubtless had good and substantial reasons for their advocacy, exerted all their influence to secure a favourable reception for Meean Jewahir Sing and his terms. Further to ensure success to his negotiations, the Rajah himself now went out among the soldiers, and he declared that he and his family were as they ever had been the creatures and slaves of the Khalsa, and that nothing should induce him to raise his hand against them. He declared, too, that though he might appear grasping and cruel in the extortion of money, it must be remembered that he sought to amass wealth only for the service of the Khalsa. He added another and a more powerful appeal to their forbearance, when he told them that he was the last of his family who knew where the vast treasures of his house lay hid, and that if he were put to death this secret would die with him. To enforce and illustrate this declaration, he would direct the Seiks to repair to certain places around Jummoo, where, by attending to the marks and signs which he gave them, they found large sums of buried money, fifteen, twenty, and even forty thousand rupees in one place, and which but for Goolaub's disclosure might have lain hid for ever. It was thus that the Rajah gained the title which the soldiers bestowed on him of the *Sona ka Kookooree*, or the Golden Hen. By such means, by flattering speeches, by promises and bribes, Goolaub Sing entirely brought over the troops to his interest, without troubling himself about the views or opinions of their leaders. The terms he offered did not satisfy the chiefs, but they pleased the soldiers, and that was all the Rajah cared for. These terms were that each man of the entire Seik army should receive a gold bangle or armlet and twenty-five rupees in cash. The first object of this offer was to attach to the interests of the Rajah, the four battalions of Avitabile's division, the Povindea division, and that of General Court, and not only to ensure his personal safety and respect, but that if he went with them to Lahore, his rank and power should be upheld, and that he should be made Wuzeer.

On these conditions the three divisions above-mentioned swore to stand by the Rajah and be faithful to his interest. On the completion of this business, Goolaub left Jummoo and encamped in the midst of the troops lately in hostile array against him. It was supposed that this arrangement, so satisfactory to both parties, was brought about chiefly by the exertions of Meva Sing Majeeteea, who was no doubt well paid for his good offices by the Jummoo Rajah. Lall Sing and the other Durbar chiefs were now in dread for their own personal safety, and lest the rest of the troops should desert them and go over to Goolaub. They therefore endeavoured to avert such a catastrophe by making promises still larger than those of their rival and by this means secured the allegiance of that part of the force which still remained with them. Thus divided into two bodies, the army marched for Lahore creating great apprehension in the minds of Jewahir Sing and his sister.

A few days before that on which Goolaub Sing entrusted his life and fortunes to the hands of the Durbar troops, Peshora Sing, at the instigation of Avitabile's and other divisions of the army had marched from Secalkote, and presented himself before the troops, when the guards of the divisions referred to turned out to salute him, while the Khalsa troops went in a body to pay their respects to him, and immediately proclaimed him their leader. In return for this he promised to increase their pay, to fifteen rupees a month for the infantry, and a rupee and a half per day, or forty-five rupees a month, for every horseman. As, however, many of the troops did not believe that Peshora Sing had the wherewithal to fulfil his promises, they would not ratify the agreement, and the consequence was that after some hot disputation among themselves, the Seiks advised the prince to return to Seealkote for the present, which he did immediately, after being in the Khalsa camp only about two hours. This visit of Peshora Sing to the army was brought about entirely by the machinations of Goolaub Sing, who believed that either the prince would be murdered, or that he would have to apply to him for pecuniary aid to enable him to bribe the troops, and who trusted to turn either event to his own advantage. The plot, however, failed, and the prince having returned safe to Seealkote, Goolaub saw that he had now nothing to do but go with the army to Lahore, trusting to his influence with the soldiery for safety and advantage. The whole body of the Khalsa, therefore, marched for the capital, where they arrived in a few days in two divisions, the one commanded by Rajah Lall Sing, and the other by Rajah Goolaub Sing. Lall Sing's division, on approaching Lahore, encamped at Shahdera, and Goolaub's at Ekrar ke Puttun, on the Ravee, at a distance of about two miles and a half from each other. A strong feeling of animosity had by this time sprung up betwixt the rival bodies. That with Lall Sing professed to uphold the Government, while that with Goolaub, which consisted of about twenty thousand men, and fifty pieces of artillery, declared that having passed their word with the Rajah they would not allow of his being molested or ill-treated by any one or in any way. While affairs were in this position, the Ranee and Jewahir Sing sent orders to the troops then with Goolaub Sing, that they should either send the chief into Lahore as a prisoner or remove to at least twenty-four miles from the city. The soldiers, however, would do neither one thing nor the other. On this Jewahir Sing ordered the troops then in and about Lahore, about twenty thousand in number, to march out and prevent the refractory body from crossing the Ravee. This force was, therefore, soon in progress for Ekrar ke Puttun, and at the same time Rajah Lall Sing's division received orders to make preparations for an attack upon the mutineers. Thus in danger of an assault on both sides, Goolaub's adherents by his advice retired to a distance of about a thousand yards from the bank of the Ravee, and took up a position in the hollow bed of a dry nullah. While, however, Jewahir Sing was so intent on attacking them, the Punches on either side were engaged in negotiations, having made up their minds that they should not come to blows. In vain Jewahir Sing went among them, taking with him the young Maharajh and all the chiefs of his court. They allowed him to seize and imprison Meva Sing Majeeteea, who, as was said, had chiefly influenced them to espouse the cause of Goolaub Sing; but they had determined that matters should be settled quietly, and what the Punches had resolved on, that the whole body of the Khalsa were ready to take for their law, such was the power and influence of these deputies. Accordingly on the fourth day it was settled that Rajah Goolaub Sing should go into Lahore and have an interview with the Ranee; and that the whole Khalsa army of all parties should guarantee his personal safety, and protect him from the enmity of Jewahir Sing and others. It was arranged that he should appear in durbar to answer any charge that might be preferred against him by the Ranee, but that Jewahir Sing should not be present on the occasion. The Punches of the army, about two thousand men, assembled in a body, to escort the Jummoo Rajah on his visit to the palace, proclaiming that the whole army was bound to protect him from insult, and intimating to Lall Sing and other chiefs, that if any thing of the kind was attempted, it should be revenged fourfold. Preliminaries being thus settled, Rajah Goolaub Sing crossed the Ravee at Ekrar ke Puttun in a boat, attended by the chief Punches; and on his landing upon the left bank he was welcomed with cheers by the whole army, who paid him all outward show of respect, and assured him of his perfect safety. On landing he was immediately placed on an elephant and conveyed under a strong escort to the Summun Boorj, where he was well received by the Ranee. After the interview he was requested to take up his abode in the palace of the late Kurruck Sing, but the Punches said that they, being security for his safety, would not allow any one to be about him but themselves, and that when the Ranee desired an interview with him, he should be escorted by them to and from the durbar, where neither Jewahir Sing nor any other chief should be allowed to appear armed while he was present.

On his first visit to the durbar Goolaub was received with the greatest respect and cordiality by the Ranee, and many compliments passed betwixt them. Her Highness even went so far as to express a wish that he should undertake the office of Wuzeer, which had not yet been formally bestowed upon Jewahir Sing. These evidences of partiality greatly alarmed and enraged the chief last named, and had it not been for fear of the troops, he would certainly have compassed the death of his rival. However, he managed by his intrigues so to undermine the Dogra in the Ranee's favour, as well as in that of the army, that he secured his own installation in the Wuzeerut. Thus firmly established, he brought Goolaub to account for his recent contumacy, and after much discussion, it was settled that he should pay to the state thirty-five lakhs of rupees, also that he should give up the territories which had belonged to his brother Suchet Sing and the property of his nephew Heera Sing. Having paid the first instalment of his fine, or whatever it may be called, the Rajah received permission to retire to Jummoo, of which, however, he did not avail himself until two attempts on his life, instigated probably by Jewahir Sing, warned him that Lahore was no longer a safe place of residence for him. He then, after a sojourn of four months, left the capital and returned to Jummoo, whence a few months afterwards he was recalled to take charge of the state, at the critical moment of a rupture with the British Government.

CHAPTER X.

THE MURDER OF PESHORA SING.

PESHORA SING on the invitation of the troops repaired to Lahore, and on his arrival there, the deputies of the army waited upon him, when some of them went so far as to desire him to place himself at the head of the Khalsa declaring that they would proclaim and support him as the rightful heir to the throne. He had not been twenty-four hours in the city when such overtures were made to him, and his cause was gaining ground. At this juncture the Ranee sent for him, and at her request he presented himself in durbar. He was there received by Her Highness with open arms and professions of regard and respect as the equal of Dulleep Sing her son. Jewahir Sing, however, did not treat him as the prince considered due to his rank, and the latter therefore left the durbar in disgust. Thence he went quietly to his quarters in the city, and immediately summoned to his presence the Punches of the Khalsa. To them he enlarged on the slight he had received in durbar, and proposed that he should leave the capital and return to his jaghire. But the deputies persuaded him from this intention, and induced him to accompany them out of the city to Buddhoo ka ava, which, since it became the gathering place of the troops on Shere Sing's accession, had been considered to have some good fortune attached to it. Here Peshora Sing was immediately surrounded by the whole body of the Punt who offered their allegiance to him in the name of the army.

Tidings of these things came to the ears of Jewahir Sing, and he thereupon repented of his conduct, and saw that it was necessary to take immediate and decided steps for the confirmation of his authority. On consultation with his sister he now, therefore, sent to the army a promise that every man should receive a golden necklace of the value of twenty-five rupees. The troops understood the meaning of his liberality, and instead of proclaiming Peshora Sing as Maharajh or even as Wuzeer, they recommended him to return to his jaghire, which they promised should be enlarged, and there to remain quietly in the hope of better times. Seeing that the tide had turned against him, the prince prudently resolved to follow their advice; and so with the good wishes of the Khalsa and some valuable presents from the Court he left Lahore.

But Peshora Sing had not lived long on his estate, when Jewahir Sing, at the instigation of Rajah Goolaub Sing, began to form plots for his destruction. The Jummoo chief was induced to encourage the Wuzeer in these designs on the life of the prince by the conviction that if he were put to death the troops would avenge his murder, and that if Jewahir Sing appeared as the contriver of the deed his doom was sealed. By this process two formidable obstacles to the extension of the Dogra's power and influence would be at once removed, and that without his having appeared to take any part in their removal.

While Peshora Sing remained on his estate, several attempts were made to assassinate him, and finding his position an unsafe one, he deemed it advisable to retire towards Attock with his followers. With these and the aid of some Mahomedans of the neighbourhood, he seized upon the fort of that place, and there took up his abode. Jewahir Sing on hearing of this movement was greatly disappointed and annoyed, and ordered off troops to recapture the place and punish the rebellious prince. But the troops sent on this service, afraid of the

Punt and unwilling to injure the reputed son of Runjeet, went reluctantly, and did not act vigorously, and so nothing came of their expedition. In the meantime Peshora Sing was gaining ground in the minds of the great body of the Khalsa at Lahore, who now declared that they would avenge any injury done to him; and the chief conspirator saw that if his purpose was to be effected other means must be employed. He, therefore, assured Jewahir Sing that it was now obvious that no man in the service of the Lahore state would act willingly or with energy against the prince, but that if he were to send Chuttur Sing Attareewalla and Futteh Khan, tools of his own, they would execute whatever orders were given them. Orders were accordingly issued for their proceeding against Attock, with the troops under their command. When these instructions reached them, Futteh Khan was at Kalabagh on the Indus, and Chuttur Sing was in the hill-country about Naoshera and Rajouri, settling some disturbances among the people, but acting rather as the agent of Goolaub Sing than as the servant of the Lahore Durbar. Having in some degree effected the purpose of his expedition, he was ordered off to Attock, which place he quickly reached. There he joined his troops with those of Futteh Khan, and with their combined force they made preparations for an attack upon the fort in which Peshora Sing with his small force had shut himself up. But Peshora Sing was daily becoming so popular among the people of the country, Patans, and the Khalsa troops who continued encamped in the neighbourhood showed such an interest in the prince's cause, that the chiefs saw there was little likelihood of much success in an assault upon the place. They therefore resorted to negotiation, and making large and seemingly sincere promises to the prince, they after about twelve days spent in discussing the terms of capitulation, induced him to evacuate the place. The conditions for which he stipulated and to which they consented were, that he should be treated with all proper respect, and that he should leave the fort at the head of his troops with all the honours of war;—that, escorted by his own forces, he should proceed to Lahore, where his interest should be attended to and all his claims considered. Thus then Peshora Sing left the fort of Attock, and was received with seeming cordiality and respect by Futteh Khan and Chuttur Sing, who repeated the most solemn professions of their good-will and fidelity. This put the prince off his guard so far that he unwarily allowed these chiefs and their troops to encamp around him and his smaller force. Thus then Peshora Sing with his troops accompanied by Futteh Khan and Chuttur Sing with their forces, marched from Attock towards Lahore. They had not proceeded more than twenty miles on the way, however, and had come to a place called Punja Sahib or Hassan Abdul, when Chuttur Sing proposed a day's halt for the purpose of hunting the wild boar. This proposal was agreed to, and the chiefs and the prince spent the day in the sport. Early the next morning, however, Chuttur Sing and Futteh Khan, with a numerous band of armed men, entered the tent of the prince, while he was yet asleep, bound him hand and foot, his troops, not above five hundred men, being simultaneously overpowered and dispersed by the numerous force of the treacherous chiefs, amounting to eight or nine thousand men. That same day Peshora Sing, heavily ironed, was taken back to Attock, mounted on an elephant, and escorted by the two chiefs with about a thousand horse. On arriving near the fort, he was dismounted from the elephant and placed in a palanquin, the better to conceal the fact of his return under such circumstances. While this arrangement was being effected, the prince addressed Chuttur Sing, vehemently upbraiding him with his treachery, yet assuring him of his forgiveness if he would only order that he should be unbound, and that his sword and shield should be given to him, that he might die—for he knew he was doomed—as became a soldier, armed, and fighting to the last. To all this, however, Chuttur Sing replied only by reiterated assurances that he might dismiss his apprehensions, for that no manner of harm was intended him. Thus then he was conveyed into the fort of Attock, where he was conducted to a low tower called the Kollboorj in close proximity to the Indus, which is extremely deep at this place. In a lower room of this tower which had a doorway opening immediately on the river, the prince was lodged. During the night he was visited by the treacherous chiefs, who placed six sentries over him, and before morning he had been strangled and afterwards sunk in the deep water of the Indus. The next day the two chiefs returned to their camp at Punja Sahib, whence they in a few days afterwards marched on different routes. Futteh Khan took his troops towards Kalabagh and Dera Ismael Khan, and Chuttur Sing returned into the hill country. They both dreaded the consequences of what they had done, when it should come to the knowledge of the Khalsa; and Chuttur Sing acknowledged his fears in the act of sending his family across the hills to Kistowar, where they might dwell under the protection of his patron, Rajah Goolaub Sing, while he himself hastened by another route to a small village near the fort of Reharsee beyond Jummoo.

CHAPTER XI.

DEATH OF JEWAHIR SING.

WHEN Jewahir Sing received tidings of the death of Peshora Sing, he was so elated that he actually ordered that a salute should be fired and the city illuminated. This ill-judged order was, however, privately countermanded by Baba Ruttun Sing and Bii Chetta, who saw the folly and danger of such a demonstration. Rumours of the event soon spread among the troops, exciting their horror and indignation; and it was intimated to Jewahir Sing that the Khalsa was likely to be in a state of mutiny, and that the soldiery were bent on mischief. A few days more served to confirm the apprehensions of the conscience-stricken Sirdar. Pirthee Sing, the son of Meean Arbela Sing, a Dogra, and his party, were busily at work exciting the troops to rise and revenge the death of Prince Peshora Sing; and so well did they play their parts, that in a very short time the Avitabile division and thirteen others had resolved on the death of Jewahir Sing. These divisions therefore marched out of their several lines and encamped about four miles from the city, a little beyond Meean Meer. Having taken up their position here, they sent orders to the remaining battalions to leave their various stations and to join them. This was done for the purpose of ascertaining whether the entire Khalsa would side with them or not, while the object of their movement was yet kept secret. They then induced the troops that were in the city to come out, that they might not embarrass them in the execution of their design; and lastly they sent a message to Jewahir Sing, informing him that if he would come forth, present himself before them, and order them gratuity, the affair of Peshora Sing's murder should be hushed up. But the Sirdar either mistrusted them too strongly to venture amongst them, or he wanted tact to seize the opportunity for making his peace with the army, and so declined to accept the invitation. He attempted, however, to negotiate, but to no purpose, as the Punches would listen to nothing that he could urge on his behalf until he presented himself before the troops.

Meantime the Punches of several battalions went into the city and took away Pirthee Sing, pretending to do so by force, and placed him at the head of the army, issuing orders in his name and that of the Punt Khalsajee. The next day Rajah Lall Sing, Buggut Ram, Dewan Denanauth, and several other principal men of the state went out to the camp and made their obeisance to Pirthee Sing. There, too, they remained, taking care, however, to make it appear that they were detained as prisoners and against their will.

There was now a clamorous multitude, under the designation of Punches, constantly assembled at the tents of the Dogra party, which were in the rear centre of Court's battalions. Word then went forth that every corps which did not join the Punt, would incur the anger of the Khalsa, and be severely dealt with. This threat had such effect, that ere the day on which it was proclaimed had past every division of the army was in line, with the exception of two battalions belonging to Jewahir Sing, which were in the fort with three or four pieces of artillery. These corps were allowed to remain where they were, but peremptory orders were sent to them to prevent the escape of their chief Jewahir Sing; and this command was enforced by the declaration, that if they allowed the Sirdar to go from among them, they should all be either blown from guns or put to the sword. This threat was so effectual that these two battalions, composed mostly of raw recruits, now thought more of guarding their chief as a prisoner than of standing by him as their leader; and during the same night a report that he intended to make an attempt to escape, threw them all into the utmost confusion. The next morning the men of the artillery, at the peremptory command of the Punt, removed their guns from the fort, being urged on and aided in the work by the Punches themselves to the number of about five hundred men.

Jewahir Sing now began to despair of bringing matters to a peaceable issue, though he and his sister were constantly surrounded by the deputies of the mutinous troops, whose object was to induce him to leave the city and place himself in the hands of the army. He went so far as to give them a written promise of twelve rupees a month to all the Punches, on condition that they should save his life and forgive his having procured the murder of Peshora Sing. His sister, too, even offered to increase their pay to fifteen rupees, and both with joined hands besought the mercy of the Punt. But their promises and humble entreaties were alike ineffectual. The Dogra party had paid ready money in large sums to several of the leading men of the Punt to insure the execution of their bloody designs.

On the 6th of Assin, corresponding to the 21st of September, 1845, about noon, Court's division, with several other battalions, all commanded by Pirthee Sing, were in motion, and stationed themselves near the Delhi gate. Jewahir Sing now saw that it was useless to keep himself shut up any longer. He therefore invited his sister to accompany him, and mounting an elephant with the young Maharajh, Dulleep Sing, in his arms, he left the fort, escorted by about a thousand men. By a circuitous route he repaired towards the spot, where the army was encamped. Pirthee Sing and his followers seeing him set forth, quickly returned by a shorter road to the camp, where they arrived before the Wuzeer had reached the spot. He entered the camp shortly afterwards from the left of the line, where one of Maun's battalions, actually received him with the customary salute. This circumstance so encouraged and assured Jewahir Sing that he directed his mahout to take him nearer to this battalion, and then to move forward. On this some Punches of the division of Lall Sing Meralia, entreated him not to go further but to fix his quarters in their lines, declaring that they would die to a man before they would allow any injury or insult to be offered to him. But the doomed Sirdar seemed confident in his belief that the main body of the army would do him no injury since he came among them in person, and had the young Maharajh with him in the howdah, while his sister, the queen-mother, followed on another elephant, scattering lavishly fair words and hard coin, in the hope of inducing the troops to spare the life of her brother. Thus he continued to move along in front of the line, receiving and returning individual salutes, while the whole Khalsa turned out to gaze on him as he passed. As he arrived on the right of Meralia's division, that of Court imbibed the idea that the former intended to assist and protect him. Thereupon ensued a great tumult, the drums on both sides beating to arms, and the artillery being dragged into position for immediate battle. Jewahir Sing himself, however, did his utmost to convince the Meralia troops that no harm was intended him, and entreated them not to cause bloodshed on his account. Having done this he again moved along the line until he came opposite the centre of Court's division. Here the procession was stopped in its onward progress, and directed towards the tents that had been pitched some days before and were intended for the Zenana. They had not, however, gone far from the lines, when Jewahir Sing's elephant was suddenly and violently brought to a halt by the soldiery of Court's division, and the mahout was compelled to make the elephant kneel. The fierce crowd of armed men now roughly demanded the boy Dulleep from the arms of his uncle, who reluctantly gave up what he had doubtless considered his best protection. Stretching forth his hands in deprecation of violence, Jewahir Sing implored them to hear him for a moment. But not a word would they listen to. He received a stab with a bayonet on the left side, which made him lean over to the right; and immediately a bullet was sent through his brain by a man who placed the muzzle of a matchlock to his forehead. He fell from the howdah, and was dragged off the elephant a corpse, but still his body. was hacked and mangled by the swords and bayonets of his murderers, while a running fire of muskets was kept up for some minutes, for the purpose of terrifying all who might be disposed to assist him or avenge his death. Baba Ruttun Sing and Bii Chetta, who were in attendance on the Wuzzeer, were killed, the former a few yards from the spot on which his patron fell, the latter was cut down by a horseman when attempting to save his life by flight. While this tragedy was being performed, the crowd of Seik soldiers were engaged in a scramble for the money and valuables which Jewahir Sing, his sister, and their now dispersed attendants, had with them. The Ranee and her slave-girls were then compelled to enter the tents which had been prepared for their reception, while the young Maharajh was kept among the soldiery for some time, when in order to quiet her alarm, he was given into the hands of his mother. The sentries placed around her Highness's tents received strict orders to see that in her rage and grief at the loss of her brother, she did not attempt to destroy herself and her son. With fearful vehemence, the Ranee upbraided and execrated the whole Khalsa, swearing that she would have her revenge upon them. Early next morning she was permitted to see the mangled body of her murdered brother, on which her curses and lamentations were renewed. She threw herself and her little son upon the body; she wept bitterly and tore her loose hair; she rent her garments until her bosom was exposed to the view of those around. It was with much difficulty that she was, partly by entreaty and partly by force, separated from the corpse, and induced to return to the city. The Punches endeavoured to pacify and console her by assuring her that the death of her brother was according to God's will,—that they could not avert it, and were not therefore to be considered answerable for it. About noon the Ranee returned to the city, whither also the body of the murdered Wuzeer was carried. That evening the corpse was burnt in the presence of several sirdars, who came to assist at the ceremony. Two of the late Minister's widows, and three slave-girls, were burnt with the body. A guard of Seik soldiers was in attendance, and the conduct of these men on the occasion was atrocious in the extreme. During the procession the unfortunate women, according to custom, carried money to scatter to the people; but it was actually forced out of their hands by the armed ruffians who surrounded them. Again, as they mounted the pile, their jewels and trinkets, their ear and nose rings, &c. with which they were adorned for the occasion, were violently torn from them by the brutal troops, who answered their shrieks with taunts and jests. One savage, more shameless, if possible, than the rest, actually thrust his hands among the smoke and flames to tear away the golden fringe and embroidery worn by one of the miserable victims on her trousers. Thus insulted and molested, the hapless women could not remain in the position which custom enjoined as proper and decent for the occasion, but were persecuted and disturbed until the rising flames acted as a barrier against further molestation. At this moment, one of them, in a transport of rage and grief at the treatment to which they had been subjected, rose erect amidst the fire and smoke, and in the loud and piercing tones of agony called down curses on the whole race of Seiks. On this one of the savages made a blow at her with the butt of his musket;—he missed her, however, and she fell, a prey to the flames alone, into the midst of the raging fire.

The troops having effected their purpose of avenging the death of Peshora Sing and removing the obnoxious Wuzeer, became all submission and repentance before the Ranee, whose grief and anger they endeavoured by all means in their power to appease. But she was yet implacable and inconsolable. Daily, attended by numbers of her women, she went on foot to renew her lamentations at the mausoleum of her murdered brother. Daily she thus walked through the city, exposing herself to the view of the multitude with her long hair all dishevelled, as she repaired to the tomb of Jewahir Sing outside the Mustee gate. As yet she would not listen to the entreaties or overtures of the troops who sought to make their peace with her, and who were now engaged in mutual recriminations against each other for the commission of the bloody deed. Some avowed their determination to inflict punishment on the corps that were accessories to the murder; while those to whose charge the act was laid, maintained that the whole Khalsa was concerned in the deed, pointing for proof of this to the fact, that every corps was in line on the occasion, with a full knowledge of the purpose for which the line was formed. However, after a few days of obduracy, the Ranee relented so far as to say that if the troops would punish those sirdars who planned and counselled the murder of her brother, she would be satisfied. She summoned the Punches and officers of the army to meet her in the Summun Boorj, and presenting herself before the assembly, she vehemently upbraided them for their treachery and cruelty. "But," said she, in conclusion of her fierce harangue, "seize my enemies and deliver them over to my will, and I will freely pardon the rest." On this some of the Punches asked her to name those to whom she referred. She then pointed out Dewan Jewahir Mull, formerly dewan to Suchet Sing, who had actually been in the plot, and had supplied all the money distributed by Pirthee Sing. Jewahir Mull, who was then in the assembly, was immediately disarmed and made a prisoner. Her Highness then intimated her wish that Pirthee Sing and others of the Dogra party should be seized and given up to her, but none of these were present, as they took care never to move out of the lines of Court's division which protected them. On hearing this demand, great murmuring and tumult ensued among the Punches, which ended in the whole party leaving the Summun Boorj and returning to the camp. Some of the troops and their deputies were for taking the members of the Dogra faction prisoners, and sending them to the Ranee, while others were strongly opposed to this measure. The French, or General Ventura's division, were most forward in counselling the surrender of Pirthee Sing and his advisers; and they, joining with several other battalions, planned an attack on Court's division for the purpose of seizing the obnoxious chiefs. On hearing of this, Court's battalions formed square to protect themselves and the sirdars, whom they placed in the centre. At this crisis word was brought that the whole army was to be reviewed next morning by the young Maharajh himself. During the ensuing night a numerous assembly of the Punches was held, at which, it was resolved that in order to prevent the Khalsa from hostile division and suicidal slaughter, Pirthee Sing and his party should be secretly conveyed out of the camp, when they could find their own way safely to Jummoo. This matter being arranged, the review came off as appointed, before the Maharajh and his mother; and while the royal cortége was leaving the ground to return to the city, Pirthee Sing and his friends, attended by a few horsemen, were allowed to quit the camp in another direction, and take the road to the hills. They reached Jummoo in safety, and Goolaub Sing wrote to the durbar expressing his sorrow on hearing of the murder of Jewahir Sing, and declaring that had he sufficient power and influence, he would severely punish Pirthee Sing and his adherents. The Ranee now seeing that there was no alternative, remained quiet for the present, and daily took counsel of her favourite, Rajah Lall Sing, by whose advice and on whose security, she in a few days, consented to the release of Jewahir Mull.

CHAPTER XII.

RAJAH LALL SING, AND THE SLAVE-GIRL MUNGELA.

THE Rajah Lall Sing, who now became a prominent character in the grand drama of Punjaub history, is the son of one Jessa Misser, originally a poor Kotree Brahmin, who kept a small shop in the village of Soongoia, formerly belonging to Jewahir Sing Puddana, but now in the hands of Lall Sing himself. Having failed in business, Jessa Misser took up the business of an itinerant trader or pedlar, wandering with his wares into all parts of the Punjaub. It was during one of his excursions that he by chance became known to Bustee Ram, the Toshakhaneea, or treasurer of Maha Sing, the father of the great Runjeet. Jessa Misser could write the Lounda character well, and to this accomplishment he was indebted for an appointment under Bustee Ram on three rupees a month and his food. From this, he in time rose to be a sort of accountant in the treasury of Maha Sing. However, on the death of that chief and during the minority of his son, Jessa Misser was compelled to throw up his employment, on which he returned to his village and re-opened his shop. When Runjeet attained to manhood, and, having risen into power, had made himself master of Lahore, Jessa Misser was again employed by Bustee Ram, though at that time all the pecuniary affairs of Runjeet were transacted by a rich merchant of Umritsir, named Ramanund, to whom the young chief mortgaged or farmed most of the districts which he conquered in different parts of the Punjaub. It was only after his first attempt to subdue Cashmere, that Runjeet formed any kind of a regular treasury. About that time Bustee Ram died, and Misser Belee Ram, his nephew, who stood high in the favour and confidence of Runjeet, was appointed chief manager and controllor of the Toshakhana. Jessa Misser was still only a petty writer or moonshee under Belee Ram, but on Rajah Dehan Sing becoming minister, that chief, who was on bad terms with Belee Ram, persuaded Runjeet to appoint Jessa Misser, whom he represented as a most upright man of great abilities, to the charge of all the money and valuables received from Cashmere, then newly conquered. Thus Jessa Misser became a protégé of the Dogra party, whom he thenceforth acknowledged as his patrons and benefactors.

In 1829 Jessa Misser died, leaving his son, the present Rajah Lall Sing, to the care of the Rajahs Dehan Sing and Goolaub Sing, enjoining the boy on his death-bed ever to remember that he had owed his rise and fortunes to the favour and patronage of the Dogra chiefs. He particularly recommended his son to consider the Rajahs Dehan Sing and Goolaub Sing as *his* patrons and protectors, and himself as their humble servant and slave all the days of his life. After Jessa Misser's death, Rajah Dehan Sing gave Lall Sing the appointment held by his father; but as the boy was too young to discharge the duties of the office, business was transacted in his name by his elder brother, the present Misser Ameer Chund, now Kardar of a large district beyond the Jhelum, and in charge of the Salt mines. Another and a younger brother, Bugwan Sing, was also ordered by the Rajah to attend at the Toshakhana for the purpose of learning the business of the office. Dehan Sing's intention was to displace Misser Belee Ram and to put this youth Bugwan Sing in his place. However the Rajah did not live to consummate his plans. Still Misser Lall Sing was acknowledged as the keeper and manager of all the cash and property that came from Cashmere; and Dehan Sing more than once exposed himself to the anger of Runjeet by too publicly, and, perhaps too strongly, advocating the cause of this youth.

Thus matters stood when Dehan Sing was killed, and Heera Sing, with his adviser, the Pundit Jellah, came into power. On this occasion Lall Sing preferred representations against Misser Belee Ram, and also against Bii Goormuck Sing, which chiefly induced the new minister and his counsellor to put these men to death. On their removal Misser Lall Sing was made chief treasurer to the Lahore Government. Thus Heera Sing and the Pundit advanced their protégé, while he on the other hand was even then forming deep schemes for the destruction of the whole Dogra party, to which he owed so much. He intrigued with Mai Chunda, the mother of Maharajh Dulleep Sing, and with her confidential slave-girl Mungela, to compass the death of Heera Sing and the Pundit, and was one of the principals in the conspiracy which brought about the murder of these chiefs. Little did the doomed men suspect that one who was a creature of their own hands was the first to turn against them.

About this time occurred the temporary disagreement betwixt Rajah Heera Sing and his uncle Rajah Goolaub Sing, which has been already recorded. On this occasion Fuzuldad Khan, chief of Rhotas and Domelia, having sided with Goolaub Sing, the Wuzeer confiscated all his lands and property to the state, bestowing them, with the title of Rajah, on Misser Lall Sing, who, backed by twelve hundred cavalry, sent by the durbar, went to take possession of his domains. On his return to Lahore, he was formally installed Rajah of Rhotas and Domelia, and it is a curious coincidence that on the very day on which this ceremony was performed, Lall Sing signed an agreement, binding him to aid in the extermination of the whole Dogra party, including his indulgent patrons. On this self same day Misser Lall Sing was with great pomp installed Rajah of Rhotas and Domelia, in the presence of all the Sirdars of the Court, summoned for the occasion by Heera Sing, who himself made the accustomed "*teeka*" or mark on the forehead of his favourite, and, as a special token of favour, with his own hand waved the chourie over the head of the new made Rajah.

About a month after this the Wuzeer and the Pundit were put to death, but during the interval, Rajah Lall Sing, one of the principal conspirators against them, was more than usually assiduous in his attendance upon them. With the Pundit he even exchanged turbans, thus becoming, ceremonially, his sworn friend and brother! During the same period too, he was in the habit of sitting up with the Wuzeer almost nightly, engaged in gambling and debauchery.

On the night before the murder, Lall Sing, accompanied by General Mathaub Sing and Meva Sing Majeeteea, who were both privy to the conspiracy, waited on the Wuzeer and the Pundit, with whom they remained for a long time, endeavouring to persuade them that they had nothing to fear, as they, the conspirators, with many other sirdars, and the whole body of the Khalsa, were ready to die in their cause if necessary. This had the effect of throwing the Wuzeer and the Pundit off their guard, and lulling them for the time into a deceitful feeling of security. They did not till too late suspect the extent of their danger, for had they done, so they might at any moment have obtained the protection of the French division, eight or ten thousand men, which was ready to turn out in their defence. The same night and just before the interview with his victims, Lall Sing had sent a message to the Ranee, with his good wishes, for the success of the enterprise, accompanying his compliments with a present of some seventeen or eighteen thousand rupees, and an offer of as much more to aid in paying the expences of the undertaking. Again, while Sirdar

Jewahir Sing, with the troops, was out in pursuit of the fugitive Wuzeer and the Pundit, Rajah Lall Sing personally paid his respects to the Ranee, by whom he was most warmly received. And finally on hearing of the death of his patrons, the Rajah Lall Sing was the first to hasten with the joyful intelligence to Mai Chunda and her adviser Mungela, whom he congratulated on the success of their enterprise and the downfall of the Dogras. On this occasion again he presented a nuzzur of eleven thousand rupees, with many valuable trinkets and ornaments of gold and jewels.

When matters settled down into something like quiet, Jewahir Sing, who was now acknowledged as ostensible head of the Government, did his utmost to break off the connection betwixt Rajah Lall Sing and his sister Ranee Chunda, and to prevent all intercourse and communication between them. His efforts were fruitless, however, but his intentions won for him the bitter though secret animosity of the favoured Rajah. It was in pursuance of these ineffectual attempts that Jewahir Sing induced Lall Sing to take the command of the troops sent towards Jummoo against Goolaub Sing. The Rajah went, but most reluctantly, and the Ranee more than once remonstrated with her brother against his being sent on this service. However, he was not very long away, and on his return in April 1845, he renewed and strengthened his intimacy with the lady, notwithstanding all her brother could do to prevent it. About this time it was known to Jewahir Sing, that the Ranee was pregnant with her fourth, or, as some say, her fifth child since the birth of Maharajh Dulleep Sing.

In this disgraceful way matters proceeded until the death of Peshora Sing, when Lall Sing seeing that the troops were bent on a bloody revenge, strove diligently not only to avert the vengeance of the army from himself but to ensure its descent on the devoted Wuzeer. He, with Buggut Ram and others, strove by giving large presents to the soldiery, and by currying favour with Pirthee Sing and the Dogra party, not only to save their own lives but also to promote the conspiracy for the murder of Jewahir Sing. The price which Lall Sing paid for his own safety and for ensuring the destruction of his enemy was twenty-five thousand rupees to Pirthee Sing, with promises of more, and some twelve or fifteen thousand rupees distributed among the troops.

To complete the history of Rajah Lall Sing up to the present time, it may be briefly stated, that on the murder of Jewahir Sing, he became, by favour of the Ranee, virtually the head of the Government;—that when the invasion of the British territories was projected, he was formally appointed and installed as Wuzeer;—that he commanded the Seik cavalry during the war on the Sutlej, without winning a reputation for skill or valour;—that having for a time given place to the commanding influence of Rajah Goolaub Sing, he was on the elevation of that chief to the dignity of an independent sovereign, reinstated in his former office of Wuzeer;—and finally that being convicted of treachery to the state in privately encouraging the Governor of Cashmere to retain possession of that province, when it should have been delivered over to Maharajh Goolaub Sing, he was, in December, 1846, sent a prisoner to Agra, since which nothing has been heard of him beyond the bare fact of his existence.

Another of the Ranee's favourites and advisers, but one of her own sex, has figured largely in the history of the Lahore Durbar. This is the celebrated Mungela, the slave-girl, as she is called, although a full grown woman on the wrong side of thirty. This distinguished personage, the confidante and counsellor of royalty, is the daughter of one Peeroo, a poor Hindoo, of the Jeur or water-carrier caste, who, with his wife and family, supported a miserable existence in a lonely cabin, five or six miles from Kangra, by cutting fire-wood and carrying it to the town for sale. This, at all events, was the ostensible means by which Peeroo and his family earned their livelihood; but they had a more plentiful though secret resource in the business of procuring and dealing in slaves. By a variety of means, some of them strongly tinged with cruelty, they collected female children for the Bunda Frashes, as the wholesale dealers in human beings are there called, who resorted to the neighbourhood to procure their supplies of slaves. Among these slave merchants Peeroo and his wife were celebrated for their skill and success in luring away young girls from their homes, and in inducing the half-starved people of the district to dispose of their offspring as a means of relieving their own necessities. The children thus collected were afterwards carried away by the wholesale dealers who sold them to the highest bidder among the Kangers, or pimps, about Lahore, Umritsir, Dewannuggur, &c. Notwithstanding this apparently profitable source of revenue, Peeroo and his family were remarkable among their neighbours for their abject poverty, which the simple people around looked upon as heaven's punishment on them for the cruel practices by which they carried on their trade. That this poverty was real and not assumed as a mask to deceive their neighbours, is testified by the fact, that about the close of the year 1825, they found themselves under the necessity of selling their own only daughter, then about ten years of age. The girl was sold to an itinerant Doom for about twenty-five rupees. The purchaser took her to Kangra, where he was compelled to dispose of her to a Kanger of the place, in satisfaction of a trifling debt of some twenty rupees. In the house of her new master the girl was initiated into all the evil arts and practices of a courtezan's life. However, about the year 1830, she being then about fourteen years old, she contrived to insinuate herself so far into the favour of one Jessa, a moonshee of Kangra, that he was induced to purchase her from the Kanger for forty rupees. According to another account, however, she absconded from the house of the

Kanger, and went to Noorpoor, whence this moonshee carried her to Lahore, where she for a while lived as his concubine. But this connection, however formed, did not last long. Her protector soon discovered that her habits, as indeed might have been expected from her training, were extremely loose and dissolute. She would absent herself from her apartments for days together, and it was discovered that on these occasions her usual resorts were the houses of some of the Kangers of the city, whither she went to obtain money, with which the moonshee did not supply her as liberally as she desired. By these means she is said to have raised funds sufficient for the purchase of a set of golden ornaments, worth perhaps twelve or fifteen hundred rupees. On discovering her true character, the moonshee resolved to get rid of her by some means or other; and she, suspecting his designs, fled from his house, and openly took up the trade of a common prostitute in the city. About the year 1833 or 1834, she became acquainted with Topee Moskee, the uncle of Gulloo Moskee, a favourite attendant on the person of Runjeet Sing, and went to live in his house. After she had remained here some time, Topee Moskee gave her over to the charge of his nephew, Gulloo Moskee, who was then engaged in his amorous intrigues with Mai Chunda. About the end of 1835, Gulloo Moskee introduced the slave-girl to Mai Chunda, by whom she was employed as a confidential agent, in the conveyance of secret messages connected with her amours. The moonshee, Jessa, the former master of Mungela, hearing that she was now in the possession of either Topee Moskee or his nephew Gulloo Moskee, went and made a demand for her, founding it on the fact that he had bought her of the Kangers of Kangra for forty rupees, and that she had absconded from his house. Gulloo Moskee, in whose hands the girl now was, disputed the moonshee's claim, and refused to give her up; this led to a dispute, which was the occasion of Mungela's being brought before Runjeet Sing. She was at this time about twenty years of age, and of a remarkably shrewd, wily, and insinuating character. She could not be called handsome in comparison with other women of her country ; but she had a pair of fine hazel eyes of which she could make a most effective use, and an easy, winning carriage and address. By means of these she attracted the attention of Runjeet so far as to induce him to give Gulloo Moskee an order that she should remain with Mai Chunda. Jessa Moonshee seeing how Runjeet had determined to dispose of the girl, had the tact to assure him that it was as a present for His Highness that he had bought her, and that he now cheerfully resigned her into the hands of the Maharajh. On this he was dismissed with a trifling present, and Mungela became a permanent inhabitant of Runjeet's Zenana, where she remained in attendance on Mai Chunda as the active and willing minister of her pleasures. It was Mungela who exerted herself to persuade Runjeet that the child borne by Mai Chunda, the present Maharajh Dulleep Sing, was his own, though none knew its real paternity better than she did. By thus aiding and encouraging her mistress in her intrigues, by sparing no means of ingratiating herself with her, and by all the arts which she exercised to gain her purpose, the slave-girl at length attained such an influence over her mistress that the Ranee could not act or decide for herself in the most trivial or the most important matter.

During the life time of Kurruck Sing and No Nehal Sing, an intimacy grew up betwixt Mai Chunda and Lall Sing, and during the short reign of Shere Sing it had ripened into the closest connection. This intrigue was favoured and forwarded by Mungela with all her power, her object being to secure to herself the gifts in money, jewels, &c. which the lovers were ready to bestow upon her most liberally,—Lall Sing then having charge of one of the toshakhanas or treasuries. When Heera Sing and the Pundit became the heads of the Government, Lall Sing was strictly prohibited from entering the female apartments in the fort, and forbidden to hold any communication with the Ranee. At the same time a particular inventory was taken of the valuable property under his charge, so that he could no longer undetected make presents to his lady-love and her confidant. This gave great annoyance to the virtuous trio, and filled them with indignation against Heera Sing and his adviser, whose ruin they thenceforth sought.

When Sirdar Jewahir Sing, the brother of Mai Chunda, was imprisoned by Heera Sing for attempting to carry away the young Maharajh Dulleep Sing, Mungela persuaded her mistress that, should she quietly submit to the incarceration of her brother, the next step would be either at once to murder her and her son, or to consign them to a lingering death in some dungeon at Jummoo or elsewhere in the hills. The Ranee was assured that the Dogra party meant no good to her or any of her family, and would certainly try by some means to get rid of her. Thus was Mai Chunda incited to appeal to the troops, whereby she procured the release of her brother, who swore vengeance on the Dogras, and immediately proceeded to lay his plans for effecting their downfall. While he was at Umritsir sowing the seeds of disaffection and rebellion among the Punches and the troops, Mungela was busy at Lahore using all her arts to induce Mai Chunda to instigate the Khalsa to rise against her enemies.

While these intrigues were working, Lall Sing contrived to insinuate himself so far into the favour of Heera Sing and the Pundit, that they, as has been before mentioned, created him Rajah of Rhotas. At the same time, however, he was, with the Ranee and Mungela, plotting their destruction; yet he acted his part so well that up to the last moment his fidelity was never suspected by his victims.

After the murder of Heera Sing and Pundit Jellah, Sirdar Jewahir Sing came into power, and at the same time became the favorite paramour of the slave-girl Mungela. He now strove by every means he could devise to put a stop to the intercourse betwixt his sister, Ranee Chunda, and Rajah Lall Sing. But his efforts were in vain, as Mungela was not so much devoted to him as to favour his views in this matter; but, on the contrary, she still exercised all her art and influence to promote and strengthen the intimacy. Nevertheless the opposition of Jewahir Sing had the effect of placing some restraint on the proceedings of his sister, her lover, and their confederate. This of course did not tend to earn him their good will, and the grudge they owed him was deepened by his refusal to bestow upon them as much of the property of the state in the shape of jaghires, &c., as they coveted. Mungela, in particular, thought herself ill-used when her entreaties, backed by those of her mistress, could not obtain for the support of herself and all her family more than three thousand rupees a-year of the public money. However she had contrived by various sinister means to collect no small amount of property entirely unknown to her mistress and her paramour; and on the death of Jewahir Sing,—for which it may be supposed she was not very sorry, whatever she may have appeared to the world,—she became virtually sole manager and controller of all the Toshakhanas, out of which she of course helped herself most liberally.

Thus the slave girl Mungela rose to be one of the most considerable persons in the state, with wealth and power almost unlimited. She had both the Ranee Chunda and Rajah Lall Sing entirely at her command, and thus through them she moved the wheels of the Government as best suited her own views and interests.

Mungela had an elder brother named Mungeloo, who was killed at the battle of Sabraon, and she has still a younger brother by name Megraj, who at the age of seven or eight years, was, by his parents, pawned or given as security for money to a Kotree Brahmin in the hills. According to the custom of the country this Kotree made the boy work as his bond servant or slave, employing him in the most menial offices in his household. This continued for some six or seven years, the parents being unable to redeem their pledge; but at length the youth was, by the money and interest of his fortunate sister, released from bondage, and was shortly afterwards made a general of artillery in the service of Maharajh Dulleep Sing.

THE WAR WITH THE BRITISH.

HAVING as they thought made their peace with the Ranee, who had apparently forgiven the murder of her brother, the troops in their gratitude promised true allegiance to Maharajh Dulleep Sing and implicit obedience to the commands of his mother. Many of them even went so far as to declare that they would receive as Wuzeer whomsover she might choose to appoint; but others, including Court's, Avitabile's, and the Povindeea divisons sent their deputies to Goolaub Sing at Jummoo, inviting him to come to Lahore to be made Minister, instead of Rajah Lall Sing, for whom the Ranee now openly evinced her preference and favour. However, even these refractory battalions so far submitted themselves to Her Highness's commands as to break up their camps and retire to their several stations. They did this the more readily, perhaps, because when issuing the order, the Ranee intimated to them, that it would soon be necessary for them to reform the line for the invasion of British India. On hearing this the troops became clamorous for stores and ammunition and the means of conveying them, which it not being convenient to supply, the Ranee chose to regard their demands as intended to embarrass the state and thus to furnish a pretext for declining to march as ordered. The troops, however, quietly repaired to their various cantonments, and for some time nothing more was heard of the projected expedition to Hindoostan. During this interval all went on smoothly, the only anxiety entailed upon the heads of the state, being that caused by the intrigues of Jewan Sing, Toshakhaneea, for the elevation of Rajah Goolaub Sing to the Wuzeerut, intrigues, however, which resulted in nothing.

The Court went to Umritsir and there remained for some time. About the beginning of November, (1845) it left that city and returned towards Lahore, but approached no nearer than to the Shalimar Gardens, where it took up its abode for a while. It was rumoured, about this time, that while at Umritsir, the Ranee and her favourite Lall Sing had formed resolutions and plans for the punishment of the army; and from the day of the Court's arrival at Shalimar, Rajah Lall Sing openly took upon himself the duties of Wuzeer, acting of course by permission of and under the authority of the Queen Mother.

Reports were now circulated of the intention of the British to take possession of the Seik territories to the south and east of the Sutlej. On several occasions, Lall Sing in open durbar produced and read papers purporting to be letters from Kardars of the country beyond the river, and in which it was stated that the British army was already advancing gradually, and was creating disturbance and annoyance in the Seik states. This intelligence, authentic as it appeared to be, of course created considerable excitement among the troops and people at Lahore, and soon formed almost the only topic of discussion and remark. When these rumours had worked their intended effect, Lall Sing summoned a council of sirdars, officers, and deputies at Shalimar. To this assembly Dewan Denanauth read a letter, which he said had been sent to the durbar by the Kardars of the states beyond the Sutlej, intimating that the British authorities really meant to seize that part of the country,—that they were causing great annoyance to the servants of the durbar, and had actually given orders to the people of several villages to pay no tribute but to the British

Government, to whom as they now formally declared, the country belonged. Dewan Denanauth also intimated to the council that great disturbances existed in Cashmere, Peshawar, &c., and that for a long time not a rupee of revenue had been paid in by the Kardars. Having thus excited the alarm and concern of the assembly, the wily Dewan went on to remind them that their sovereign was but a child, that there was no recognised head of the state, and that unless arrangements were made for the government of the country, ruin must speedily ensue. He then informed them that it was the wish of the Ranee that Rajah Lall Sing should be Wuzeer, and Sirdar Teja Sing Commander-in-Chief, and that she was willing to sanction the march of the army across the Sutlej for the protection of the national honour, and would, if they thought proper, order all the necessary preparations to be made. All she wanted, said her representative, was the advice of the assembly for the guidance of her conduct at this critical juncture of affairs. Hereupon the council unanimously and by acclamation confirmed Her Highness's choice of Rajah Lall Sing as Wuzeer, and of Sirdar Teja Sing as Commander-in-Chief, declaring that the wishes of the Ranee were to them commands that must be obeyed. On this Rajah Lall Sing thanked the assembly for his appointment, promising to do all in his power for the good of the Khalsa ; and when he sat down, Sirdar Teja Sing rose and made a similar speech. Dewan Denanauth now intimated to the assembly, that the Ranee would appoint a certain day on which they should all assemble at the mausoleum of Runjeet Sing, there formally to install the new Wuzeer and Commander-in-chief in their respective offices. He also announced, that on the day appointed, it would be settled when and whither each division of the army was to march, and that the necessary orders would then be issued.

This meeting at Shalimar took place in the beginning of November, and two or three days after the Maharajh and his mother, with the whole Court, returned to the palace in Lahore. Preparations for the projected invasion were now commenced in earnest, and each corps and battalion was directed to send in an account of all that it required for the march. Henceforth the expedition and its anticipated results formed the grand subject of discourse in camp and city. The soldiers expatiated on the booty they were to bring back from Delhi, Muttra, Benares, &c., and some were forming plans for keeping and ruling the country they were to conquer.

The astrologers having named an auspicious day, the grand assembly for the installation of Rajah Lall Sing and Sirdar Teja Sing was held at the *summood* or tomb of Runjeet Sing. The first thing done on this occasion was to read some passages from the Grunth, their sacred book, preparatory to their partaking of the *Gurree Persauth*, or holy bread and wine,* a ceremony observed at all their solemn assemblies. This performance over, a discussion ensued on an order for the French division (Ventura's) to proceed towards Peshawar, where troops were required to quell some disturbances in the province. The Punches of the division however declared that they would not march in that direction until the war with the British was over, and so the matter dropped.

Now all the sirdars, officers, and Punches were requested to lay their hands on the Grunth and on the hem of the sacred canopy over the shrine of Runjeet, and thus to swear allegiance to Maharajh Dulleep Sing, and obedience to Rajah Lall Sing as Wuzeer, and to Sirdar Teja Sing as Commander-in-chief. Then orders were issued for the march of the army torwards the Sutlej. It was made known that Lall Sing in person would command the Gorechar cavalry,

* The *bread* used on this occasion is rather a fine dough, sweetened with sugar and raisins, and rather heated than baked. There is generally a great scramble for this Seik sacrament, and the officiating Gooroo is sometimes trampled down by the rude and impatient mob of soldiers.

then about twenty-two thousand in number, with three or four camps of artillery, which were well inclined towards him. The rest of the army, about forty-two thousand infantry, with about ten regiments of regular cavalry and great part of the artillery, was to march in divisions towards Ferozepore. Lall Sing would follow in a few days, and Teja Sing would remain to complete the necessary preparations, the troops under his command being conducted on the march by their respective officers.

The preliminary arrangements completed, the meeting broke up, and the sirdars, officers, and deputies returned to their several corps to communicate the result.

The troops, allured by the hope of the expected booty, exhibited much eagerness for the order to set forward towards and across the Sutlej; every one seemed full of confidence and high spirits, and the preparations for the march were carried on with the utmost vigour and despatch. Many of the soldiers sent word to their relatives to join and accompany them in their advance across the river, in order to be ready for the purpose of assisting them in carrying home the property of which they were to become masters in Hindostan.

On the 23rd November, Rajah Lall Sing left Lahore and encamped with his twenty-two thousand Gorechars and about forty guns a little beyond Shalimar. Thence he marched to about ten coss from the city, and halted for five or six days. The Rajah was a bad soldier, and personally not very eager for the fray, but he affected a great confidence in the invincibility of the Khalsa, and seemed very eager for their advance across the river. About the 23rd of November, the infantry made its first move towards Ferozepore on various lines of march, under the orders of Sirdar Teja Sing, who still remained at Lahore, or rather those of the Ranee herself, of which that chief was merely the channel of communication. When the entire army had reached the right banks of the Sutlej, Teja Sing was written to by many of the chiefs and deputies to come and head the troops in person. It was not however till the 16th of December, that he left the capital, and hastened the camp. The main body of the army had already crossed the river at two or three different points above Ferozepore, and was encamped on the left bank of the stream, at some distance from that place. Rajah Lall Sing was still encamped with hisc avalry, about six coss from Hurree-ka-puttun, seemingly intent on continuing his march towards Loodiana. But Teja Sing, as also the officers and Punches, now wrote to him entreating, or rather commanding him, to form a junction with the infantry near Ferozepore.

It was now proposed that the army should advance by regular marches on Umballa; but Lall Sing seemed disposed to demur to this arrangement, as he dreaded to be in the neighbourhood of the infantry, by whom he was cordially hated. He was however in a manner compelled by his troops to accede to it, and he accordingly crossed at or near Hurree-ka-puttun, taking care however to keep wide of the infantry.

The Seik force now on the British side of the Sutlej may be computed at eighty thousand fighting men, but the number was swelled up by followers and hangers-on to at least two hundred thousand. Most of these followers, however, were armed men and capable of doing much damage in an enemy's country, or even in their own, by plundering and murdering.

The question of an attack on Ferozepore was now mooted. Both Teja Sing and Lall Sing were in favour of an attempt on the place, but the troops were irresolute. They had imbibed a belief that the fort was mined to a considerable distance all round, and would be blown up on their taking possession of it. They believed in short that it was a huge trap, baited for their destruction with some lakhs of treasure; and they regarded the exhortations of their chiefs to proceed to the assault as evidence of a desire for their slaughter and ruin. Moreover the British garrison put on a bold front and astonished the Seiks with the sight of a handful of men with fortifications at their command, turning out to offer battle to overwhelming numbers in the open field.

Thus Ferozepore and its garrison remained unmolested by the Khalsa force, which lay encamped in the neighbourhood for several days. Early on the morning of the 17th December, however, news reached Lall Sing's camp of the approach of a British force of no great strength, with the intention of joining that already at Ferozepore. On this the entire body of Gorechars immediately prepared to advance, supported by sixteen horse artillery guns, ordered from the camp of Teja Sing, those with Lall Sing being all heavy ordnance, drawn by bullocks. Thus the cavalry and artillery advanced some ten or twelve coss, and again came to a halt in the forenoon of the 17th December. Lall Sing evidently had much difficulty in making up his mind to attack the British force that was approaching his position; and it was not until the Seiks had reproached him with cowardice, and declared their determination to fight whether he led them or not, that he advanced to meet the British column, which was then drawing near to Moodkee, about five coss in his front. In the afternoon of the 18th, as the Seiks came within two coss of the main body of the enemy, they stumbled on a picquet of about a hundred horse, which retreated before them with great coolness and regularity, although attacked by the Gorechars with much impetuosity, and vigorously followed in their retreat. The Seik cavalry was thus lured on until it came close to the main body of the British, when the picquet which acted as a decoy galloped forward and joined the advancing ranks. On finding himself in front of the enemy, Lall Sing commenced a fire of round shot from fourteen of his guns, the other two having been left on the road. The British troops then formed in columns with their artillery in front, and first slowly and then at a rapid pace advanced upon the Seik line, which, by order of Lall Sing, awaited their attack. Presently, however, the British began to fire shells, which did great execution, and caused much confusion in the ranks of the Gorechars. The Seik artillery now began to fire grape, but without the expected effect of checking the onward progress of the enemy, who still continued steadily and rapidly to advance. On coming within range of small arms, the Gorechars commenced a desultory fire, but on the fierce attack of the British they gave way and fled, leaving most of their guns behind them,—Lall Sing, their leader, being one of the first to turn his horse's head towards the Sutlej. The British force did not pursue the fugitive Seiks, but encamped on the ground. During the whole of that night, the Gorechars came dropping into their camp from the different directions in which they had fled. Lall Sing himself did not make his appearance till after day break the next morning, having, it was reported, been hid in a bush for some time.

The next day, the 19th, the gallant Rajah sent to Teja Sing for a reinforcement of twelve battalions, whereupon the French division (late General Ventura's) was ordered to join him, as also those of Mathaub Sing and the Misser, or in all the required twelve battalions, with fifty-two guns.

By the 21st December, Lall Sing had again screwed up his courage for another attempt to arrest the progress of the British force. He therefore advanced in front of his entrenched camp at Ferozeshuhur for nearly a mile, but thinking better of the matter, he then, partly by commands and partly by persuasion, induced the troops to turn back and re-enter the camp. On arriving within their entrenchments again the soldiers got leave to take off their regimentals and accoutrements, and to cook and eat their victuals. While thus engaged and thus unprepared, the British force was seen coming down upon them in column from the right. On this the drums beat to arms and the troops were promptly in line. They were scarcely in their ranks, however, when the enemy opened a murderous fire upon them, and immediately bore down upon and broke the French squares, the Ventura division being on the right, and unsupported by their comrades. The Gorechars were on the left, and were furiously attacked by the British cavalry, which turned their flank and completely routed them. The artillery was thus left unprotected, and such of the artillerymen as had not sought safety in flight were cut down at their guns. Soon after this the divisions of Mathaub Sing and the Misser retreated, and thus only the French division, which had re-formed, was left to keep up a desultory fire, which continued throughout a great part of the night.

Before daylight however, even this division, finding itself unsupported, and in fact deserted, deemed it best to retire after the others, so that by sunrise not a man that could get away was to be seen in the Seik camp. The British, who it was said, had also retreated during the night, now, hearing that the Seiks had fled to the river, advanced and took possession of their camp and artillery. At this moment Sirdar Teja Sing, with some twenty-five or thirty thousand fresh troops, arrived from the camp at Ferozepore, and presented himself before the British force, which, tired and exhausted with its previous exertions, was unable to attack him, and would, in all likelihood, have been found unable to repel a vigorous assault from an army of fresh men, in overpowering numbers, like that led by him. The usual good fortune of the British prevailed however, and instead of seeing the Seik reserve advance to the attack, they had the satisfaction of beholding them turn back without firing a shot and follow their defeated comrades towards the Sutlej. The British force was thus left in undisputed possession of the field of Ferozeshuhur, with the entrenched camp of the Seiks and all their artillery.

That portion of the Seik army which had advanced under

Lall Sing, and had been routed and driven back by the British, fled tumultuously across the Sultej, many men being drowned in the hurry and confusion of passing that river. Arrived on the opposite bank some ten thousand of them, including many officers, dispersed and fled to their houses. It would however have been better for them to have held together, even at the risk of an attack from the British, for the straggling fugitives received very rough usage at the hands of their countrymen and even of their countrywomen, the inhabitants of the district through which they fled. Those who reached their houses had to encounter the taunts and reproaches of their friends and neighbours, and in many instances even of their wives, who bitterly reviled them for the cowardice. They were robbed and abused and beaten, even the women of the villages turning out to rail at them and strike them as they hurried along. At Lahore the gates were shut against them by order of the Ranee, and an order went forth that all fugitives from the camp should be imprisoned, and their property confiscated. This had the effect of checking the desertions and even of inducing many of those who had retired to Lahore and the places adjacent, to return to their posts on the banks of the Sutlej. Rajah Lall Sing, who was one of the first to flee from the fight, made his way to the camp of Runjoor Sing near Philoor, whence he hastened to Umritsir, where he secreted himself for some time.

The Seik army under Teja Sing now lay encamped on the right bank of the Sutlej, in the neighbourhood of Hurree-ka-puttun; the British on the opposite bank, meanwhile, waiting for reinforcements and supplies, which were fast pouring in. The Khalsa soldiers entertained strong suspicions that their late defeats were brought on by the treachery of their chiefs, prompted by the Ranee, who sought their destruction in revenge for the death of her brother Jewahir Sing. These suspicions were loudly expressed even in several messages to the Ranee, accompanied by threats of their vengeance. Their conduct had such an effect on the mind of Her Highness, that she began to fear they would march back upon Lahore and put her and her son to death. She therefore stationed strong guards at every gate of the city, with strict orders to prevent the ingress of any Seik bearing arms.

She also sent orders to Teja Sing to use every exertion to keep his men together, and to prevent them from returning to Lahore in a body. Further, to divert their attention from their designs of vengeance on her and her advisers, she caused a report to be spread that Runjoor Sing had crossed the Sutlej, and captured and burnt the town and cantonments of Loodiana, that chief being in reality quietly encamped near Philoor all the time. However, the rumour reached the army at Hurree-ka-puttun, accompanied by a message from the Ranee, in which she contrasted their cowardice and inactivity with the good conduct of Runjoor Sing and his force, a taunt by which Her Highness hoped to inspire the troops with a determination to cross the river immediately and to attack the British. It had not, however, its expected effect. At this time Rajah Lall Sing returned to the camp, but took care to keep the river betwixt himself and the Khalsa, who, he believed and probably with truth, would have murdered him had he trusted himself in their hands.

The army meanwhile was not idle. Two European engineers, Signor Hurbon, a Spaniard, and Monsr. Mouton, a Frenchman, were called to the camp to advise and assist in strengthening it against an assault from the British. By them a field-work of great strength was designed on the left bank of the Sutlej, at the head of the bridge of boats. On this work the whole army laboured night and day, with great diligence and assiduity, and it was not long ere what seemed an almost impregnable *tête du pont* was completed.

Thus the opposing armies lay watching each other for many days, ere the preparations of the British for the attack were completed. In the interval, the battle of Aliwal was fought, where Runjoor Sing was routed with great slaughter by a detachment of the enemy's force which had been sent to the relief of Loodiana. The news of this reverse created a panic among the Seiks, both in Court and in camp. The troops, notwithstanding their strong position and superior numbers, lost all heart and regarded themselves as doomed to defeat and slaughter. They had no confidence in their leaders, and their only hope of safety lay in the promise of Goolaub Sing to place himself at their head. This chief had, on the first out-break of hostilities, been summoned from Jummoo, whence he had come with no great alacrity. He made, however, a great show and many promises of assistance, which were never to be realised. At length he reached Lahore, with about three thousand men and large quantities of supplies ; but though his troops were sent forward to join the army, he himself remained at the capital, on various pretences, for some time. He was now surrounded by about five hundred Punches, who spoke of making him Wuzeer, and of carrying him to the camp to lead the army against the British. He, however, evaded compliance with their wishes, making them satisfied for a while longer with promises and professions. He would, he said, shortly proceed to take the command of the army on the banks of the Sutlej, and he urged the necessity of abstaining from an attack upon the British until he should have placed himself at the head of the troops.

But, as possibly may have been anticipated by the sagacious chief of Jummoo, ere his time for taking the command arrived, the British had acquired strength sufficient to become the attacking party instead of waiting to be attacked. Goolaub Sing was yet at Lahore, when on the morning of the 10th February 1846, the Seik army was assailed in its works on the left bank of the Sutlej, and after a desperate resistance, driven across the stream with great slaughter. The troops had resolved on one last struggle, even though they had in reality little hope of success, and now that struggle had resulted in their defeat and repulse, they lost all heart for further efforts. The British army, victors in the battle of Subraon, immediately crossed the Sutlej, and advanced directly upon Lahore, not a shot being fired in opposition to their triumphant progress.

Meantime at Lahore, the Punches who had taken charge of Goolaub Sing, had almost by force installed him as Wuzeer, he day by day promising at such a time to proceed to the Sutlej and take command of the army. These Punches were engaged also in bandying abuse with the Ranee and her advisers, Mungela, the slave-girl and others, whom they accused of treachery and wickedness of all kinds. Thus matters stood at the capital, when the news of the battle of Subraon arrived there, closely followed by intelligence of the advance of the British into the country. On this the Ranee called a council of the Sirdars and Punches, &c., who were on the spot, and intimated to the assembly, that with the consent of the army and on receiving a written assurance of its readiness to obey all her orders, she would depute Rajah Goolaub Sing to meet the Governor-General, and offer the submission of her son the Maharajh and herself, as the only means of averting the entire subjugation of the country. The promise was readily given, and the next day Goolaub Sing marched for Kussoor, where the British camp now lay. Here he had an interview with the British Chief, and in a few days afterwards the young Maharajh Dulleep Sing was brought from Lahore and instructed to make a formal submission before the Governor-General. Thus perished the independence of the once powerful state founded by Runjeet Sing.

It has been already remarked, that the troops who formed the Seik army on the Sutlej, strongly suspected that they had been betrayed into the hands of the enemy by their own chiefs, acting under secret instructions from the Ranee. The conduct of those chiefs, and especially that of Teja Sing, was, it must be owned, such as to strengthen, if not confirm, these suspicions. There was but too much reason for them to believe that the whole or nearly the whole of their sirdars and officers, were combined in a treacherous scheme to entrap them, and deliver them up an easy prey to the British army. Instead of watching for opportunities to employ the force to the best advantage against the enemy, it seemed as if the leaders of the Seiks were intent only on placing their troops in such a position as might render them an easy and complete conquest to their foes. Notwithstanding, however, that the Seik soldiery more than suspected these designs and intentions of their chiefs, they were unable to extricate themselves from the position into which they had been thrown. They gave vent to their alarm and indignation in fierce reproaches on the treachery of their leaders, but that was all they could do. "We know," they said to their leaders, "that you have leagued with the Court to send us against the British and to pen us up here like sheep for them to come and slaughter us at their convenience; but, remember, that in thus acting, you play the part not only of traitors to your country, but of ruthless butchers and murderers. You destroy a whole army, which, whatever its faults and crimes may have been, has always been ready to obey the orders of the state and its officers. We might even now punish you as you deserve, but we will leave you to answer to your Gooroo and your God, while we, deserted and betrayed, as we are, will do what we can to preserve the independance of our country." By language such as this, many of the officers were induced to assume an appearance of fidelity, while they nevertheless continued their endeavours for the betrayal of the army.

It has been said that the conduct of Teja Sing, in particular, savoured much of treason to the Khalsa. His strange conduct in ordering a retreat before the wearied and almost defenceless British force at Ferozeshuhur, on the morning of the 22nd December, is inexplicable on any other supposition than that of treachery. It was on this occasion, while he was haranguing the troops, and persuading them of the necessity for retiring, assuring them that unless they did so, their bridge of boats and the whole line of the river in their rear would be immediately occupied by the British,—while he was thus discoursing, an old Seik horseman, a soldier of the times of Runjeet, galloped up to him, and drawing his sword, strove by threats and fierce invectives, to induce the Sirdar to order the advance instead of the retreat of the army. He pointed to the exhausted British forces unable to fire a shot, and asked what was to be feared from them, who, he declared, would not be able to stand a vigorous charge from the fresh troops now opposed to them. The conduct and language of this brave old trooper induced Teja Sing with joined hands solemnly to protest and swear by the name of God and his Gooroo, that he had no other intent in retiring than that of saving the troops by preventing their retreat from being cut off by the British. But the old horseman, still convinced of the treachery of the Sirdar, cursed him as a traitor and a coward before the whole army, and then quietly returned to his post in the ranks.

The troops however, though convinced of the treachery of their chiefs, could only follow where they led; for no one came forward from among themselves to lead or advise them, and without a head they could do nothing. They therefore returned with Teja Sing to the banks of the Sutlej, and thence across that river.

It is reported, as an illustration of the personal character of Teja Sing, that while the army was lying in the entrenched camp, on the banks of the Sutlej at Hurree-ka-puttun, or Subraon, he, being in a manner compelled by the troops to take up his quarters in the midst of them, sought to secure himself from the consequences of the anticipated cannonade, by erecting a small but strong circular tower to which he might retire for safety. It is said also, that just as he had completed this triple-walled fortalice, a Brahmin astrologer persuaded him that it would be no defence for him unless constructed according to certain rules and proportions, which he, on consultation with the stars, had discovered. The disinterested seer added, that on being duly rewarded for his pains, he was willing to communicate the secret of construction on the proper plan; and on receiving five hundred rupees as earnest money, he declared that to ensure the requisite strength, the walls must be equal in thickness to the length of three hundred and thirty-three long grains of rice, or about three English yards and a quarter, while the inner chamber to which the Sirdar was to retreat, in case of need, was to be a regular circle, the diameter of which must be thirteen and a half spans of Teja Sing's own measurement. Report says further, that the gallant Sirdar might have been seen day after day engaged in vain attempts to lay down the plan and dimensions of his little fort on the prescribed scale,—idly busied in spanning over a certain spot of ground, while the soldiery were hard at work forming and strengthening their entrenchments. While he was thus employed, one of the European engineers then in camp happened to pay him a visit, and on learning, to his great amusement, what the Sirdar was so anxiously engaged upon, pulled forth an English foot-rule, and with the greatest expedition and precision laid down the plan, of what, after some trouble he convinced the Sirdar, would be quite as secure a retreat as any the stars could devise. So effectually indeed did he at length instil into the mind of the gallant Sirdar a persuasion, that in his advice alone was security to be found, that thenceforward scarcely an hour passed in which he was not summoned into the presence of the Commander-in-chief to advise and report upon the construction of this castle.

It is asserted also, that on the first intimation of the attack by the British, Teja Sing sent about fifty of his most attached and trusty followers to secure the ghat and the approach to the bridge of boats connecting the camp with the right bank of the Sutlej, thus providing as far as possible for his safe retreat in case of need. While the battle was raging, the Commander-in-chief was, it is said, securely ensconced in his own peculiar fortress, watching only for an opportunity of making good his retreat unobserved across the bridge. While he tarried for this purpose, some horsemen gallopped up to his castle, and demanded that he should come forth and repair to the spot where the troops under Sham Sing Attareewallah were beginning to waver, that he might rally and strengthen them by his presence and commands. —He thereupon dismissed the messengers with his compliments to the gallant chief Sham Sing, desiring him to hold his ground as long as possible, and assuring him that after he had secured the bridge he would hasten to his assistance and support. Soon after this he found his way down to and across the bridge, attended by fifteen or twenty horsemen in waiting upon him, and was thus, if report does him no injustice, the first to quit the bloody field of Subraon. It is said, moreover, that having got safely across the bridge, he ordered up eight or ten guns, and had them pointed on the bridge as if ready to beat it to pieces or to oppose the passage of the defeated army. To this is attributed the crowding and confusion among the retreating troops that led to the breaking down of the bridge and the fearful slaughter that ensued. Some even assert, that having made good his own retreat, the ropes by which the bridge was held, were, by the Sirdar's orders, cut or cast loose, whereby it became impassable to the retreating masses. It is possible, however, that many of these stories, attributing treachery and cowardice to Teja Sing, may have had their origin in the distrust and ill-will with which he was regarded by the army, and therefore they are not to be implicitly relied on.

MISCELLANEOUS NOTICES.

PHOOLA SING, THE AKALEE.

PHOOLA Sing Nahung, an Akalee of the Jat Sing caste, and the son of a poor Akalee attendant of the Akal Boongah at Umritsir, first distinguished himself as the leader of the attack on Mr. Metcalfe's escort, in 1809, at Umritsir. Soon after the unsuccessful termination of this exploit, Phoola Sing, with a few of his comrades, forced himself into the presence of Runjeet Sing, and drawing his sword, demanded vengeance on the band of strangers who had been the cause of so much loss and disgrace to him and his class. This unreasonable demand he endeavoured to enforce by threatening to wreak his own revenge and that of his comrades on Runjeet himself and all his family, if it was not complied with. Runjeet was astonished, and possibly somewhat alarmed at this intrusion of the bold and desperate young man and his followers. Compliance with their demand for the slaughter of the British envoy and his retinue was, however, out of the question, as it would have ensured his own political and perhaps personal destruction. He, therefore, with that coolness and tact for which he was distinguished, told his rude visitors that if they were bent on vengeance, he offered himself as their victim, for that they might as well slay him at once as ensure his ruin by causing him to break faith with the British, and to insult or injure their ambassador. After a long parley he induced the young Akalee and his followers to lay aside their desire of vengeance, at least for the present, and presenting the leader with a pair of gold bangles, and distributing gifts of smaller value among his companions, sent them away in good humour.

From this time Phoola Sing became very popular among the Akalees, and ere long became an acknowledged chief of the class. At the head of three or four hundred Nahungs, horse and foot, he scoured the country as a free-booter, plundering villages and committing depredations of various kinds. However, like the Robin Hood of English history, or the Deesoo of his own country, he was noted as much for his kindness and forbearance towards the poor as for his ravages upon the rich and well-to-do. It is probable that he lost nothing by pursuing this line of conduct; for by sparing the poor, who were in truth hardly worth robbing, he made them his friends, and in some measure his allies, they often reciprocating his kindness by affording him useful information and sometimes assistance or shelter when required.

The fame of Phoola Sing's exploits soon reached the ears of Runjeet in the complaints of those who had suffered loss at the hands of the Akalee chief. Runjeet, however, knew the man too well to think of resorting to extremities with him on slight provocation. He therefore politely requested his attendance at court, and when he came, gently remonstrated with him on his conduct, endeavouring by presents and persuasions to induce him to adopt a more orderly and honest mode of life. But all the eloquence of the Maharajh, backed as it was by costly bribes, failed to lure Phoola Sing from his evil courses. Runjeet now tried to frighten him into propriety by sending after him large bodies of troops, but the Akalee was not to be caught, and was not to be frightened by a vain pursuit. He still therefore continued his career as a robber-chief on a large scale, his band swelling out on occasion to the number of four or five thousand desperate and greedy men. Even in the court and camp of Runjeet, the Akalee free-booter was an object of dread; and he, pre suming on the terror which his name inspired, would enter the houses of the most powerful sirdars and openly carry off the choice of their goods and horses, or whatever he took a fancy to. He also levied "black mail" on the chiefs, demanding large sums of money for the expences of himself and followers; and if his demand was not immediately complied with, the contumacious sirdar might expect to be plundered of all his property. Even Runjeet himself was not exempt from this impost, which he was content to bear in common with his sirdars. The Maharajh, however, prudently strove to conciliate the powerful free-booter, by yielding to his demands with a good grace, and sometimes indeed by anticipating them. He frequently bestowed gifts of money and jaghires on the Akalee leader and his followers, and thus in some degree secured their forbearance and friendship.

At length it occurred to the sagacious Runjeet to turn to his own advantage those qualities and propensities of the Akalee band, under which he had suffered so long. This purpose he attained by taking them into his service, but without insisting very strongly on the enforcement of regular military discipline. It was indeed the prudent policy of Runjeet, whenever he knew of any famed and dreaded robber to send for him to his presence, and by presents and the promise of good pay, to attach him to his own service, thereby converting to his own use and benefit, the courage and the rapacity which would otherwise be exercised at his expense. Thus it happened that in most of the battles which Runjeet fought with his Affghan or other foes, the tide of victory was turned in his favour, by the daring and impetuous onslaught of some of these desperate spirits, whose predatory habits while they had given them an utter disregard for all discipline had inspired them with a thorough contempt for death and danger.

Phoola Sing with his small band of Akalees, when taken into the service of the Maharajh, contributed largely on more than one occasion to win victory to his cause. It was an Akalee and one of the picked men of Phoola Sing's band, that, without orders, first mounted the half-formed breach at Moultan, in 1818, with about forty of his comrades at his back, and by this desperate assault made way for the entrance of the whole besieging army, which otherwise might have lain before the place for many days longer. It has been commonly said that this Akalee, whose name was Jussa Sing, was drugged with opium; but this is a mistake, as it is well known this man was a fanatic of such pretensions to sanctity that, contrary to usual practice, he strictly denied himself the use of *bhang* or *sookah*, the only intoxication drug in use among the Akalees. So pious was he reported to be among his comrades, that he was commonly known as Maullah Sing,—the *maullah* being the beads which the Seiks use in prayer. However, it was to the desperate bravary of this man and his followers that Runjeet owed the early and easy captive of Moultan, his troops being so much annoyed by the fire from the fort that they had been compelled to keep close in their entrenchments, where but for this exploit of Jussa or Maullah Sing, Akalee, they might have lain inactive for some time longer. This achievement, however cost the lives of Jussa Sing and thirty-four of his forty followers, who were found, on the capture of the place, lying dead or mortally wounded within the walls.

In 1819, Phoola Sing signalised his courage at the capture of Cashmere, on which occasion Runjeet rewarded his bravery with many gifts and favours, and raised him to the rank of a sirdar. He was now a constant attendant on Runjeet's person, and accompanied him in all his campaigns against the Affghans, &c., contributing, not a little to their successful results. In 1823, a battle was fought at Teree on the northern bank of the Loonda or Cabul river. Victory at first seemed to have declared against the Seiks, for in spite of all that Runjeet with his European generals Ventura and Allard could do to prevent it, a panic spread among the troops, who were on the point of turning to flee before their Affghan foes. Several unsuccessful attempts to drive the enemy from his position on the hill of Teree, in which they had been repulsed with great slaughter, had exhausted their strength and broken their spirits, and a shameful defeat seemed inevitable. In vain Runjeet threatened and implored, in vain he adjured them by their God and their Gooroo to advance, in vain dismounting from his horse he rushed forward sword in hand calling on his troops to follow him,—his threats, his entreaties, his adjurations, and his example were alike disregarded. The troops would not advance, they were beginning to retire in panic flight, and the day seemed lost. Runjeet was in despair and as a last resource was about to betake himself to his prayers and his beads. Just at this critical juncture, however, he saw, to his great joy and equally great surprise, the black banner of Phoola Sing and his Akalees moving along the foot and then up the side of the disputed hill. The Akalee chief at the head of his five hundred desperadoes was advancing against the enemy. Runjeet had himself seen Phoola Sing, in the heat of the engagement, struck from his horse by a musket ball which shattered the cap of his knee; he had seen him borne to the rear to all appearance utterly disabled. But there was Phoola Sing seated on an elephant actually leading his little band to the assault. On went the Akalees after their leader who from his elephant shouted an invitation to the whole army to follow them. The army did not respond to his call, but up the hill and towards the foe went Phoola Sing and his men, determined to decide the fate of the day by a desperate assault. The Affghans waited not for their attack, but rushed down the hill to become the assailants. At this moment, Phoola Sing ordered his men to dismount and let their horses go. This was done, and at the same instant the Akalees shouted their war-cry of *Wah Gooroojee!* which the Affghans as loudly answered with their *Allah! Allah!* The horses set at liberty, either from habit or alarmed by the tumult, rushed wildly forward and into the ranks of the enemy. This strange and unexpected attack caused some confusion in the Affghan host, observing which the Akalees, throwing down their matchlocks, rushed forward sword in hand with such impetuousity as to drive back the enemy, and to secure themselves a footing on the hill. The main body of the Seiks witnessing this success of the Akalees, now took heart, and with a loud cheer rushed forward *en masse* to take advantage of it. By this movement, a body of twelve or fifteen hundred Affghans was placed betwixt the Akalee band and the advancing Seik army. Finding themselves thus exposed on both sides, they took to flight, endeavouring to elude the Akalees who were above them, and to make their way towards the summit, where their main body, some eight or ten thousand men, was strongly posted. But Phoola Sing was not the man to permit them to escape so easily; he turned and attacked them with such vigour that they were speedily brought to a stand, and in the attempt to check his advance, lost above six hundred men. The Akalee force, however, was by this time reduced to little more than one hundred and fifty. Yet this exploit of theirs, had so inspired the main body of the army with courage and spirits that hastening to the support of the little band of heroes, they completely routed the Affghan detachment, and followed up their advantage by a desperate effort to dislodge the more powerful body of the enemy from its position on the summit of the hill. Phoola Sing mounted on his elephant led the advance undeterred by the receipt of another musket ball in his body. His Akalees rushed on, in front of the attacking army, eager to close with the enemy. As they approached the position of the Affghans, they were met by a most destructive fire of matchlocks and musketry, which greatly thinned the small party of Akalees who now remained. At this moment the mahout who conducted the elephant on which Phoola Sing was seated, having already received three balls in his body, and being terrified at the close and destructive fire, hesitated to advance. In vain the chief urged him to proceed directly towards the enemy, the man was panic-struck and seemed rather to meditate a retreat. On this Phoola Sing drew a pistol from his belt and shot him through the head. He then with the point of his sword urged the elephant forward towards the enemy. He had not, however, advanced much further when a bullet from an Affghan matchlock entered his forehead, and he fell back in his howdah a corpse. The death of their leader so infuriated the Akalees, that though their first charge was repulsed, they again and again returned to the assault with more desperate resolution, and in the end made a way for the Seik army into the midst of the enemy's position, and dislodged him from the height with great slaughter. Runjeet, now rejoined by many of his troops who had fled at the first reverse, followed up his advantage, and falling on the Affghans who had again formed at the foot of the hill, put them to flight in the greatest tumult and confusion, numbers of them hiding themselves in the long grass of a neighbouring swamp where they were cut to pieces or shot down by the victorious Seiks. The loss on the side of the Seiks was upwards of five thousand men, and it was thought that the Affghans lost nearly double that number.

This battle of Teree was won for Runjeet, after all hope of victory had fled, by the bravery of Phoola Sing, so gallantly supported by his little troop of Akalees. The heroism of the Akalee chief won the applause of both Seik and Mussulman, and the tomb erected over his remains, on the spot where he fell, although watched and attended by a party of Akalees, has become a place of pilgrimage for Hindoos and Mahometans alike. It stands at Naoshera, on the Yuzoofzie side of the Loonda or Cabul river.

Since the days of Phoola Sing, the Akalees have greatly degenerated, and are to be found intermixed with men of low castes, as Mujbees, &c., a practice, which their distinguished chief never countenanced or permitted. A true Akalee of the original Jat stock is now rarely to be met with, except at the different Akal Bhoongabs, as at Umritsir and elsewhere. The real Akalee was bold, free, and assuming to all, but in particular haughty and audacious to those who dared to call or think themselves his superiors in rank or station. He ever strove to win the character of a friend to the poor, and an enemy of the rich and powerful. He was a fanatic in his religion, which was nearly a pure deism, and followed strictly all the rules laid down for his guidance by the great Gooroo Govind Sing. He made no scruple to seize or demand from even a friend whatever he required; but he was equally ready to overpay an obligation. He cared little for wealth, but was content with the mere necessaries of existence. He was regardless of life and willingly exposed his own to danger at the call of duty. Such was the true Akalee of the stock which produced a Phoola Sing; but the race is now nearly extinct. Before the war with the British, they had much fallen away, and since that campaign, in which they suffered severely, little has been heard of them.

THE MUTINY IN CASHMERE.

About a month after the accession of Shere Sing, and when intelligence reached Cashmere that the troops at Lahore had mutinied and were murdering their officers, the two Seik battalions there under the command of Meean Sing, the Governor, made a demand for their arrears of pay. This demand not being immediately complied with, the troops conspired together to put the Governor, Meean Sing, to death, and to set up a member of their own body in his place. They believed that they could hold possession of the valley, and prevent any force that might be sent against them from entering, by opposing it in the passes through which it must advance.

Meean Sing was warned of this conspiracy, and informed that it would actually break out in an open mutiny if measures were not promptly used for its suppression. He, however, heeded not the warning and advice, regarding the danger described by his friends as purely imaginary. Thus he remained in false security, until one night he was rudely aroused from his sleep by a band of about fifty Seik soldiers, who had broken into his house, even into his chamber, and who told him, in terms which he could not misunderstand or disbelieve, that they had come for the purpose of putting him to death. They bade him rise and dress himself, promising him a short time to prepare for death by reading a few passages from the holy book. On this, Meean Sing calmly replied, that as they were considerate enough to give him time to read the Grunth, it would be only a necessary indulgence that they should allow him a light for the purpose. His request was granted, a light was brought, and he composedly read some appropriate passages from the Seik scriptures. Having thus prepared himself, he told his murderers that he was now ready to die, and was thereupon most deliberately cut down with a sword. His body was then handed over by the assassins to his friends that it might be disposed of in accordance with the ceremonies of their religion and custom.

Meean Sing had a Bungee, or slave, to whom he had shewn great kindness and favour, even making him the Under Kotwal or Deputy Superintendent of Police in Cashmere. When this man heard of the murder of his master and friend, he went in disguise and marked out the leader of the assassins. He then on the next night, taking with him a trusty follower, made his way into the house where this chief of the murderers was sleeping with some thirty others around him. Having effected their entrance, the Bungee and his comrade slew the leader and his second ere the rest of the party took the alarm, and having thus fulfilled their purpose, made their escape as they came. They then hastened from the valley and into the Punjaub, and gave information at Lahore of what had been done and was doing in Cashmere. Thereupon a body of about five thousand men was sent into the valley under the nominal command of Pertaub Sing, the son of Shere Sing, who was placed under the charge of Rajah Goolaub Sing. The object of this expedition was of course to punish the mutineers and murderers, to restore order and quiet in the country, and to instal a new Governor in the place of Meean Sing. The troops advanced to the very city of Cashmere without meeting the least opposition; but it appeared that the mutineers were here resolved to stand their ground. They refused to deliver up their arms on being summoned to surrender, and though Rajah Goolaub Sing condescended to negotiate with them for some time, it was to no purpose. On this, the order went forth that they should be attacked in the intrenchments which they had formed on the south bank of a small stream, there called the Dood-Gunga. On hearing that the assault had been determined on, the mutineers sent their women and children to a place of safety, and gave away all their property, even their clothes and shoes, to the Brahmins, thus significantly intimating their resolution to conquer or to die in the battle that was to ensue. Some of them, however, waited on Rajah Goolaub Sing, as though to make further propositions for their surrender, and by deceitful representations induced him to mount his elephant, and proceed towards their entrenchments. As he approached, fifty of the band suddenly rushed out upon him sword in hand, and attacked his escort of five hundred men with such desperate fury that the Rajah had to seek safety in a precipitate flight to his own camp.

Enraged at this treachery and its effect, Goolaub Sing ordered an instant attack by his whole force, which was already drawn up in line on the opposite bank. Ere, however, his troops could get into motion for the assault, a party of about two hundred and fifty of the mutineers rushed upon them with such impetuosity, that the four battalions of the Rajah's force were for the moment broken and put to flight. But the troops thus surprised and temporarily discomfited, soon rallied again, and opened so heavy a fire on their assailants that the latter had speedily to retire to the shelter of their entrenchments. By this sally of the mutineers the Durbar force lost about two hundred and thirty men.

Now the Rajah's four battalions, with about a thousand Gorechars, advanced to attack the main body of the mutineers in their entrenchments. The ground to be passed over was the half-dry bed of the stream already referred to. The troops marched over it in regular order, until they came within about twenty-five or thirty yards of the entrenchments, when the mutineers,—about five hundred only were present, the rest having escorted the women and children—fired a most destructive volley into the advancing ranks, then throwing down their matchlocks, rushed out sword in hand upon the enemy and drove the whole line back to a distance of about a hundred yards. Again, however, the heavy and continued fire of overpowering numbers compelled the mutineers to retire to their entrenchments,—all but about fifty of them, who broke desperately into the midst of the Durbar troops and sold their lives most dearly.

On this occasion the standard-bearer of the mutineers distinguished himself greatly. He was seen to rush forward with his colours,—to plant them in the sand,—to leap in among the troops, laying about him with his sword,—to return to his standard,—advance with it to another spot,—again plant it and again cut his way forward. Thus he acted for about a quarter of an hour, making great havoc among the Durbar troops, of whom he killed about twenty with his own hand. At length he fell, shot through the head by a matchlock ball. The loss of the Rajah's troops in this affair was about five hundred men, the mutineers losing about half that number.

The mutineers who yet remained, having re-assembled, now retreated towards the Peer Punjal Pass, intending to make their way out of the valley and into the Punjaub. They were however, met by Meean Jewahir Sing, the nephew of Goolaub Sing, who with about four thousand men, had been left to guard the pass and to prevent their egress. By this force they were attacked just as they had reached the southern side of the Peer Punjul range, and being unable to resist the assault of numbers so superior, they were dispersed with considerable loss. Those who escaped fled towards Lahore, where when all had come in they assembled about five hundred men. They now sought to be reinstated in the service of the Maharajh, but Shere Sing ordered that they should be disbanded and discharged, and on this they dispersed to their respective homes.

Goolaub Sing having thus effected the object of his expedition to Cashmere, left Shaik Mohee-ood-deen as Governor of the province, and departed with his troops for the Hazareh and Trinoul districts, by the Mozufferabad road. The object of his march in this direction was to put down the disturbances that were just then created by Paindha Khan, the chief of the Trinoul district, an old and inveterate enemy of the Lahore Government.

The Rajah encamping at Chumkaree, was engaged in settling matters in that quarter, about a month before the Cabul insurrection broke out. At the beginning of October, secret despatches reached him from his brother Rajah Dehan Sing at Lahore, and some Patan messengers arrived in his camp about the same time from the same quarter; it was, apparently, in consequence of these communicaations, that the Rajah moved down into the Hazareh country. He was heard about this period to throw out hints of things to come, which afterwards tended to excite a strong suspicion that he was privy to what was to take place at Cabul. However, when the outbreak did occur, and the news of it was made public, he professed to consider it quite a matter of course, and what must in the nature of things have occurred sooner or later.

When the first two battalions of the British force sent to the relief of their countrymen in Affghanstan reached the Indus at Attock, Goolaub Sing, who was in that neighbourhood, and who had orders from the Durbar to render them every assistance in his power, did his utmost to delay their passage across the river. He secreted all the boats, with the exception of some two or three, and these he contrived to keep from them for some time, on the plea that they were urgently required for the use of his own troops, then engaged, as he said, in active operations against the insurgents under Paindha Khan.

WUZEER ZOROVEROO.

THE celebrated Minister and military leader under Goolaub Sing, who is sometimes but improperly called Zorover Sing, but properly Zoroveroo, was a native of Kussal, near the fortress of Reharsee in the hills beyond Jummoo. He began his career as a private soldier in this fort, and being well acquainted with the country and people around, soon rendered himself particularly useful to, and so won the favour of, the Killadar. This officer finding Zoroveroo more intelligent than most of his comrades, frequently employed him in carrying messages to his master the Rajah at Jummoo. It was on one of these occasions, that Goolaub Sing first became acquainted with the merits of his humble follower. Zoroveroo, with an eye probably to his own advancement rather than to the interest of his chief, informed the Rajah that he was a great loser by the manner in which rations were distributed to his troops. He said, that every man in the hill-forts received one pukka seer of flour a day, that this being more than they could eat, at least one-third of the quantity was sold by them. He therefore proposed, that if the Rajah would authorise him, he would effect for him a yearly saving of at least a lakh of rupees ; and Goolaub immediately gave him a writing to the effect that he, Zoroveroo, was appointed inspector of commissariat supplies in all the forts north of Jummoo.

Zoroveroo had not promised what he could not perform. He speedily effected a saving to the Rajah's coffers of the full amount he had mentioned, and thereby won the admiration and gratitude of his master. As may be supposed, he soon became a favourite with the Rajah, who was as much astonished as pleased to find that he had a servant who could resist alike the temptations of presents from himself and bribes from others. Zoroveroo was quickly raised from one appointment to another, until he became Governor, with almost irresponsible power, over all Kussal and Kistowar. In this office he was strict even to cruelty; so much so, that the people of the country dreaded him even more than they did his master, Goolaub Sing. It was, moreover, useless for them to complain to the Rajah, who invariably confirmed his decisions, and in fact refused to interfere in any thing which he had done.

Eventually Zoroveroo received the title and office of Wuzeer, with full power to levy and direct forces as he pleased for the conquest of the independant states around. Not long after this new dignity and power had been conferred on him, Goolaub Sing heard that his Wuzeer had conquered and seized a large tract of fine fertile country belonging to Chumba; and soon after this, he learnt that the valley of Iskardo had in like manner come under his rule. The victorious leader seldom wrote to the Rajah to tell him of his successes, he knew it would be more pleasing to his master to learn the results of his expedition by the loads of spoil which almost daily arrived at Jummoo; and it was chiefly in this very agreeable and unmistakable manner, that Goolaub traced the progress of his General.

Zoroveroo had studied the character of his patron to good purpose. He knew that his master-passion was avarice, and in all things he sought, by the gratification of this ruling passion, to secure and extend his credit with the Rajah. Hence it was that he refused all presents and even all pay from his master; hence it was that he sent to that master all the bribes and presents that were offered to himself; and hence it was that instead of boastful despatches, he sent loads of booty to announce his conquests. In all this he simply bartered wealth for power, as, according to his hopes and anticipations, the Rajah reaping the fruits of and delighted with the display of his self-denying integrity in money matters, rewarded it in the manner most acceptable to Zoroveroo, namely by the grant of additional powers and the further extension of his confidence and trust.

It was, however, at the expense of the most fearful suffering to the people around, that Zoroveroo courted his master's favour. Goolaub was surprised as well as delighted to find that where he formerly received a thousand rupees of revenue, he now received fifteen hundred; and he was not, it may be supposed, very careful in his inquiries as to how the increase was effected. He did not know, or knowing did not care, that much of this increased revenue was raised by the exercise of the most frightful cruelty on his unfortunate subjects. Zoroveroo made no scruple to seize the children of those who could not or did not pay up their contributions to the revenue at the moment it became due or was demanded, or the fines which he arbitrarily laid upon them. These children he actually sent about the country in droves, like sheep or kine, their unfortunate parents following them with cries and lamentations. Even young infants were thus carried away for the satisfaction of a cruel avarice; and married women were taken when children were not to be had. When one of these herds of wretched captives amounted to a large number, it was driven down to the plains about Noorpoor, Denanuggur, and other towns in the Punjaub, where the miserable slaves were sure to find a ready sale. Inexorably cruel and pitiless was Wuzeer Zoroveroo in pursuing the interests of his master, and he has been known to have captives cut to pieces for either attempting to escape, refusing to proceed, or even for fainting on the road.

Thus did Zoroveroo extend his master's sway over the greatest part of the hill-country north and north-east of Jummoo. Thus too did he with the most heartless cruelty exercise his delegated but practically irresponsible authority over the subjects of Goolaub Sing. While he was thus winning provinces and hoarding wealth for his patron, he exercised the most rigid self-denial towards himself. He had never drawn pay from the time of his first interview with the Rajah; he wore no clothes but those sent him by his master; where bribes or presents were offered to him, he invariably sent the money to his chief. Even his wife and children he left dependant on the Rajah for their daily subsistence. But he had his reward in the favour and admiration of his master, and in the unlimited confidence which that master placed in him. It is possible too, that he might have had ulterior views for his own aggrandisement, in the exercise of the power which he thus acquired, but as the time or the opportunity for effecting his purpose, whatever it might be, never occurred, nothing is known on this point.

The conquests of Zoroveroo in the north rendered him an object of dread among the people inhabiting the countries that lie along the further base of the Snowy Range, and it was not without reason that they regarded his progress with alarm. At his suggestion, Goolaub Sing formed the project of an expedition for the conquest of Ladakh, and this plan was carried out by the Wuzeer, though at the expence of much difficulty and loss. His army marched by the way of Kistowar, and penetrated the Snowy Range, through passes of the most difficult and almost inaccessible character. On his return from this first expedition to Ladakh, however, he greatly improved the communication with that province, repairing the roads and removing some of the obstacles to his advance through the passes.

It was not long ere he proceeded on a second expedition in this direction, marching by the same route to Ladakh, where he was joined by a force from Cashmere. Thence he advanced and took Iskardo and Little Thibet from Ahmed Shah. This conquest however, he owed less to his military skill or prowess than to the exercise of bribery, and to the disunion existing among the members of Ahmed Shah's family. After plundering the country which thus fell under his power, Zoroveroo returned by his old route, and sent the spoils of his late campaign to his master at Jummoo. At the same time he informed the Rajah, that if he were reinforced to some extent he would, in another campaign, overrun the whole Champa country, and plunder the holy places of the Lamas, whose shrines, as he told the Rajah, were of solid gold and silver. He also informed his master, that not far to the eastward of Ladakh, there was a gold mine worked by the Chinese Tartars, which he should be able to secure for his patron. Dazzled by the splendour of these prospects of unbounded wealth, the covetuous Rajah directed his Wuzeer to hasten to his presence, when they could discuss the arrangements for a campaign of so much risk and so much hope, more conveniently. Goolaub had so much confidence in the skill, courage, and prudence of his Minister, that he doubted not for a moment his ability to execute the bold plan which he had formed. It was therefore only for the purpose of arranging as to the means and manner of the expedition that he requested the attendance of Zoroveroo at his capital. Thither the Wuzeer hastened at his patron's call, and it was not long ere the plan and arrangements for the campaign were settled in consultation betwixt him and his master. The force destined for the service, was to consist of five hundred Meeans or Rajpoots, and eight hundred Rohillas, with nine thousand hillmen to be collected from the provinces under the Wuzeer's government; while a battalion of infantry, with two guns, was to go by the Cashmere road to Ladakh, there to join the main body under Zoroveroo. The Wuzeer would proceed by his former route to Ladakh, and thence towards the Champa country and the lakes of Manserawara.

Matters being thus arranged, the Wuzeer left Jummoo in high spirits to execute his bold design. In May 1841, his whole force was assembled at Leh, the capital of Ladakh, whence after settling some disturbances in the neighbouring districts, it set forward in the latter end of June. Leaving the Cashmere battalion and its two guns at Leh as a reserve, and to keep the country quiet, Zoroveroo, with the rest of his force, about ten thousand men, marched along the north bank of the Scinde river. When he had thus advanced for some days, they took prisoners some Bhoteas or Thibetans, and some Tartars from the plains of Changthong, and these men led the army to a large plain to the north or north-west of Rudakh, where the Tartars used to dig for and find gold in small pieces or grains. Zoroveroo was thus induced to halt in this district for about twenty days, during which time he had numbers of men employed in searching for the precious metal which his master loved so well, and the result was that a weight of about two seers and a half was collected. The price of this gold was the destruction of Zoroveroo and his army. While the Wuzeer was foolishly lingering about the spot that yielded the vile dross, the people of Champa, the Chinese Tartars, and a large force from Lassa, had united and were advancing to check his progress and to give him battle. Learning this he hastened forward rapidly, and ere he met the enemy came upon three or four Lama shrines, which he plundered of all that was valuable. He then pushed forward towards the lakes, where he promised himself much rich booty. He had not, however, proceeded many days in this direction when the Champa cavalry and other hostile forces became so annoying to his army on the march that he found himself compelled to halt. Having done this he was soon surrounded by the overwhelming force that had collected to oppose him, and being compelled to give battle was completely defeated. Zoroveroo himself, and his five hundred Rajpoots, were among the slain, and the whole army was dispersed with great slaughter. Only a miserable remnant of the force, which found their way through the hills into the British territories by way of Almora, returned to Jummoo, to tell the tale of their defeat and the death of their leader, the Wuzeer Zoroveroo.

THE SOODHUN REVOLT.

About the year 1832, several independent hill-tribes inhabiting the north western regions of the Punjaub were reduced into subjection to the Lahore state. These were the Doondh, Soodhun, Suthee, and Murdiall tribes. The Doondh tribe lived chiefly on the banks of the Jhelum, especially on the western bank, from the point where the river leaves the Kukka Bumba hills for about twenty-five or thirty miles down the stream. This tribe was in number about fifty or sixty thousand. The Soodhun tribe inhabited a large tract on the eastern bank of the same river opposite the country of the Doondhs, and numbered about forty thousand souls. The Suthee tribe dwelt chiefly in the lower hills to the south of the tribes above mentioned, and was estimated at about twenty thousand. Lastly the Murdiall tribe lay to the east of the Sudhun, and was reckoned at about eighteen thousand people.

About the period above mentioned the Dogra brothers of Jummoo endeavoured to bring these wild clans into subjection, nominally to the Lahore state, but really to themselves. Finding, however, the conquest less easy than they had anticipated, they prevailed upon their master, Runjeet Sing, to march with his whole army towards Rawul Pindee, and thus to aid them by making a demonstration against the tribes whom they in vain sought to subdue. Runjeet accordingly marched with some sixty thousand men in the direction indicated, and encamped with this force at Kooree, in the plains, but just at the entrance of the hilly region inhabited by the doomed clans. Seeing so overwhelming a force, under the famous Runjeet Sing, apparently coming against them, and startled by the thunder of a hundred and fifty pieces of ordnance echoing among their mountains day and night, the people readily submitted to the yoke which the Dogra chiefs sought to impose upon them.

One of the head-men of the Sudhun tribe when it submitted to the Dogras, was Shumass Khan. This man, as a hostage for the fidelity of his clan and family, was kept about the person of Rajah Dehan Sing, whom he actually served as a private Gorechar trooper. In this capacity he so far won the favour of his master, and was taken so far into his confidence, that he incurred the jealousy and dislike of the elder brother, Goolaub Sing. This feeling of hostility induced Goolaub on several occasions to remonstrate with his brother, on what he chose to consider the folly and impropriety of reposing his confidence in a man so circumstanced as was Shumass Khan. The younger brother, however, could never see the matter in the same light, and he accordingly continued to display his favour and partiality to the fallen chieftain as before. Shumass was to all appearance duly grateful to his patron and reciprocated his regard; and thus he remained in close personal attendance on Rajah Dehan Sing at Lahore, until near the end of the year 1836.

About this time Rajah Goolaub Sing was summoned from Chiniote, where he was just commencing a campaign against Dewan Sawun Mull of Moultan, and compelled to hasten with all his troops towards Peshawur, where the Affghans had won a temporary success over the Seiks, and had killed the Governor, Sirdar Hurriett Sing. Rajah Dehan Sing had already hastened to the point endangered, having left Runjeet Sing encamped at Ramnuggur; and, attended by a few horseman, made so rapid a march that he arrived at Peshawur in little more than three days. Goolaub, as has been said, broke up his camp at Chiniote, and, without any warning or previous arrangement, his army was directed to hasten, every division as it best could, towards Peshawur. His force consisted of about six thousand men, horse and foot, with twelve light guns; yet with the exception of some three hundred men and two guns, which broke down on the rapid march, the whole body was re-assembled on the further bank of the Indus near Attock, on the morning of the fifth day.

Here Goolaub Sing rejoined his troops, and here he received a letter from Dehan Sing, now at Peshawur, informing him that as matters there had changed for the better, there was no occasion for him to advance upon the place; but that his services were required in the Yuzoofzye country, north of the Loonda or Cabul river, where all the people were up in arms to claim their independance. Accordingly the army immediately proceeded towards the troubled districts, crossing the Cabul river at Jehangerah, seven or eight miles to the north-west of Attock.

It was while engaged in the suppression of these disturbances in the Yuzoofzye districts, that Goolaub heard of a revolt in his own hill states, among the Sudhun, Suthee, Doondh, and Murdiall tribes. It took him, however, two months and some hard fighting to reduce the Yuzoofzyes to subjection, nor was it till he had laid waste a great part of the country, and had driven most of the inhabitants to the hills that order was in any degree restored. After all, the country was in a very unsettled state when his anxiety for the suppression of the revolt in his own dominions induced him to hasten thither, leaving the Yuzoofzyes to the management of one Ursulla Khan, whom he made Kardar of the district. This man was devoted to the interest of the Jummoo Rajah, and was greatly favoured and trusted by him. He is the same Ursulla Khan, who lately caused much disturbance by exciting and heading an insurrectionary movement in the country entrusted to his charge.

It was by the wide-spread intelligence of the Seik reverses at Peshawur, and a rumour that these disasters were of so serious a nature that they would require for some time all the power of the Dogra brothers to repress them, that the hill tribes had been induced to hope that they might by a vigorous effort shake off the yoke which they so reluctantly bore. This hope was strengthened by the prevalence of another rumour which spoke of Rajah Goolaub Sing as being badly, some even said mortally, wounded, in one of the skirmishes with the Yuzoofzyes. Hence it was that the tribes rose in rebellion, and being at first but feebly opposed by the Seik garrisons, carried all before them.

It happened that Shumass Khan, the former chief of the Sudhun clan, and who, as has been related, had since the subjugation of his tribe, continued in attendance on Dehan Sing, had just before this time obtained leave to return for a short time to his home in the hills. Goolaub Sing, as it has been mentioned, held this man in bitter enmity, and on hearing of the reports which were circulated in the hill country, and which were exciting the people to rebellion, he immediately wrote to Dehan Sing at Peshawar, informing him that Shumass Khan was the treacherous enemy who was spreading these rumours so prejudicial to their interest. He furthermore strongly advised his brother to leave the supposed traitor entirely in his hands, and not to interfere in any way with the measures to which he should resort for punishing him and restoring order in the country.

A short time after this, instructions were sent to some of the Kardars and other dependants of Goolaub Sing, to have Shumass Khan, with all his family, taken prisoners at his residence in the hills, where he then was. The chief, however, received intelligence of the design for his capture, and knowing the fate that would await him should he fall into the hands of Goolaub, made his escape with all his family into the fastnesses of the hills, thus placing himself beyond the reach of the Rajah's power.

This was the signal for the hitherto smouldering flame

of rebellion to break out. The whole country rose in arms against the authority of the Dogra Rajahs, and as they at first met with little opposition, the insurgents had in less than a month, and before Goolaub could extricate himself from the Yuzoofzyes, taken and destroyed all the forts and strongholds of their rulers, from Poonch almost to the walls of Jummoo itself, and from the borders of Cashmere to the base of the hills. All the troops which Goolaub could as yet send against them were repulsed and obliged to return with heavy loss, leaving the triumphant insurgents in possession of the whole country. And this although the Jummoo force numbered about five thousand men, and was commanded by Meean Oottum Sing, the eldest son of the Rajah, one of the bravest of his race, and by Dewan Hurree Chund, Goolaub's principal minister and commander.

At length the Rajah himself left the Yuzoofzye country, and marched his troops to Kohoutee, at the foot of the hills to the north-east of Rawul Pindee. Seeing, however, that if force alone were used, the result would be at least doubtful, he halted at Kohoutee for some time, and commenced a course of intrigue and bribery for the purpose of creating disunion among the insurgents, and bringing some of them over to his side. Shumass Khan had now openly placed himself at the head of the insurgents, and it was by intriguing with and bribing the enemies of this man among the hill chiefs that Goolaub wrought his purpose. Having succeeded by such means in detaching many of the insurgents from the common cause, and secured their aid or at least their neutrality, the Rajah at the head of about eight thousand regular infantry and twelve thousand irregulars, a sort of militia raised in the hills about Jummoo, ascended from the plains at Kohoutee and marched towards Mung and Pelundheree. In order at once to strike terror into the insurgents and to distress and punish them, he devastated the country as he advanced, permitting his troops freely to plunder and to practise every excess. More than this, he offered a reward of five rupees for the head of every insurgent or any of those connected with him, man, woman or child; and in consequence a cool systematic massacre ensued, likely to lead to the utter extermination of the miserable people. Panic struck by this display of ferocity, and hopeless of being able to resist the overpowering force led by the Rajah, the insurgents dispersed and fled to hide themselves and their families among the rocks and mountains, and in the pine forests and jungles, leaving their houses, cattle, and property to the mercy of the advancing army.

Often the troops came upon their hiding places, and discovered a wretched family pent up together in some den or cavern, where they were, without respect to sex or age, savagely massacred for the sake of the paltry reward put upon their heads. However, after some few days of this exterminating slaughter, the Rajah issued an order that the women and female children should be spared, and when taken captive, brought and delivered over to certain officers whom he appointed to take charge of them. Thus in a short time each separate division of the army had in its train a drove of unfortunate women and children, driven about like cattle, in the most miserable condition, half starved and scarcely half clad—whatever little clothing they had carried with them in their hasty flight from their homes having been taken from them by the greedy and merciless Dogra soldiers. Sometimes for days no rations were served out to these wretched captives, and they were left dependant for subsistence on what chance threw in their way, or what the rude soldiery might be disposed to give them. On the re-assemblage of the army at Pelundheree, these prisoners were gathered into one large herd, consisting of about five thousand females of every age. They were now regularly penned in a sheep-fold secured by a strong hedge of prickly bushes, and here kept without any proper provision being made for their subsistence. The troops themselves, at this time, lived chiefly on the grain called *Mukh* or *Mekoi* which they eat raw; and a bundle or two of this was daily thrown among this herd of five thousand human beings, as all that was considered necessary to preserve them from actually dying of hunger. To quench their thirst they were once a day loosed from their fold and led to some neighbouring stream, and then like sheep driven back again. To such barbarous treatment, and other ill-usage, which it is not necessary to describe, no less than fourteen or fifteen hundred of these poor wretches fell victims during the halt at Pelundheree.

The males of the insurgent tribes had been almost entirely exterminated, some five or six thousand of them, whose heads were tossed about the encampment in the sight of their captive relatives, having been hunted down and slain during the halt of fifteen or sixteen days at Pelundheree. Altogether not less than fourteen or fifteen thousand people of these small tribes perished in this campaign.

During the stay of the army at Pelundheree, some of the enemies of Shumass Khan, for whose head Goolaub Sing had offered a very large reward, promised to lead the Rajah's forces to the spot in which the insurgent chief was secreted with a few of his followers. Accordingly Meean Oottum Sing, with a strong detachment, was guided to the very house in which, by the advice of his betrayers, Shumass Khan had taken up his abode. He was there surprised while he and his attendants were asleep, and of course was immediately put to death. His head with that of his son, who was killed at the same time, was afterwards exhibited in an iron cage, at the top of the Adha Dek Pass above Poonch, where it remained for some years.

With the life of Shumass Khan ceased the last hopes and efforts of the insurgents. No further resistance was offered to the triumphant progress of the victors; and satisfied with the amount of punishment which he had inflicted, Goolaub withdrew his troops, retiring by various routes through the hills to Jummoo.

On his departure for his capital the Rajah ordered that the drove of captive females should be sent thither after him. During the march to that place, about seven hundred of them died from want and fatigue, while many more were privately carried off by the soldiery as their share of the booty. Thus of the five thousand females that had been collected in the sheepfold at Pelundheree, only about eight or nine hundred reached Jummoo. From these some forty or fifty of the youngest and best looking were selected for the Rajah's zenana, in which some of them are still living. The rest, with the exception of about a hundred who died from ill-treatment at Jummoo, after being kept in the neighbourhood of that city for some time, were sold to the highest bidders, and thus many of them were consigned to hopeless slavery.

Thus was the Sudhun insurrection suppressed and revenged, and such was its immediate but not its only result. Those who had escaped the sword of the conqueror, and were left at liberty in their hill-fastnesses, on returning to their homes found that they had yet an enemy to encounter more formidable than the Jummoo troops and their merciless leader. The fields having remained uncultivated and unsown during the occupation of the country by the enemy, Famine, with all its horrors, raged throughout the land. The wretched people were, therefore, again compelled to fly, and some thousands of them sought the means of subsistence in the nearest lowland districts, where, however, many of them perished of hunger, perhaps after selling their children for a rupee or two each to purchase food to preserve their lives and the lives of their offspring.

Such was the fate of a people who dared to take up arms in an attempt to free themselves from the power of Rajah Goolaub Sing.

FUTTEH KHAN TEWANAH.

FUTTEH KHAN the chief who, in conjunction with Sirdar Chuttur Sing Attareewalla, effected the murder of Prince Peshora Sing, and who has lately given the Lahore Durbar so much trouble in the Yuzoofzye country, was a Chowdrie and the son of a Chowdrie of Mitha Tewanah, a place on the banks of the Jhelum, fourteen or fifteen miles to the north-west of Kooshaub. From the place of his birth and abode, he is commonly called Futteh Khan Tewanah.

About the year 1821, when Runjeet Sing took the fort of Monkera, and brought into subjection the Nawaub of that district, he advanced and returned through the district of Mitha Tewanah, which was before that time divided into a number of small estates, altogether independent of the chief of the country. Each of the Chowdries, possessing a small Ghurrie or fort, with four or five villages around it, regarded himself, and was regarded by his neighbours, as a sovereign potentate on a small scale. As might be expected these petty princes were constantly at war with each other, bloody conflicts were of frequent occurrence, and the people of the country from their habits of strife were notorious for their depredations, and became in short little better than a race of mere robbers and free-booters. Their country had long been famous for its excellent breed of horses, and the people were celebrated from their good horsemanship and their skill with the spear. It happened thus, that when Runjeet conquered the country in 1821, Futteh Khan and Khoda Buksh, his brother, with their father and about fifty or sixty horsemen of the clan, accompanied the Maharajh to Lahore, he having invited them to follow him in consideration of the assistance which they had rendered him in the subjugation of Monkera and even of their own country.

It was, however, chiefly through the instrumentality of Rajah Dehan Sing that these men were first introduced to Runjeet's special notice. On their arrival at Lahore, Dehan Sing frequently exhibited them and their followers before the Maharajh, displaying their wonderful skill in the management of their horses and arms. One feat, which particularly pleased Runjeet, was that of striking a tent peg from the ground with the spear while at full gallop. It was thus that the Maharajh was induced to take favourable notice of the Tewanah brothers, and to retain them in his immediate service, with a jaghire in their own district of about six thousand rupees, enlisting also their fifty or sixty followers at about three hundred rupees each sowar yearly.

Khoda Buksh was placed in command of the little troop of horsemen, the father being appointed Chabook sowar, or rough rider, in attendance on Runjeet, in which capacity his skill and adroitness earned him many marks of the Maharajh's favour. Futteh Khan, being a particular favourite of Rajah Dehan Sing, became his right hand man, and chief councillor in all his hunting expeditions, an office for which his previous habits of life peculiarly suited him.

Thus the family advanced their interest and influence at Lahore, until about the year 1832, when the father died. On his death, Futteh Khan and his brother, at the intercession of Dehan Sing, received a considerable addition to their jaghire, which already amounted to twelve or fifteen thousand rupees a year. A district worth twenty or thirty thousand rupees, in the Hazareh country, was given to them in farm. Sirdar Hurriett Sing, Nellowa, then Governor of Peshawar, was an implacable enemy of the Tewanah family, and had hitherto been the sole obstacle to their rise and advancement, judging that as he held the greater part of the Hazareh country in jaghire, they could rise only on the ruin of his fortunes. Ere long, however, Hurriett Sing was slain by the Affghans at Peshawar, and soon after his death, the brothers received, through the favor of Dehan Sing, another large addition to their estates in the Hazerah, being a district worth above a lakh of rupees yearly. At court, also, the Tewanah brothers had, through the influence of their patron, become sirdars of great dignity and influence.

Thus matters stood at the death of Rajah Dehan Sing, on which occasion Futteh Khan, with his son a lad of fourteen or fifteen years of age, was in attendance on the Minister. It is said, however, that when Dehan Sing was met on his way to Shahbelore by Ajeet Sing Scindawalla and his band, and by them turned back towards Lahore, Futteh Khan, who till that moment had been riding close by the side of the doomed Minister, seeing that something was wrong, dropped behind the cavalcade and so only arrived at the gates of the fort in time to be shut out from the scene of murder. On finding the gates closed betwixt himself and his patron, and knowing that Ajeet Sing's party could mean no good to him, Futteh Khan prudently retraced his steps, and hastening into the city there concealed himself until the death of the Scindawallas made it safe for him to re-appear. His young son, who was by the side of Dehan Sing when he was about to enter the gateway of the fort, was despatched by the Rajah, who suspected danger, to summon a band of three or four hundred armed followers from his Havelee or palace, but, as might be supposed they did not arrive at the fort until the gates had been closed against them, and when the adherents of the Scindawallas mustered strong enough to frighten them from all attempts at a rescue of their master.

On emerging from his retreat, when matters had somewhat settled down, leaving Heera Sing and the Pundit Jellah at the head of affairs, Futteh Khan found that the new Wuzeer and his adviser were any thing but favourably disposed towards him. He was taxed with treachery and unfaithfulness on the occasion of Dehan Sing's assassination, and soon found that evil was in store for him. Heera Sing and the Pundit, as a pretext for laying their hands on him, demanded a lakh of rupees as due for the country held by his family in the Hazareh, and claimed from him thirty thousand camels, which they said Rajah Dehan Sing had given into his charge. Compliance with these demands being out of the question, and their fulfilment being insisted on, Futteh Khan, by night and in disguise, fled from Lahore and retired to his patrimonial estate of Mitha Tewanah. Thither he was ere long followed by a body of troops sent from Lahore to take him prisoner. He had, however, got the start sufficiently to be able to flee with his family and the greater part of his moveable property across the Indus, where he found a safe retreat. Finding their pursuit ineffectual, the troops sent against him returned to Lahore without having fulfilled the object of their journey. On their retirement, Futteh Khan recrossed from his hiding place, and was able to collect a large force of Moolkeeas or inhabitants of the surrounding districts. Putting himself at the head of these insurgent bands, he began to lay waste with fire and sword the whole country within his reach. Plunder, rapine, and revenge being his only objects, he was too prudent to attempt to meet the regular troops that were from time to time sent from Lahore against him. This predatory warfare he kept up during nearly the whole administration of Heera Sing and Pundit Jellah; but on receiving news of the death of these his enemies, he hastened to Lahore, assured of a favourable reception from Jewahir Sing, who now came into power. His hope of favour with the new Wuzeer was founded on the encouragement which he had received from that Sirdar in his measures for the annoyance of their common enemies, Heera Sing and the Pundit. Nor was his confidence misplaced. Jewahir Sing, on his appearance at Lahore, presented him with a valuable *Khelut* and additional jaghires in Hazareh worth ten or eleven lakhs a year, including Dera Ismail Khan, Golatchee, Bunnoo-Tank, and Mitha Tewanah, with all their dependencies. His son, also, a mere youth, was made a general of artillery, with a salary of twelve hundred rupees a month.

Khoda Buksh, the brother of Futteh Khan, died at Mitha Tewanah, of cholera, when this disease was raging throughout the Punjaub. Soon after this event, a private perwanah from Jewahir Sing, instructed Futteh Khan to proceed with all his troops against Peshora Sing, then at Attock, whom he was to capture and put to death. In this affair, which has been detailed elsewhere, he was joined and assisted by Chuttur Sing Attareewalla, and in the murderous business they both acquitted themselves greatly to the satisfaction of their employer. On the death of the Prince, Futteh Khan hastily retired to his domains of Dera Ismail Khan and Bunnoo-Tank, where he knew he would be safe from the apprehended vengeance of the Khalsa on the murderers of their favourite Peshora Sing. He thus avoided the retribution which fell on his patron and employer, Jewahir Sing, who became a victim to the rage of the troops.

Elated with his former successes and the impunity with which he had hitherto escaped, Futteh Khan now determined to rid himself of some of his principal enemies in the country about him. In fulfilment of this design, he, while living at Dera Ismail Khan, invited certain Patans, his intended victims, to a great feast, and when his guests were off their guard, he had the whole party put to death by the swords of his followers. The clansmen of the murdered chiefs, however, enraged at this bloody and treacherous act, united for the punishment of the murderer, and, attacking him with a considerable force, he was compelled to flee across the

Indus to his own district of Mitha Tewanah. It was while residing here that he learnt, seemingly to his great astonishment, that his conduct at Dera Ismail Khan was regarded at Lahore as so heinous, that he had been proclaimed a traitor and a rebel, and that troops had been sent towards Mitha Tewanah for his apprehension. Knowing, however, that at the capital craft and money could do any thing, he sent in his submission by the hands of his mother, accompanied by large sums of money as presents to the Ranee and her confidential adviser, the slave girl Mungela. His ambassadress, thus accredited and recommended, was of course well received. She was provided with a residence in the palace, and taken into the favour of the Ranee, and what was more to the purpose of the all-powerful Mungela, whose good offices had, it is said, been purchased by no less than a lakh of rupees. It hardly need be said, after this, that Futteh Khan was relieved from all fear of present molestation, and allowed to remain in quiet, for a while. Subsequently, however, affairs turned so much to his disadvantage that he found himself deprived of a great part of the country to the west of the Indus, which was made over to the son of Dewan Lekhee.

THE

LORDS OF THE HILLS;—

A

GENEALOGICAL HISTORY OF THE JUMMOO FAMILY.

CHAPTER I.

ACCORDING to various old Sanscrit manuscripts, corroborated by numerous incidents and historical facts in the traditional legends of the family, about 471 years before the time of the great Vikramadita, and about the time of Kyroo (Cyrus) and his vast and great conquests,* at which period a great commotion and stir seems to have been excited throughout all Ind or Hind, and bold adventurers to have been enticed from different parts of the far South and East:—about this

---

* Numerous native traditions and fables speak of the wars of Kyroo, and by all those accounts he may be supposed to have extended his conquests somewhat more eastward than the Indus. We may appropriate some of the native names of his successors as follows:—Cyrus, B. C. 536, Kyroo Badsha; Cambyses, B. C. 529, Kome Badsha; Smerdis, one of the magi, B. C. 523, Moordoo; Darius, son of Hystaspes, Daroo Badsha; Xerxes the Great, B. C. 486, Keeroo or Keroon;—Artaxerxes, B. C. 665, unmentioned. Xerxes 2nd, B. C. 424, unmentioned; Sogdianus, B. C. 424; Sooje Badsha; Ochus or Darius the Bastard, B. C. 423, Daroo Nauk, or Na Hok; Artaxerxes. Ochus, B. C. 405, unmentioned; Arses or Arsames, B. C. 306, unmentioned; Darius Codomanus, B. C. 336, Daroo Shuko or Shukust, being beaten and conquered by Alexander or Secunder Badsha, B. C. 331.

period two Rajpoot brothers, Boogjoo heroes,* emigrated with their families and followers (about forty in number) from a small village called Oopa or Oop, the original hereditary jaghire of their family, and in the vicinity of the present Oude. Some family dissensions appear to have been the main cause of this emigration, and a fortune-seeking and adventurous spirit seems to have induced them to leave their paternal home and make their way towards the North West, then the supposed scene of strife and a promising field for the heroic adventurer. On their way thither, they, while performing their devotions at the holy Ganges, were advised by some astrologers (Jothushee and Nejume pundits) that they should proceed on their route to the banks of the second next large river they should meet with. Thus they crossed the Jumna, and seem to have met with opportunities sufficient to induce them to settle on the east banks of the Sutlej, where those two brothers, the elder named Bajoo Sirb, and the younger Dulleep, formed a kind of settlement in some dense jungles. However, it was not long before they disagreed, so as to induce the younger, Dulleep, to leave the elder; and he is supposed to have, at this juncture, crossed the river, and with his own family and a few followers, to have settled in the present Punjaub. From this date or period there is no further notice of Bajoo Sirb left on record, except some

* It must be supposed that in those ages, there were different kinds of soldiers and weapons, and the heroes were called after their different weapons,—thus the Boogjoo warrior was he who could wield in battle the heavy Boogjoo or mallett, at present in native use only among wrestlers. The Moon or Moonghy is still different from the Boogjoo or Goorj, &c. The Goorg or Goorj was he that could wield the heavy mace in battle. There were several kinds of Goorj, from the heavy and large headed mace—iron and metal imitations of which may be at present seen among natives, down to the lat'h or iron-headed dong or bludgeon, at present in use among natives. The Kumannee is perfectly out of use except in ripe grain fields, where the sling is now only used to frighten away birds, &c. The Tereendauz or archer is in some parts as yet to be seen with his poisoned rrows, as about Kukka Bumba, Kaabaan, &c. &c.

slight and faint hints that he was the founder of the present much-famed Rajwara dynasty, or the supposed head and founder of the Joudpore and Jeypore families. Dulleep is said to have served as a soldier (or Boogjoo hero) under Rajah Seenoo of the principality and fortress of Rhahuk (supposed to be the site of the present Sull, or Seealkote*) and possessed then by a Hindoo tribe or race called Rhahauks or Rauks; not the Kokuss or the famed giants so called, but their supposed descendants. An immemorial hatred caused a long and continued series of feuds between the Rhahauks and Khaundores,† the then mighty princes forming the N. W. barrier of India, and in those feuds Dulleep and his Rajpoot successors gained both fame and credit, and were the renowned Boogjoo-daurs of the Rhahauk faction.

Thus passed six generations or 180 years, and the lineal descendants thus:—Dulleep 1st or founder; 2nd, his son Dehu Chund; 3rd, Sooruj Ther; 4th, Bridd Bull; 5th, Purin Ther; 6th, Therm Kurn. Some short space after the death of the last mentioned, Therm Kurn, great consternation and excitement was caused throughout all India, and especially in the present Punjaub, and in all the Rhahauk states, by the victorious advance of the invading Unan forces, and their renowned chief Sekunder (then by the Hindoos generally called Oondroo and sometimes Koohoondroo) who after a series of rapid successes seems to have ultimately formed a standing camp, or became stationary on the west banks of the Abba or Baba Sceen or Sceend (Indus) and just in the centre

---

* Raja Sull, he that is said to have built the present Sull Kote or Sealkote, was a Rhahauk Chief and Prince, and his descendant Rajah, Resaollah, who lived about the latter end of the last century, was, or is supposed to have been, the last of that race of princes. He at one time conquered as far as the Indus.

† The Khaundores were ultimately driven from the country and afterwards settled about the present Candahar, which it is said they founded, and the place took its name from that race.

of the Khaundore territories, whose three great seats of government were then, the first or greatest at the present Maa Buun, a great mountain on the west bank, and twenty miles north east of the fort of Attock; the second at Khond or Khaund, formerly a great city, as yet to be seen, about twelve or fifteen miles north or north west of Panahthaur, all curiously cut out of the solid rock into caves and apartments of different kinds, round and all over a large mountain of bare black flinty rock, and its present extent and circumference may be said to exceed 4 or 4½ miles. The third was Dheroo or Droogh, (the present Gund-e-ghur, a large mountain, and to this day an obstinate stronghold held by the Gundaghurries, on the east bank, and just to the east of the town or village of Hazeroo. Besides these there were several other but smaller principalities and strongholds of the Khaundores. The Khaundores conceived that they could not act better than to enter into a close alliance with Koondroo or Koohoondroo, and by this alliance they hoped to crush, or usurp the power of their eastern enemies, the Rhahauks, Gethes and Nazoos,* whose country and numerous wandering hordes were the southern and south-western neighbours of the Rhahauks or southerly or south westerly Punjaub, and their wild tracts, with some few exceptions, extended to the sea (Beloochistan) and were always in friendly alliance with the northerly Rhahauks, and though much more numerous, a wild and wandering race, were mostly graziers, shepherds, &c. and acknowledged a kind of supremacy in the heroic lords of Rhahauk. The Gethes were plunderers and wanderers, and the present Jat may be supposed to be the descendant of the Nazoos and Gethes, roving shepherds that inhabited and wandered along the different banks of

---

* The Nazoos and Gethes were the supposed aborigines of the Punjaub, and the present Jum Loke or inhabitant herdsmen and shepherds, with the Gudgers of the lower jungles, may be supposed to be their descendants. The Jats, who always intermarry with the Gudgers, may be considered of the same race; and perhaps their appellation Jat may be a corruption of the former Geth or Géte.

the five rivers; or they may seem the forefathers of the present Sepaide, or the famed *Kurls* and the wandering *Junn,* and all those called or coming under the denomination of Barr Loke—all or most of whom to this day just lead the same kind of life as did the former Nazoos and Gethes, and may be said to be still the most able and active race in the Punjaub.

To return to the subject, the son of Therm Kurn, Arathunge Kurn, under his leader, Rajah Maanaa or Mahnahook, distinguished himself by many feats of valour, and much blood was spilt on both sides in defending their country and resisting the invaders who had sent at different times large bodies of troops from the Indus to invade the Rhahauk territory. The east boundary of the Rhahauk country was the Sutlej, and its west the Jhelum—or the low range of hills on which the present fort of Rhotas stands, where the Khaundores joined it;—on the north the mountain range, and on the south the Nazoo wilds and wastes, whose northern bounds may be considered about the present Amenabad, Lahore, Kussoor, Gujerawalla, and Guzerat. However the Rhahauks were, by the numerous and powerful attacks of their allied enemies, obliged to give way, and at this juncture it was to them a happy circumstance that by the arrival of three different great and powerful princes at different periods from the east and south, their country was partially saved, and a strong check put on the advance of the invading army. However their cavalry were still accustomed to scour the country as far as even the very gates of Rhahauk. But ultimately all this and Mahnahook's dread of their presence subsided on the arrival from the far east of, it is said, 30,000 Goorjberdaurs and Boogjoods, chiefly mounted on buffaloes, with a like number of Teerendauz, chiefly mounted on elephants, and a numerous body of slingers (Kummanees), spearmen, &c. &c. and all headed in person by the great Porso or Phorso, supposed chief or Rajah of Adjudea, a great, powerful and warlike prince of a large dominion in the far east. Now, with this great reinforcement, the whole army as it was encamped on the east bank of the Chenaub, and a day's march from the fort of Rhahauk (at the present Kooloowall-ke-puttun) amounted to about 200,000 fighting men, and the entire number, followers and all, would exceed 500,000. It was not long before Secunder, assisted by the Khaundores and several other tribes, advanced from the Indus to give battle, but his force altogether fell somewhat short of the number of his opponents, while his own countrymen, or all the foreigners, did not ammout to above 50,000. Now the tract between the Chenaub and Jhelum, or about the present Gujerat, Minore, Doulutanuggur, and certain other spots, where many coins, relics, &c., are as yet to be found, became the scene of many bloody skirmishes and actions, all which tended to drive the invader to the west bank of the Jhelum; where now Secunder had concentrated all his forces on the heights of the Rhotas range, and along its east base, while the Indian army proudly pitched its large camp on the east bank in the hilly tract and broken ground that runs east of the village of Quarr. It was not long before Secunder gave battle by crossing at or a little below the present Quarr-ka-puttun, with numerous boats he had collected and newly made (said to be 5,000 in number) and though he did not effectually rout the Indian army, still they were driven back and disheartened so as to allow him not long after to take most of his troops along with him, and to march and sail down the river. He however left, unprotected and unprovided for, about 10,000 of his own Greek troops encamped as a rear guard or reserve on the west bank of the Indus, where his fixed and entrenched camp had been, about where the fort of Oud or Ode now stands, and, where many vestiges of it may be found in the bed and on the west bank of the stream. It may be supposed that Secunder was somehow anxious to retreat, and perhaps his proceeding down the river was only in fulfilment of a clause in some conditional treaty. He took most of his boats, and part of his troops lined each bank of the river, while he is said in a manner to have forgotten his unfortunate followers, the nine or ten thousand men left on the west bank of the Scind or Indus. However this may be, on his retreat the attention of the Indian army was called towards this small body of Greek troops, who had among them all the sick and weakly, or those that were unable to attend their leader down the Jhelum. Soon, therefore, this body of his troops was attacked and routed, the greater part of them flying in the direction of the city of Khaundore, and thence northward towards the snowy range, which they entered, and whence they are supposed never to have returned. Some of them retreated into Kafiristan, and in this country under the different names of Seer Post or Posht, &c. the present descendants of this unfortunate relic of the Greek army may be supposed to exist; while all those that were scattered in various directions at that period, and those that became intimate with and mixed with the natives by intermarriages, &c. are those which now may be supposed to go under the well known name of Gukkers.

Arethunge Kurn, in the seventh generation from Dulleep, is said to have been killed in some of those bloody engagements; and now his son Keerut Kurn, the eighth, left the service, of the Rhahauks, and his posterity down to the twenty-eighth generation followed their warlike occupation, and served under different masters, but always in or about the Punjaub. The twenty-eighth Bija Sing or Bija Ther, who is said to have lived about the year 369 of Vikramadita, is put down as the first who settled in the hills about the present Noorpoor, while himself and the male part of his family served under different chiefs in the Punjaub. But henceforward the Rajpoots collected their families, and formed a small colony at or near Noorpoor, in the hills north of Lahore.

Sooruj Dehu, the fiftieth in succession, lived about the year 1009 of Vikramadita, and was but a lad of about ten years old when his father died, and a young man of about twenty when, as tradition says, on the second day of the month of Ramjaun in the year 271 of the Hejira, Sultan Mahomed (commonly called the Ghuzneewalla) fought a bloody engagement, close to the walls of Ghuznee, thereby deciding the fate of that fortress, which in a few days after fell into his hands. Mun Bown, Envoy from the Sirhind court, was then (with about forty followers, mostly Rajpoots) on a mission to different Hindoo Rajahs (Authush and Pruth and Prest) then reigning in that quarter ; and actually Mun Bown and one of his followers were all that returned to Sirhind alive, the rest having been cut up or made prisoners in the general massacre at Ghuznee, being then and there present.

The capture of this famed fortress struck terror into all the chiefs and people around, as it was from days immemorial considered impregnable. It was believed (as tradition had it) to have been originally built by a great Deuh (giant) called Nahor or Nauhour who was said to have come there from the far west, some thousands of years before, and who is perhaps the same as Chedorlaomer,* supposed first prince of Persia, and cotemporary of Abraham, B.C. 1915. But in after ages the walls being greatly shaken and partly demolished by an earthquake, it is said to have been rebuilt (about 2000 years before the time of Sultan Mahomed) by Rajah Kuss, Kash, Kishna, or Kussna, but commonly afterwards called Kizu or Guzu, and from whom the place ultimately took its present name of Ghuznee. This prince was an Autushprest or fire worshipper, and his territory extended from the sea in the south, to a month's march beyond the great snow ranges of the present

* More probably Nahor the *brother* of Abraham.—Ed.

Hindoo Koosh—and from the Indus in the east to the Tigris in the west; and this great Empire, though afterwards much curtailed, and brought down to the state of a small principality, still in some manner existed until the time of Cyrus. However, Kuss or Kish is supposed to have rebuilt this fort, and the walls, or their remnants, as they stood in the time of Sultan Mahomed, are said to have been 10 musaatheir high (ten mens' height) and 15½ hat'h broad (7¾ yards) at top, built of immense blocks of stone cut and properly faced.

The Sultan's forces made many unsuccessful attempts to reduce and subdue the neighbouring princes around, especially those of Nire (supposed to be the present Logurut) Rajnah (the present Rajgull) Lugh (or the present Lughman) and Oorch—a large fortress, near the site of the present Cabul. The chief of the last mentioned place was a Rajah Oorg or Urj (properly, perhaps, Urgin) who as well as most of the chiefs around was a fireworshipper. However, after a long series of campaigns, Sultan Mahomed succeeded in subduing the country as far as Lughman and the places before mentioned, with the exception of the strong hold held by Urj or Urgin, who obstinately stood out and kept himself independent until about the year of the Hejira 392, when Sultan Mahomed (it is supposed at the instigation and invitation of some of Urgin's relatives and friends who had betrayed him) was induced to send one of his Generals, Abdul Ruheem, with a large force to reduce that now last remaining fortress. The site of the fort was on the summit of one of the hills, and near where stands the present Balla Hissar. After some hard fighting on both sides, Urgin and his followers were compelled to shut themselves up in the fort, where after some days they were so reduced as to be compelled at last to agree to all Abdul Ruheem's terms. Among these, the first was that the Rajah himself should embrace the Moslem faith and become the dependant of Sultan Mahomed. Though repugnant to all this, Urgin agreed to it, on condition that he should retain his former station, with his fortress and principality. Matters being thus so far settled, the Sultan was written to for advice by his Wuzeer, and in a few days a laconic answer was received, that as the Kaffir has been *qubool,* so he might now be Qubool Shah. Thus this chief was henceforward by the Moslems called Quobooll Shah; and in course of time the Mahomedans took care to do away with the former name, and in its stead called the city and fort itself, Qubool or Kubool, or, as at present, Cabul. These and some other such facts have been by tradition, as in the present instance, brought down to the present day, most likely to commemorate and corroborate the traditional story of the cruel death of the Rajpoot, Sooruj Dehu, (the fiftieth in the line of ancestry, and son of Bujer Ther) and the determined conduct of his heroic wife, commonly called Neila Ranee. The best of those traditions says, that Sooruj or Surj Dehu, leaving his son and family behind him in the Punjaub, was induced to visit Rajnauth (Rajgull) probably in search of employment. However he was there taken prisoner by Abdul Shureeff Khan, son to Abdul Ruheem, about twelve or fourteen months previous to the fall of Cabul; and though he was put to all sorts of torture, still he obstinately refused to embrace the Moslem creed. Shureeff Khan, therefore, ordered him (as an example and to terrify others of the same mind) to be enclosed in a strong cage, and thus hung up near Rajgull. Thus caged, he was by a certain treatment made to linger out a wretched existence for twelve or fourteen months; during which space the news of his sad fate reached the ears of his faithful wife, then residing in some humble capacity near the present Noorpoor. Neila quickly resolved to proceed to her husband and either save or perish with him. Sutteeism has been always considered as a rite to be strictly observed by all true Rajpoots females. So she, with two younger brothers and a female attendant, set off on her pilgrimage, and arrived at Rajgull, where she saw her husband in his cage, only the shadow of what he had been, a mere skeleton fit to inspire terror and dismay. All he could mutter out to his beloved wife was to tell her in a dismal and horrified yet resolute tone, that he expected to linger but a few days more. She then proceeded towards Oorch or Cabul, where both Shureeff Khan and his father were busily engaged in operations against the place. But the pilgrims had not proceeded far before news of the fall of Oorch reached them, and shortly after, the return of Shureeff Khan to Rajgull induced them likewise to retrace their steps. At this moment, all Neila's hope and expectation was merely to obtain an interview with this Moslem chief, and to soften his heart so as to obtain the release of her husband. However, immediately on the return of Shureeff Khan, and before she had an opportunity to put her resolution into effect, Sooruj was dragged forth by order of the Khan, and in the very presence of his wife placed still living in a pit where a pillar of strong stone masonry was built close around him, leaving only the head or part of it exposed. All this was done in the presence of the disconsolate but then silent wife, who is said to have been seemingly one of the most unaffected and apathetic spectators of the scene. However, Sooruj Dehu in a few hours breathed his last, still refusing to comply with the wishes of Shureeff Khan, who not only personally attended, but even to the last did his utmost to induce or compel his obstinate victim to change his resolution. But up to this moment, and even afterwards, it was unknown to Shureeff and those around him, that the Rajpoot's wife or any of his family were then present.

That very day, Neila with the help of her brothers (but unknown to any one else) contrived to form a funeral pile of the driest materials procurable, opposite and close to the spot where her husband's corpse was now entombed in the pillar. Every thing having been thus privately got in order, she warned her brothers to secrete themselves for some short period near the pile, while she with her female companion departed, under pretence of ablution at some holy stream or fountain in the vicinity. She thus left her brothers in charge of the pile, while she by some wily policy and under some proper guise, contrived to be introduced to the presence, and in no small degree to attract the attention, of the licentious and unwary Shureeff. The fascinating, winning, yet simple and graceful part which she acted, aided by personal charms and attractions proverbial even to this day, and all set of by a well-assumed female hauteur, a particular reserved, lofty air, seen only in females of the highest rank, gained so far on the unworthy Shureeff that even on their first and introductory acquaintance, a private interview was appointed; and on the night of the second day after the death of Sooruj Dehu, Shureeff Khan proceeded, unattended as agreed on, to meet the unknown fair one. The heroic Neila, anxiously yet coolly watching her opportunity, soon found means to consummate the bloody deed on which she had resolved by plunging deep in the heart of her enemy a *Katar* which she had procured and kept concealed for the purpose. So mortal and true was the heroine's blow that Shureeff Khan never rose or even made any resistance to his fair murderess, who actually leaving the *Katar* (a curious kind of native poignard) deep sunk in his heart, instantly, with more than even a masculine intrepidity and coolness, severed the head from the body, and quickly yet silently issuing forth, flung it at the feet of her murdered lord. She then with blood-stained hands and covered with gore, the marks of victory and success, quickly repaired to her brothers at the pile, where now (all proud of the glorious deed) affairs were so quickly managed that before the morning dawned, and even before the Moslem chief's death was discovered, the dead corpse of Sooruj Dehu was extracted from its recent position, and underwent the ceremony of incremation; while the faithful and heroic wife, having so well avenged the blood of her lord, now felt doubly happy and proud in sacrificing herself on the same pile with the murdered body of him for whom she had staked her honour and her all. Their ashes, in charge of her brothers, and according to her own orders, were before morning far from the scene of these deeds, on the way homeward, or to the Gunga, where ultimately those of both husband and wife were sacredly deposited.

The date of this tradition is put down at about 392 of the Hejira, and now the line of succession is resumed at the 51st member, the son of Sooruj Dehu, named Boje Dehu, 52d Oodum Dehu, 53d Peler Dehu, 54th Urjin Dehu, 55th Oothar Dehu, 58th Jess Dehu, who had two sons, the elder Kirpal Dehu, and the younger Singram Dehu, these were the 59th generation. As it has been before stated, most or all of the Rajpoot families made a kind of temporary settlement near the base of the hills, somewhere in the nighbourhood of Noorpoor. But from some unknown cause, about the year 589 of the Hejira, these two brothers the sons of Jess Dehu, left that quarter, where there seems to have been a general breaking up or emigration, as the Rajpoots were scattered in different directions. Both Kirpal Dehu and Singram Dehu with some others of the family fought under the banners of the 588 much famed Raat Pithoura at the battle of Thanessur, and on their return to their homes, in the following year this small Rajpoot colony about Noorpoor, &c. broke up and became scattered in different quarters.

It was at this time that one of the distant branches of the family settled in Chumba and another about or at Teera-Kangra. The first of these is called now the Chummiall Rajpoot, the second the Katochee family; and other members of the house became the founders of different principalities at present known by divers names, such as Patancote, Mandote, Seeba, Samba, Jesrota, &c. while the two principal or head members of the family wandered for some time in search of a proper and suitable place of rest for their families. Ultimately Kirpal Dehu and his brother Singram Dehu settled in the then thickly-wooded and almost uninhabited hills of Dhahman, and about the spot where the present fort of Bhow stands. This occurrence is put down at about 591 of the Hejira, or three years after their return from the battle of Thanessur. These hills were then but a wild, mountainous, thickly-wooded tract, very thinly peopled by a few Meghs, a poor race of low caste, and by yet fewer of a Hindoo race called Tukkers. But these hills, though wild, still afforded good pasturage, which was enticement sufficient to ensure the annual visits of the northern and eastern Ghaddees,—herdsmen and shepherds who generally live in and about the snowy ranges, north of Chumba, Kistowar, &c. and who were then a bold, independent and wandering race, who for ages past had been in the habit of proceeding with their flocks and families to the southern and milder parts, and to pass the severity of winter grazing their numerous flocks of sheep, goats, &c. in the hills now described. A long continued animosity existed between the bold and hardy hill shepherds and their neighbours, the poor and helpless Meghs, and each year's visit only brought on a new succession of quarrels and sometimes bloody affrays. The Ghaddees in their annual visits monopolized and partly destroyed the best pasture spots, and even sometimes encroached on the small tillage fields of the Meghs, who, too weak openly to resist, sought to avenge themselves and their wrongs by nightly thefts and attacks, in which they carried off the wives and children of their enemies, whom they usually sold afterwards in the Punjaub, &c. But the wild herdsmen always with fury, bloodshed and desolation, revenged these barbarities. Such was the state of the hills when these two brothers came among the Meghs, and chose the place near Bhow for their future residence. This poor and hitherto unprotected race were soon brought to consider the Rajpoot settlement among them in the light of a blessing, and as a token of the favour of Heaven; and they willingly acknowledged their claim to the title of lords and masters. The Rajpoot community, including the families of both brothers, numbered only about twenty persons; but still their very name seems to have become a terror to the Ghaddees, who were brought by the superior prowess and policy of the Rajpoots to enter into certain agreements and conditions, and to respect the rights of the now protected Meghs. Thus in course of time all animosity between these tribes was partly lost and forgotten, until the Rajpoot race grew so strong and numerous that at last even the very Ghaddees were obliged for their own security to acknowledge the superiority and power of the new colony, whom they in a few years were constrained to look on in the light of their temporary masters. However about the year of the Hejira 602, or nine years after their arrival, these two brothers are said, for some unknown reason, but most likely for their mutual interest, aggrandizement, and power, to have separated. The elder, Kirpal Dehu, remained at or near the present site of Bhow, where he had erected some huts with thatched roofs; while his younger brother erected a small habitation of the same kind on the opposite hill to the west, and just on the opposite bank of the small stream, called the

Thovee, which divides the two hills, on the site of the present Jummoo, the places being less than a mile apart. Thus were the seeds of the present great and promising Hill principality sown, and thus those two brothers and their descendants slowly but steadily became Lords of the Hills and of those around them.

The 58th in the line of succession of the Jummoo or Jumwall family was the son of Singram Dehu, the elder branch, or that of Kirpal Dehu, being called the Bhow family, of which mention will be made hereafter in its proper place, The sixty-third chief of the family was the great Mal Dehu, who was the eldest of nine sons of Jey Dehu, and lived about the year 1389 of Vikramadita, or, as is mentioned, 749 of the Hejira, and is supposed to have been contemporary with *Timor* or *Timorlung,* Timor the Lame. He was the first of the family who had ever in those parts aspired to the title of Rajah. For this purpose he is said to have taken a large stone (of about half a ton weight, and to be seen at the present day) from the bed of the stream that flowed round the hill on which his humble habitation stood, and thence carried this immense weight in his arms, up the steep paths to his home, where at a suitable spot he laid it down. Then collecting thither all his kinsmen and relatives on his side of the Thovee (then supposed to be about 500 in number) he, in the presence of these and of the neighbouring Meghs, was unanimously declared Rajah, by his own brotherhood and the people of all the hill territory, from the Thovee, westward to the Chenaub, an extent of about fourteen or fifteen miles of a wild hill tract, and then very thinly inhabited. He was now formally installed, and the ceremony was enacted, while he proudly sat on the huge block of stone, which was thenceforward considered a most necessary point in the creation or installation of his successors. It was to the story of his having (by the will and favour of Heaven) carried this great fragment of rock the distance he is said to have done, that he owed his own title of Rajah.* Henceforward this Rajpoot colony was treated with greater respect by the country people around, while the Meghs and numerous other new-comers and temporary inhabitants, Hindoos, who had fled from the Moslem rule and emigrated from the Punjaub hither—all now looked up to the Rajpoot chief as their rightful lord, prince, and protector.

---

* This will remind the reader of the famous stone so important in the coronation of the Scottish Kings.—ED.

CHAPTER II.

All the institutions and appendages necessary to a princely court and government were now called into requisition in the little state of Jummoo; and though but little understood, still in this young and self-created principality, things and matters, as well as Rajahs themselves, must be allowed to go on in a rude, plain, simple manner of their own. However, Mal Dehu seems to have known and heard sufficient of men and manners, kings and courts, to introduce and to make known and respected, his royal seal and signature. But he is said to have had in his principality or at his court only one writer, who acted at once the part of Moonshee, Dewan and Wuzeer. He either knew little of or did not wish to establish any thing like an Adawlut or court of justice, so that he was in himself the sole judge and jury of the state. Leases of lands, grants, jaghires and tenements were now legally and systematically drawn up and signed in his name, and in which he was entitled Soorj Bunse Rajah Maha Rajah Mal Dehu, (descendant of the son and rajah of rajahs) whose orders were to last for ever and ever, &c. &c. He was now able when occasion required to assemble round him three or four hundred armed followers; nor did he, with such instruments at his command, lose the opportunity of making himself known and dreaded all over the neighbouring lowlands, where by plunder and rapine, nightly inroads and surprises, the burning of villages, with their sleeping inhabitants, and other such acts, he showed that he little respected and even defied the great Moslem power of the age. However, the disturbances of the times gave him and some of his descendants opportunities to ravage the lowlands on different occasions for some forty or fifty coss.

To Rajah Mal Dehu succeeded five generations of his descendants, whose reigns extended over a period of one hundred and fifty years. The last of these, Beeram Dehu, is said to have flourished about the year 1539 of Vikramadita, and was a contemporary of the Emperor Baber. This is ascertained from the following tradition and the occurrence which it records. The Cashmere fruit *dallies* (loads or baskets) having been more than once plundered on their way to the Court of Delhi by some of the numerous predatory clans and tribes then infesting and inhabiting different parts of the route, such as the Jelall tribe, at or about Rajouri, the Chib tribe at Bheembur, &c., a royal purwannah, signed and sealed by the Emperor Baber, was addressed to all the Zemindars, Ryuts, and inhabitants of the Dhaman Hills, in which district no Rajah was yet known or acknowledged at Delhi. The bearer of this order, perhaps not finding a more proper person in the range named, brought the purwannah to Jummoo and presented it to Rajah Beeram Dehu. The order was simply to act as *Mooffzuth*, or to afford an escort and safeguard to the fruit dallies coming from Cashmere and going to Delhi, for which service the persons addressed would be favourably regarded by the Court of Delhi. Beeram Dehu seemingly took this into his head as being a special compliment paid to himself personally by the great Baber; and he felt so proud of it that he took some three or four hundred armed men, and brought the fruit dallies safe through the dangerous passes, as far as Gujerat or the Chenaub. Here he was informed by the Delhi officer that as now, by his good services, the fruit was safe for the Emperor, there was no further fear. This was a polite way of informing him that his services were no further required, and that he might, with his followers, return to his home. However all the hints the Emperor's officer could give were of no avail, as Rajah Beeram Dehu seemingly had some higher schemes in view; and all that the officer could do was to induce him to send back the greater part of his half-naked followers, whom he was told would make but a poor show at the Emperor's court. Thus with about twenty-five followers, Rajah Beeram Dehu kept close to his charge of some fifteen dallies or loads of fruit, and with them he entered Delhi, where he was by the officer, his travelling companion, ultimately introduced to the court and presence of the Emperor. Beeram Dehu expected to meet somebody of but little higher rank and power than himself, and kept up his spirits on his long march with the idea that he was going to meet a kind of half brother, a Rajah something like himself;—that he would be received with open arms and be treated in every manner as an equal. Great, therefore, was his disappointment and chagrin on finding himself coolly received by the Emperor, who seeing the Hill-man and his train, all dressed much alike (some half naked, with only coarse dirty leather breeches) and the chief with but little to distinguish him from his followers, considered him and them entitled to but scant courtesy. Beeram Dehu did not let slip the opportunity of letting the proud] Baber know, what he most likely never before suspected, that he too was a Rajah; and as a proof of his assertion he recounted many feats of himself and his predecessors, spoke much of his high rank, fame, and caste, and ultimately had the good fortune to receive a written acknowledgment of his dignity from the Emperor, who now humorously styled him Rajah. The Hill chief was so perfectly satisfied with this; that he asked no more, and considering that he had attained the pinnacle of his ambition, he, with further promises from Baber, in case of good behaviour towards the lowlands of the Punjaub, in a few days left Delhi and the

Emperor's court, to go and keep his state at his own. There more important business awaited him; for on his arrival he found his little territory almost in open insurrection. He arrived, however, in time to prevent mischief, and the very sight and even mention of the great Baber's seal and signature, was more than sufficient to quiet and put down all rebellious spirits. Henceforward the Rajah and his successors were treated as the allies of the mighty rulers of Hindostan. Beeram Dehu considering it but right to spread around him a just idea of his distinction and rank among princes, and to keep up and ensure a continuance of that friendship which should always exist between allied monarchs and princes, he yearly sent to the Court of Delhi, for Baber's especial use, a well-stocked bag of wild walnuts, onions, &c.; and in one rare instance he is said to have gone so far as to send 101 head of goats. He seemed much perplexed and surprised (but perhaps was the only one that was so) at never receiving any return for either his presents of rare dainties or his earnest professions of friendship.

Many such traditions and anecdotes of Beeram Dehu and his successors have been handed down, all tending to display their moral, social and political condition in their several generations. It is now necessary, however, to pass over these almost purely traditional times and to come down at once nearer to the present day. It may therefore be briefly mentioned that to Beeram Dehu succeeded many generations of his descendents until we find the Rajahship vested in Drupe Dehu, who died about the year of the christian era 1742. This chief had four sons, Runjeet Dehu, Kousar Dehu, Sooruth Sing and Bulwunt Dehu. The first of these succeeded his father and died about the year 1780, when he was succeeded by his eldest son, Bijerei Dehu, who had rebelled against his father some years before the death of the latter. Bijerei Dehu died about 1786, leaving an only son, who after reigning little more than a year died at the age of fourteen. On this Jey Sing, only son of Delele Sing, a younger brother of Bijerei Sing, became Rajah, and so continued until his death in 1809. On the occurrence of this event his sons and family fled across the Sutlej, leaving their territories to the Seiks, who retained possession thereof until the year 1818, when the present Golaub Sing, the eightieth in descent from the founder of the family, was made Rajah of Jummoo by Maharajh Runjeet Sing.

The second son of Drupe Dehu, was, as before mentioned, Kousar Dehu, whose lineal descendant and rightful heir is the present Meean Laub Sing.

The third son of Drupe Dehu was Sooruth Sing, who had three sons, the 1st, Zorover Sing, 2nd, Meean Mota (who acted as Wuzeer to Jey Sing) and the 3rd Meean Jellah. The first of these, Zorover Sing, had an only son, Meean Kosour Sing, the father of the present Golaub Sing and his brethren. The second, Meean Mota, had one son, Bupe Sing, who died, leaving an only son, Bujer Dehu, a young man at present living, a poor dependant on the Lords of the Hills. The third, Meean Jellah, died without issue.

The fourth son of Drupe Dehu, Bulwunt Sing, died without issue.

Thus these eighty generations embrace a period of about 2371 years, beginning about 527 before our era, and by computation about 29½ years to each member, which may not be considered too much, considering the plain simple life and generally moderate habits of the Rajpoot tribes.

We now return to Rajah Runjeet Dehu, and commence a more minute relation of facts and incidents down to the present day. Runjeet Dehu was born about the year 1724, and was but a lad of eighteen, when his father, Rajah Drupe Dehu, died in 1742. Runjeet Dehu in a few years after his father's death showed himself to be an able and active Hill chief; and certainly he was much more so than any of his predecessors, and did more for his family and tribe than did all the long line of Rajahs before him. It may be said, that he lived and reigned at a time when better opportunities were afforded him; however, he remodelled the state, and all this much for the better, he instituted proper and wholesome regulations for the benefit of all classes, and by many like acts gained himself the name of a just chief. His reputation extended even as far as Lahore, and numerous families from different quarters, including some persons of high rank and large fortune, fled to his territory and stronghold. Most of these brought with them the great bulk of their fortunes, while all their rights and persons were invariably respected and protected. By this and such like means, in the year 1775, or five years before his death, the town of Jummoo had increased to about three miles and a half in circumference, being about twice as large as at the present day. Its inhabitants then numbered about 150,000 souls, more than four times as many as now inhabit the town. It was considered an opulent, wealthy, flourishing, and promising place, having for its residents numerous wealthy men from the Punjaub. One of these alone is said to have brought with him upwards of a crore of rupees. Runjeet Dehu was certainly poor, but still he was able to commence the building of the present palace at Jummoo, where in the time of his father some miserable huts stood, sufficing for the habitation of himself and his predecessors. Most of these huts were thatched with long grass, and termed *chunns*, and differed but little from the *chuggees* of the villagers. It should be mentioned, that in the time of Drupe Dehu, the Bhow family, then in the height of its power, carried on a long and bloody war with its neighbours and kinsmen, the Jumwalls. On several occasions in the time of Drupe Dehu and his predecessor, the Jumwalls made nightly assaults on their neighbours, burnt their houses, carried off their cattle and murdered all those that fell into their hands. Such treatment roused the Bhows to inflict a heavy retaliation. Thus no less than seven different times in Drupe Dehu's reign were the Jumwalls' huts, and even those in which the Rajahs themselves resided, burnt to the ground, and the village made a desolate heap of smoking ruins and ashes. It was mostly for this reason that Jummoo was so thinly inhabited before the time of Runjeet Dehu, and that his father and his predecessors considered temporary huts the fittest for their own residence and that of their people. The fort of Bhow was commenced by Goolaub Dehu, in the beginning of Drupe Dehu's reign, and ultimately finished by Rajah Runjeet Dehu, who not only pacified his inimical brethren, but ultimately reduced them to a state of subjection.

About the year 1743, or a year after his father's death, Rajah Runjeet Dehu commenced a desultory kind of warfare with the lowlands and the hilly tracts on the west, where he took several forts and in a manner conquered the country as far as the present Runjeet Ghur, where he built a temporary mud fort as his boundary to the south. In one or two instances he surprised and plundered the town of Seealkote, and overran the country on both sides of the Chenaub as far as Gujerat. He even attacked the forts of Koolowal, Kotelee, Minore, Bejewath, Oknoor and Reass, all on the banks or line of the river Chenaub, burnt the villages and left the rest to their fate. He almost put a stop to the communication between Cashmere and Lahore, and his troops or hill rangers often plundered and slew the Kassids and Hurkaras on their way between Lahore or Delhi, and Peshawur and Cabul, &c. He himself and his three brothers were continually and actively engaged in hostilities with the lowland people, and in the year 1745 they mustered a force of about 1,000 matchlocks.

In the year 1746, the general consternation and confusion

consequent on the first Affghan invasion, materially assisted Runjeet Dehu in forwarding his ambitious views. During that year and the two following, he made himself at least nominal master of all the forts, ghurrees, and strongholds abovementioned; and his band was now reinforced by numerous Hindoo emigrants and refugees from the Punjaub, who fled with their families through fear of Ahmed Shah. In 1747 he plundered a Kafila or Caravan, with about 100,000 rupees worth of Pushmeena, going from Cashmere to Lahore for Meer Munnoo, who wrote to and remonstrated with Rajah Runjeet on this and other like acts but to no avail. However, in the latter end of 1748, or the beginning of 1749, he seems to have been so closely pressed by his Bhow brethren (they being the descendants of the elder branch of the family, Kapoor Dehu, who always claimed superiority) that he was induced to visit Lahore, in hopes of having this family quarrel properly adjusted; he previously having received some promises and invitations from the Lahore Court. But he had no sooner presented himself at the durbar than he was put in irons, and kept a close prisoner in one of the vaults or dungeons within the fort or citadel of Lahore. During his absence Kousar Dehu, the next eldest brother, acted as the Rajah of Jummoo. Rajah Runjeet remained a close prisoner at Lahore until the year 1760. In his absence Kousar Dehu was but slightly respected by his own clan of Jumwalls, while his enemies the Bhows daily gained strength and made several successful attacks upon the tribe. During this time they burnt, four or five different times, the *chuggees* and *chunns* or huts of Jummoo, there not being even at this period a brick or stone built house in the place. Runjeet Dehu's imprisonment and absence helped to increase and ferment the old broils and feuds between these two branches of the family residing close in the vicinity of each other.

Nothing worthy of particular notice occurred until the year 1760, when Rajah Runjeet Dehu not only obtained his release but also gained the good will and favour of the governor of Lahore. It appears that the Bhow Sirdars or Rajpoot chiefs of the time, Komul Dehu, Budj Dehu, and Gool Dehu, had entered into close alliance with the Seik chief, Churuth Sing, the grand-father of Runjeet Sing, and by this intrigue they incurred the displeasure of Adeena Beg, then governor of Lahore, who threatened their destruction. Kousar Dehu, his brothers, and their party found opportunities to increase this hostile feeling of the Lahore Court towards the Bhow faction. It happened that about this time two Mahomedan chiefs, Bahadoor Khan and Affzull Beg, were sent by the Court of Delhi to Lahore and the N. W. parts of the Punjaub, to purchase some Toorkistan horses, and to look after and report on the state of that soubah. About the year 1760, these two officers were at Lahore as Acting Governors, when a famous horse arrived there, which they had procured from Toorkistan, and for which they are said to have paid forty-eight thousand rupees in ready money. However, no one then about the Lahore Court could be found bold or skilful enough to train or ride this fiery steed. On this the long-imprisoned Rajah Runjeet Dehu, being well known as a most able and daring horseman, was brought forth from his dungeon, his fetters were knocked off, and he was instructed as to the duty imposed on him to break in the untamed steed.

The mountain chief gladly undertook the task, and such was the skill and courage which he brought to bear upon it, that in an incredibly short time, the wild and unmanageable horse became gentle and tractable under his hands. It must not be supposed that those who kept the Hill Rajah in custody, entrusted him with such a means of making his escape as the possession of this fleet steed afforded, without taking precautions for preventing his availing himself of it. To this end they would not trust him to exercise the horse outside the fort, but kept him within the walls, causing him to perform his task in the enclosed area of the Hazooree Bagh. At this time the Ravee washed the north and west angles of the fort, and as it partially served as a defence on this side, the walls there were not more than six or seven feet high. One day while Runjeet Dehu, on the noble steed which he had so completely subdued to his will, was careering about the Hazooree Bagh, exciting the wonder and admiration of a crowd of spectators, he suddenly wheeled about,—charged at the six feet wall,—cleared it, alighting in the deep stream of the river that ran beneath. For a moment horse and rider sunk;—for an instant they were seen on the opposite bank,—and then they were off and away. A thousand cavalry were soon on the track of the fugitive, but mounted as he was, their pursuit was vain. A reward of twenty thousand rupees was proclaimed for any one who should recover the gallant steed,—the recapture of his rider being, in comparison with this, hardly worth a thought. But Runjeet Dehu and the good horse were away to the hills, and ere the day had passed, the chieftain stood amidst his family at Jummoo. Scarcely, however, had he received their embraces and congratulations than, to their grief and astonishment, he set forth on his return to Lahore, where about forty hours after his departure he again presented himself to those who had given up all hope of seeing him or the animal which he bestrode. He had been seized, he said, with a sudden desire to try the speed of the horse and to pay a short visit to his home, and having accomplished his purpose, again committed himself and his steed to the hands of their keepers. It is gratifying to have to read that the Mussulman chiefs appreciated the conduct of the brave and honorable hill-man sufficiently to induce them to grant him his liberty. In further token of favour a reward of twenty thousand rupees was bestowed upon him, he was invested with a *khilut*, and received a written acknowledgment of his rank as Rajah of Jummoo, and furthermore was escorted back to his principality by a body of eight hundred cavalry, charged with the task of reinstating him in all his rights and possessions. Under such auspices and so assisted, Rajah Runjeet Dehu speedily quelled his enemies of the Bhow faction, and even compelled the members of that branch of the family to come in and reside under his rule at Jummoo. Here he established for them a separate *Mundee* or Court of Justice, which to this day is known as the *Kull Mundee* or Lower Court, the lower part of the hill having been assigned for the residence of the Bhow people. But few descendants of that family, however, are now distinguishable from the general population of Jummoo. Among these may be mentioned Meean Sumba and his family, and the Khona Chuck family, so called from the place of that name which they received as a jaghire. Of this family also were Durga Sing and his brother Arbela Sing. The first of these left two sons, the eldest of whom, Rae Kisseree Sing fell gallantly fighting by the side of his master, Rajah Suchet Sing. Arbela Sing had three sons, Pirthee Sing, Jewahir Sing, and Balloo Sing, the last of whom was killed with Rae Kisseree Sing. These were some of the members of and descendents from the Bhow branch of the Jummoo family.

Thus the fort and town of Bhow came into the hands of Rajah Runjeet Dehu, and the people of that branch of the tribe became subject to his authority. He repaired the fort, and to the people he gave grants of land on the Jummoo side of the Thovee, in lieu of those which they had held beyond the boundary stream.

From the year 1761 down to 1773, nothing worthy of note occurred in the little principality, except that during this period Rajah Runjeet built for himself and family a large house or palace on the foundations which had been laid by his father. It may also be noted that the fame of his mild and just sway having spread far and wide, many people from the lower districts of the Punjaub and elsewhere came to settle in his territories. He had also, during this period, extended his dominions by the conquest of the hill country as far north as Reaschun.

In the year 1773 Bijerei Dehu, the eldest son of the good Rajah Runjeet Dehu, rebelled against his father, and sought to dethrone him. In this wicked design he was aided by the Seik chiefs, Churut Sing Sukerchuckia and Jey Sing Kunnia, whom he invited to Jummoo. The Rajah was, however, so well supported by his subjects and showed so determined a front, that with the aid of a little money bestowed on the mercenary auxiliaries of the rebel son, they were induced to withdraw. After this event Runjeet Dehu reigned in peace and prosperity until the year 1780, when he died. His name is to this day greatly respected throughout the hill-country, and his grants, regulations, &c., have still the force of law. He had extended his dominions greatly, but at his death, their total annual revenue did not exceed eighty thousand rupees, the country being but poor and thinly peopled.

Runjeet Dehu was succeeded by his weak and dissolute, yet ambitious and intractable son, Bijerei Dehu. When the news of Runjeet's death and Bijerei's succession reached the plains, Maha Sing, the son of Churut Sing Sukerchuckia, went as far as Seealkote on a visit of condolence to the new Rajah whom he there met. While they were at Seealkote together, the wily Seik chief so insinuated himself into the friendship of the hill-man, that by the ceremony of exchanging turbans he became his *Bii bund* or *Paggree Bra*, that is they were thenceforward sworn brothers. On the authority of this close alliance, Maha Sing, in the winter of 1781, visited Jummoo, with a band of twelve hundred men, and finding the Rajah and most of his followers laid up with an epidemic fever, he sacked and burnt the town, and withdrew only on receiving an engagement for the payment of an annual tribute.

Bijerei Dehu died in 1786, and was succeeded by his son

Sefurin Dehu, a young boy, who after a reign of seventeen or eighteen months, died at the age of fourteen years. On this, in 1788, Jey Sing, the only son of Delele Sing, was created Rajah, and had Meean Mota, the uncle of Goolaub Sing and his brothers, as his prime minister and principal adviser. Jey Sing was an imbecile and incompetent chief, and was unable to act for himself. About the year 1806, Runjeet Sing, who had succeeded his father, Maha Sing, and was extending his power over the Punjaub, sent a body of cavalry to take possession of Jummoo, but the invaders were bought off, and retired without having effected the purpose of their visit. Again, in 1807, Runjeet sent one of his lieutenants, Misser Dewan Chund, with a strong force to reduce the place. But the combined influences of a stout opposition and heavy bribes once more preserved the independance of the hill state. It was during this attack on Jummoo, that the present Goolaub Sing so distinguished himself by his bravery, that Misser Dewan Chund on his return spoke to Runjeet Sing very highly in his favour.

Kussour or Kussoora Sing had three sons and four daughters;—the latter, it is said, were secretly put to death by their brothers in 1811 or 1812. The eldest of his sons was named Goolauboo, and was born about the year 1788. The second was Dehanoo, born in 1797. The third was Suchethoo, born in 1801. Goolauboo and Dehanoo lived with their uncle Meean Mota at Jummoo, while their father and younger brother resided at Ismailpore Deully, a village seven or eight coss from Jummoo in the plains, and on the road to Lahore, deriving their subsistance from the produce of a few acres of land. In the year 1807, when the Seiks under Dewan Misser Chund attacked Jummoo, Goolauboo and some other Rajpoot lads of his own age distinguished themselves in a hand to hand fight with the Seik horsemen in the stony bed of the Thovee. This conduct so pleased Misser Dewan Chund, that on his return

Golab Sing
Dihan Sing
Heera Sing
From Native Paintings. C.G.

to Lahore he described it in terms of glowing eulogy to his master Runjeet Sing. Hearing of this, Goolauboo, then about nineteen years of age, taking with him his next brother Dehanoo, who was ten, left Jummoo and hastened to Lahore in the full hope of building his fortunes on the favor of the Seik Maharajh. Great was the disappointment of the ambitious stripling on finding that after idling away three months in the vain expectation of procuring an introduction to the great chief through the favor of Faquir Azeez-oodeen, he had nothing for it but to return to Jummoo as he came. And now leaving his young brother in charge of their father, Goolauboo went to seek service in some other quarter. In this pursuit he was so far successful, that in the course of the year 1808, he obtained military employment, on three rupees a month and rations, under the Killadar of Munjela, a fort on the west side of the Jhelum. He did not, however, stay here long, being compelled through some quarrel with his fellow soldiers to leave the fort, upon which he took service under Sultan Khan of Bheembur. He was now stationed in the fort of Kotelee, about fourteen or fifteen miles to the west of Minore. Hence, however, he was ere long compelled to remove owing to some dispute with his chief. He now returned disappointed and destitute to his family and their humble home at Ismailpore, where he remained until the year 1811.

The two elder brothers married while residing at Ismailpore, being snpplied with the pecuniary means of doing so by a Hindoo named Doolo to whom they were consequently deeply in debt. However, in the beginning of 1811, this man was again called on by Kussour Sing to advance money sufficient to enable his two eldest sons to purchase horses and outfit, that they might proceed to Lahore, to enter the Seik service as Gorechars under Runjeet Sing. Doolo, though with but faint hope of repayment, cheerfully advanced the required sum, and, provided with credentials from Meean Mota to

Misser Dewan Chund, the brothers repaired to Lahore. On arriving there they presented their letters of introduction to Misser Dewan Chund, who treated them with due respect and made them many promises of assistance. Just about this time, news arrived that Meean Mota had been murdered by Damoother Sing and Gal Sing of the Bhow faction. The brothers hereupon determined to revenge his death, but as it was at present out of their power to do so, they were compelled to defer their design till an opportunity for its fulfilment should present itself. Misser Dewan Chund, meantime, introduced them to Runjeet Sing as two of the gallant Rajpoot youths whose conduct he had before described and extolled. The Maharajh pleased with their character and appearance, directed them to remain in attendance upon him, on a subsistence allowance of three rupees each per diem. Thus loitering about the court for some months they acquired all its habits and manners, and became accomplished courtiers. In 1812, however, they were made Gorechars in Meean Sing's Missee, Dehanoo, being the greater favourite with the Maharajh, receiving five rupees a day, while Goolauboo, the elder brother, had only four. Their pay was, however, ere long doubled and tripled, so that of their savings from this source and from the presents they frequently received from the Maharajh, they were able by the latter end of the year to send home to their family no less than three thousand rupees. While they were dangling attendance on the durbar, their father died, leaving his sons to the care of his brother Meean Mota.

The two brothers were the most favoured of all Runjeet Sing's favourites; it is supposed, however, that Goolauboo would not endure the Maharajh's intimacy as his brothers did. In 1813 they, at Runjeet's request, sent for their younger brother Suchetoo, now a lad of about twelve years old, whose handsome face and graceful person immediately won for him the entire regard of the Maharajh. The Rajpoot brothers were now all in all at court. Both Dehanoo and Suchetoo were well instructed by their elder brother Goolauboo, in the part they had to play for securing the affections of him who had even then become their dupe.

In 1813 or the following year Damoother Sing and Gal Sing, the murderers of Meean Mota, happening to be in Lahore, the two elder brothers considered this a favourable opportunity for carrying their long-deferred scheme of vengeance into execution. They, therefore, watched for a suitable occasion, and having found one, they both, well mounted and armed, rode towards Anarkullee, where their intended victims, who were Gorechars of the Seik Cavalry, then lay encamped. They had not, however, proceeded far from the city when they met Damoother Sing riding towards Lahore. They saluted him with apparent civility, but as soon as he had passed, Goolauboo turned and fired at him, wounding him in such a manner as to prevent his escape, and the brothers dismounting quickly despatched him with their swords. At this moment Gal Sing, the other murderer, came in view, and received a mortal wound from the matchlock of Goolauboo. On this several persons who saw what was done raised the cry of murder, which prevented the despatch of their second victim, who escaped for the moment to die elsewhere. And now the brothers were attacked by the mob which had collected, and had they not wisely retreated, would have been put to death. They fled to the artillery camp of Misser Dewan Chund, where they received present protection; and on the affair being represented at court in a light favourable to them, the Maharajh, who, as may be imagined, was well disposed to leniency, readily pardoned them. It now became apparent to all in what relation they stood to the Maharajh, and neither he nor they seemed to deem it necessary to keep the connection secret. The murder of Damoother and Gal Sing seemed only to have raised the brothers higher than before in the favor of Runjeet, and now their allowance, exclusive of the presents they received, was eighteen rupees a day.

In 1809 when Jey Sing, the last of the rightful Rajpoots of Jummoo died, and Runjeet Sing sent his Dewan, Bowanee Doss, surnamed Khooba, or the humpbacked, with Bii Ram Sing, and a body of 2,500 men, to take possession both of Jummoo and Bhow. On the appearance of the force, the family of the late Rajah, unable to offer resistance, fled across the Sutlej, on which the Seiks took quiet possession of the state, its capital and government. In 1811, however, an occurrence trivial in itself but important in its results, disturbed them greatly in the possession of their ill-gotten prize. Hawking has ever been a favourite amusement of the Seik chiefs, and many of the birds employed in this sport were caught on or near the Tri Nokur a Devi, a lofty three-peaked sacred mountain, about twenty miles north of Jummoo. The birds caught here were considered the property of the Jummoo court, and on that place going into the hands of the Seiks were claimed by that of Lahore. It happened, however, that sometime in 1811, it was reported at Lahore, that one Deedoo, a Rajpoot living near the sacred hill, and about sixteen miles from Junmoo, had caught a remarkably fine hawk. The Seik authorities of the district regarding the bird as the property of their masters or themselves, demanded it from its captor. Deedoo, however, stoutly refused to surrender his prize. On this an officer and twelve men were sent to take it from him by force. They arrived at the hut of Deedoo and demanded the surrender of the bird. On this a parley ensued, and Deedoo proposed to accompany them to the Durbar at Jummoo, carrying the hawk with him. This was agreed to, and time was given him to prepare for his departure. The hospitable Deedoo hereupon provided them with the raw materials of a meal, which they proceeded to cook in a small area adjoining the hut. While they were thus employed, Deedoo committing the hawk to the care of his wife, the only other inmate of his dwelling at the time, sent her off with it from the rear of the hut to hide herself and the bird in some thick jungles that were near. He then, watching his opportunity when his unwelcome visitors were busily engaged with their meal, rushed upon them sword in hand, and before they could recover from the surprize and confusion into which his sudden assault threw them, he had despatched seven and mortally wounded four of the panic-stricken party. Only two of the thirteen returned to Jummoo to tell the tale. Deedoo now rejoined his wife in the jungles, and as he could no longer live in that neighbourhood, he took to the hills, an outlawed robber, carrying murder and rapine through the country, but reserving his special attentions for the district subject to the authorities at Jummoo.

Sometimes in these exploits he was at the head of two thousand armed men, outlaws like himself, and sometimes he was alone. He was favoured, and when need was, sheltered and protected by the people of the country, who were well disposed towards any one who had the will and power to harrass and annoy the Seik intruders. There was a garrison of about two thousand men in Jummoo, but Deedoo hesitated not to attack the place on several occasions by night or by day, though his force sometimes numbered only fifty or sixty men. In one of these assaults he burnt down nearly the whole place and carried off a great part of the moveable property of the Seik inhabitants. After these exploits he would disappear as suddenly as he came, and the Seiks never ventured to pursue him a musket shot from the walls. It is said that seldom fifteen days passed without an achievement of this kind, and according to tradition, Deedoo, from time to time, slew, with his own hand, above three hundred of his enemies, the Seiks. On more than one occasion, this bold brigand has been known to enter Jummoo at the dusk of the evening with a band of two or three hundred men, the garrison offering no resistance, but hiding themselves wherever they would find places. After putting to the sword all the Seiks they met with, the robbers would spend the night carousing round fires, which they had lit in the Mundee (the *forum* of the place) and on which they cooked their evening meal. At dawn of day they would decamp unmolested, taking with them whatever they thought worth the carriage.

In 1812, tired, probably, of his unquiet life, and allured by promises of pardon from the Seik authorities at Lahore and Jummoo, Deedoo surrendered himself into the hands of his enemies; but no sooner had he done so than suspecting treachery he set upon his guard, and made his escape after killing five men of his escort. He again returned to his wild predatory mode of life, and for above a year more, kept the country in so unquiet and disordered a state, that the Seiks found it impossible to govern it or to realise their revenues from it. Thus in the latter end of 1813 or the beginning of 1814, Runjeet Sing found an excuse for displacing the Jemadar, Kooshial Sing, to whom he had committed the charge of the district, and for delivering the country over to his favourites, the Rajpoot brothers. This measure was the result of an intrigue of the elder brother Goolauboo, who had managed to fill his master's mind with distrust of the Jemadar by describing him as engaged in schemes for establishing himself as the independent chief of the hill-countries. With the aid and support of Misser Dewan Chund, the wily brothers found little difficulty in persuading the too partial Maharajh that in their hands only could the government of their native district be satisfactorily carried on. As preliminary to their formal establishment in the hills, Goolauboo was presented with a jaghire of about forty thousand rupees a year, near Jummoo and Bheembur, which latter place had lately been taken from Sultan Khan, its former chief. Leaving his two younger brothers, the special favourites of Runjeet, to push the family interest at Court, where they jointly held the much coveted office of Doudeewan or keeper of the King's gate, a title and office almost synonimous with that of Wuzeer, Goolauboo set off for Jummoo, assuring the Maharajh that he would never return but to lay the head of the terrible Deedoo at his master's feet. To enhance the value of their prospective loyality, the brothers gave it out that the free-booter, whom out of regard to their sovereign they were about to put down, was their near relative. Goolauboo or, as he was then called, in virtue of his Rajpoot descent, Meean Goolauboo, took with him to Jummoo five or six hundred men to reinforce the body of two thousand strong, which were in garrison there already. He did not venture, however, to rely on his military strength for the capture of the formidable Deedoo and the destruction of his armed bands. He put in practice all his wiles and spent large sums in bribes, and by such means succeeded so well that ere long he was able to return to Lahore, on the condition which he had himself imposed, that of laying the outlaw's head at the feet of the Maharajh. After receiving large rewards of money and jaghires for himself and family, in acknowledgment of the service he had done to the state, Goolauboo was sent off again with about fifteen hundred horse to subdue the Kuss country about Kistowur and to the north of Jummoo. In 1817, he returned from this expedition in which he had been highly successful and was of course lavishly rewarded for his services. It must be observed here that the younger brothers, from their good looks and more compliant disposition, were personally more in favour with the Maharajh than was Meean Goolauboo. On them Runjeet was desirous of confering the title and dignity of Rajah, but they, well tutored in the part they were to play, declared that they could not consent to receive honours, which were withheld from Goolauboo, their wise, brave and well-deserving elder brother. They prayed, therefore, of their kind master, their father, as they now styled the Maharajh, that in any honours and favours which he had to bestow upon the family, Goolauboo might have that preference to which his merits, as well as his seniority, entitled him. A slave to his own vile passions, which had driven him into the toils of these cunning and unscrupulous youths, Runjeet, rather than forego his design of ennobling his minions, Dehanoo and Suchetoo, at length consented to include the less favoured elder brother in the patent of nobility. Thus, in the year 1818, the three brothers were created Rajahs. The eldest, to whom precedence was reluctantly given, became Rajah Goolaub Sing of Jummoo, the second Rajah Dehan Sing of Bheembur and Kussal, the third Rajah Suchet Sing of Sumba, Ramnuggur, &c. To these titles were appended territories to the annual value of about three lakhs, one a lakh and a half, and one lakh, respectively. But this the brothers considered as mere out-fit money for the career of profit which they now saw before them.

Taking leave of Runjeet and the court of Lahore, Rajah Goolaub Sing now repaired to Jummoo to take possession of the seat of his ancestors, as an almost independent prince. His allegiance was limited to the maintenance of a small force of horse and foot at the service of the Durbar, to be presented annually at the Dusserah festival for review at Lahore, and certain promises of obedience to all the orders of the Maharajh. Thus Goolaub departed from Lahore, leaving his younger brothers still there in high favour and close intimacy with their royal master, and well instructed as to the use they were to make of their opportunities for the aggrandizement of the family. Henceforth he paid only occasional visits to the capital, seldom making his appearance there except when summoned by his brothers to consult on some matter in which their interest was involved and in which his advice was required. Thus these three Rajpoot brethren in time monopolized all the power and influence of the Lahore court, the

Maharajh being little more than the instrument of their will. Rajah Dehan Sing, in particular by his superior abilities, obtained such an ascendancy over Runjeet that while seemingly the humblest of his servants, he was in reality the regent of the Punjaub during the latter years of its aged sovereign.

When Rajah Goolaub Sing was settled in the government of the hill territories committed to his charge by the Maharajh, the Seik troops were withdrawn from Jummoo, together with the civil officials that had been employed in the management of the district. Thus left to himself, the young Rajah ruled his subjects with an iron rod and extended his power over all the petty independent chiefs of the neighbouring states. His avarice and cruelty were boundless, and both found free scope. Yet though loud complaints were raised against his tyranny, none of them reached the ear of his master, the Maharajh, it being an important part of the duties of his brothers, and especially of the more influential Dehan Sing, to arrest them in their progress to the durbar, where through his vigilance not one of them obtained a hearing.

The character of Goolaub Sing as exhibited in these early days of his power, was one of the most repulsive it is possible to imagine. Ambitious, avaricious, and cruel by nature, he reduced the exercise of his cruelty to a system for the promotion of the objects which his ambition and avarice led him to seek. He exercised the most ruthless barbarities, not in the heat of conflict or the flush of victory only, nor in the rage of an offended sovereign against rebellious subjects; he deliberately committed the most horrible atrocities for the purpose of investing his name with a terror that should keep down all thoughts of resistance to his cruel sway. With all this he was courteous and polite in demeanour, and exhibited a suavity of manner and language that contrasted fearfully with the real disposition to which it formed an artfully designed but still transparent covering.

He would be all things to all men, and displayed a readiness to adapt himself to the circumstances even of the humblest of his subjects that would have won all hearts, had not the tiger-nature that crouched beneath this fair-seeming exterior rendered him an object of distrust and terror. His character is thus sketched by the rude but vigorous hand of one who knew him well :

"He is an eater of opium, he tells long stories, keeps irregular hours, sleeps little, has a mind unsettled, offers little, promises less, but gives his word ; of good memory ; free, humorous and intimate even with the lowest and poorest classes of his subjects. The partaker and often the companion of their toils and labour, seeming or acting their very diligent, careful and instructing father, their sorrowful and heart-broken mother, their very intimate and laborious village brother, their free, jocose and humorous neighbour, their kind and continual visitor,—yet with all this, in reality a very leech, sucking their life's blood, the shameless slave-trader of their sons and daughters, brothers' sisters, wives and families. The would-be great merchant of the east ; the very jack of all trades, the usurer, the turn-penny, the briber and the bribed. The Jew shopkeeper of both old and new shoes, cloths, &c. The very pawnbroker, the very purchaser and retaker of his own alms."

In explanation of this last trait, it may be necessary to state, that it is the custom of Hindoos of all ranks and castes to bestow alms, according to their ability, on certain classes of Brahmins on stated occasions. Now in the dominions of Goolaub Sing this source of profit was in a great measure monopolized by the Rajah, for whom, in reality, the Brahmins were collectors of revenue, holding in farm from him the right of collecting alms. Thus the alms which he himself gave in accordance with custom, came back into the hands of the donor.

The authority already quoted, thus describes the other side of the chieftain's character:

"Still with all this he must be accounted the very best of soldiers, and, for an Asiatic and an unlettered, uneducated man, he is an able, active, bold, energetic yet wise and prudent commander. He is anything but strong-headed and hot blooded;—prudently making slow but resolute and judicious movements; thinking more of his resources, reserves, &c. than most of his country are wont to do. Looks more to the future, its wants and requisites, than either to the present or past—slowly goes on and feels his way as he goes—always ensuring supplies and resources—quick in taking opportunities,—fond of the defensive though ready to take the offensive when opportunity offers or requires—always considering arms as his last resource. He possesses great self-reliance on his political and subtle powers,—is slow but sure, and anything but forward in the field of battle. *There,* self-composed, prudent and careful and ever suspicious to the last. But at the breach, storm or charge, he freely though yet reluctantly expends his men, while he himself is just the man to be at their head if required, but generally the cool and able commander is in the rear."

The character of the second brother is thus sketched by the same hand:—"Rajah Dehan was active, enterprising, brave, energetic and intrepid to a degree; unconscious of all personal danger, but ever ready to repulse any; despising the habits of the indolent Asiatic life; ever employed in bold and manly pursuits; well accustomed to endure all sorts of privations and fatigue; remarkable for his adroitness in the use of all warlike weapons; expert, quick, agile in all his movements; of a most determined and resolute disposition, but when required to yield no one could do so with a better grace; the master of a most winning, gentle, affable, sedate, yet manly and commanding address ; ambitious to a degree that knew no bounds ; quick of parts ; of deep discernment ; discreet, prudent, careful, and ever scrupulous of offending without just cause ; always studying, and seldom failing to gain the respect and good wishes of all around ; mild and polite even to the meanest class ; extremely laconic in speech ; impatient of delay ; deaf to all long, round-about, or shuffling explanations, speeches, petitions, or harangues ; off-handed and concise in all orders, judgments, and sentences for punishment ; bashful and seemingly with an inward consciousness of the degradation of his original rise at court ; ever passive with inferiors ; high, haughty and distant with equals, and respectful to superiors, but polite to all ; occasionally humorous, witty and sarcastic ; but generally silent, thoughtful and reflective ; an enemy to the sensualist, libertine, or debauchee, and of regular and moderate habits himself.—In religion Rajah Dehan Sing in his heart was more a Deist than anything else ; and though outwardly following the rules prescribed to his caste, &c. he was often known to rail at the whole as made up of Brahminical deception. He believed but little in either the Jothushee or Nejumee. He despised Brahmins and their tenets, as false and foolish, and more than once speaking in private on caste and religion, &c. he acknowledged that be believed the Europeans knew more about the right way than any native. He considered all Europeans as Deists, aud often, when going through some long, holy, and sacred ceremony, he would order the Brahmin to make quick work of it, smiling and saying, 'We have now had enough of it.' He was often known to ridicule the whole as a farce, and really had the same opinion of Hindoo deities, as Europeans have. He could write a good and quick hand in his own Dogra character, and was extremely apt in learning Persian, &c. But though he may be said to possess, as he certainly did, all those and many other qualities, still the good traits in his mysterious character seemed to be but as a well-assumed and well-worn, befitting, mystic cloak, to screen a Machiavelian spirit, made up of a most diabolical, wily, deceptive, crafty, dissembling, faithless, subtle, deep, dark, designing, and ruthless disposition. And all for what? Ambition! He was ever determined and indefatigable to gain his end, but blind to the sacrifice it required, even to his own life, person, honour and character, and even to that of his wife, sons, and family; all were shamefully sacrificed to the one consuming passion—ambition and the thirst for aggrandizement."

Of Rajah Suchet Sing we have the following account:—

"Rajah Suchet Sing, though possessing but few of the qualities of his brothers, still was, at the first view, esteemed polite and courtly to a degree. He was certainly master of all their bad traits, or was as deep and dark spotted. Without possessing a whit more bravery or intrepidity, he assumed the tone and air of a Bravo amongst them, always considering himself and his handsome person to have been the chief cause, and means of their rise and power. He was the bully at court, and the desperado of the Punjaub; knowing better how to fight than to command; a capital soldier but no officer; utterly careless of life; wild, furious, proud, fiery and impatient in the midst of slaughter; always wishing to signalize himself and become the hero of some desperate and daring exploit; —a would-be Deedoo—with a proud, high, domineering spirit to both equals and superiors; irregular habits, and hard living; a most licentious debauchee and shameless defiler of women, and robber of the peace of many husbands and fathers. The handsome, dangerous, insinuating lady's man. The court dandy, ever conscious of his beauty of person and figure; jealous, to a degree of his nephew, Rajah Heera Sing, whom he well considered as his successful rival and successor in the affections of his master. In few words his character may be depicted thus—

for the first half of his court life, high-mettled, easily ruffled, never persuaded, over-petted, hot-blooded, light-headed ; and for the last few years, by freedom broken, by lust satiated, by jealousy embittered—a crest-fallen, broken-hearted desperado."

Of Rajah Heera Sing, the son of Dehan Sing, and who succeeded to his father's place and power at the court of Lahore, our authority thus writes :

" Of Rajah Heera Sing, at one time the virtual ruler of the Punjaub a few words may be said. He was twenty-three years of age and was what might be called a spoiled child when he died. The pet of Runjeet, or Runjeet's own last darling chicken, perhaps his last and most loving victim ; made up of many of the most curious and contradictory ingredients ; still addicted to low cunning, pride, effeminacy and licentious debauchery—the shameless intruder and Paul Pry of the court harem. Crouching, mean and timid to superiors, or those to be dreaded ; silent and suspicious to equals ; proud, supercilious and arrogant to inferiors ; subtle and deceitful to all :—too proud and high to take notice or even to return the salute of men of higher rank and certainly of better character than himself ; reared and brought up as the lap-dog of Runjeet and his dissolute associates ; with a little smattering of English, Persian and Sanscrit, and pretending to a perfect knowledge of all ! In person somewhat handsome, and approaching to his father's likeness ; always rectifying his dress, whiskers, beard, mustachios, and invariably chewing or seeming to chew something. Clean, neat, and showy in appearance, the would-be copy of his father—but too effeminate and proud ; unstable, or seemingly dare not walk, stir, sit, rise, eat, drink, or sleep, or even speak, answer, think, suggest or decide, *without what ?* A trifling sign —a careless nod—or some such other sufficient token of consent from the magic finger of his mystrious jailor, his old and original guardian spirit, his grand secret keeper, his sole adviser, his powerful magician, his sworn friend and protector, his preceptor, master, tutor, father and brother,—inferior and superior, Misser Jellah Pundit !"

The later history of the three brothers, the death of the two younger and the exaltation of the eldest, are recorded elsewhere in this book, and need not, therefore, be further noticed here. It is enough to say, that Maharajh Goolaub Sing, through favor of the British Government, sovereign of Cashmere and Jummoo, is now sole and undisputed LORD OF THE HILLS.

APPENDIX.

From Sir J. Malcolm's "Sketch of the Sikhs."

"Amera Das died in the year A. D. 1574, and of the Samrat 1631, at the village of Gondawal, in the province of Lahore, and was succeeded by his son-in-law, Ram Das, whom he had initiated in the sacred mysteries of his holy profession, and who became famous for his piety, and still more from the improvements he made at Amritsar, which was for some time called Rampur, or Ramdaspur, after him. Some Sikh authorities ascribe the foundation of this city to him, which is not correct, as it was a very ancient town, known formerly under the name of Chak."—*Page* 11.

NOTE.*

The proper word is *Chuck* not Chak. Chuck in Punjaubee means literally the foundation part of a Well, there being always a large circular ring of wood set or sunk down as far as they can make it reach in the water or mud beneath. This large ring which is made of several pieces of wood rudely but strongly attached together is called the Chuck of the well. Thus several idioms have sprung from this word, such as when a man is about to form or erect a new village he is said to be about sinking a *Chuck* in such a place. Again when a man inquires about some small Village or Hamlet, he asks what *Chuck* is that? Thus also the word Chuck is found applied, instead of the word Grom or Gom (a village) in many parts of the Punjaub, and several villages are actually called *Chuck* with the name of the founder added to it, as

* All these notes excepting three or four " by the Editor are by a Mr. Gardner, an officer of the Seik Artillery, one of the few who have not grown rich in that service for the last *thirteen years*, he has I believe held the rank of *Colonel*, but as his pay has been much reduced of late, and he has now only charge of six guns, I have merely given him the rank of Captain, he long foresaw in the Political hemisphere of Lahore, the storm that has taken place, and after the death of Heera Sing, when Colonel Courtland was anxious to *return*, and Colonel Mouton actually *did return to the Seik Service*, Colonel Gardner was most anxious to *leave it*, and Major Lawrence kindly endeavoured to procure him an appointment, but as he did not succeed, and I knew it might be said if the man on whom peace or war depended.

What tho' with war the maddening nation rung,
Peace when he spoke was ever on his *tongue*.

I unfortunately recommended Colonel Gardner not to leave the Punjaub, he however managed to remain at Lahore, during the late Campaign, and thereby avoided the necessity of either deserting from the Seiks or fighting against us.—*(Editor.)*

a

" *Beekoo ko Chuck*"—the Chuck or village of *Beekoo Mull*, the latter word Mull being left out for abbreviation's sake. Thus, also is the name of the old but well known village of '*Sooker Chuck*,' the cradle of Runjeet's family; and thus the present Amritsar was once occupied by a village known by the name of Sooa Chuck.

"The Sikhs, under one of their celebrated leaders, called Jasa Sing Calal, immediately took possession of the vacant Subah of Lahore."—*Page* 42.

NOTE.

Jussa Sing, the founder or head of the present Kollolwalla family; "Collol" or "Kollol" means a distiller and vender of spirits, and is considered one of the lowest castes in the Punjaub; Jussa Sing was of this caste, and a native of a village at present called Kollol Walla.

"The cities of Lahore and Amritsar are both in this province (Bari Duab or Manj'ha) and it becomes in consequence the great centre of the power of this nation. Ranjit Sing of Lahore; Fateh Sing of Alloowal; and Jud'h Sing of Ramgadia; are the principal chiefs of this country."—*Page* 51.

NOTE.

Ramghurria, not *gadia*:—all Ramghurria Sings are carpenters by caste;—so that now even the very word Ramghurria Sing, signifies a Sing carpenter. In mentioning the name of any Sing it is the usual custom to add or mention likewise, either the name of his village, district, occupation, or family, by which he may be recognized from any other of the same name. Thus Futty Sing, *Alloowalla;* Khan Sing, *Mulwai;* Sham Sing, *Attareewalla;* Panjoo Sing, *Nekeii, &c. &c.*

"The inhabitants of the country between the Ravi and Chanab are called D'harpi Sing, from the country being called D'harpi. The D'hanigheb Sings are beyond the Chanab, but within the Jeelam river."—*Page* 51.

NOTE.

It should be *Dhunnee-Gebe*, which words are the names of two large distinct districts south of the Puttwar country. But I have never known a Sing to be called Dhunnee Gebe Sing; Sings from that quarter are generally plainly mentioned thus, Ameer Sing *Gebee*, or Omer Sing *Dhunnee Kan;* those of Puttwar are called thus, Preme Sing *Puttwarree, &c.*

"The order of Sikhs have a place or Bunga on the bank

NOTE.

There are several *Bungas* in the Punjaub, but the principal of the sacred reservoir of Amritsar, where they generally resort, but are individually possessed of property, though they affect poverty, and subsist upon charity; which however, since their numbers have increased, they generally extort, by accusing the principal chiefs of crimes, imposing fines upon them, and in the event of their refusing to pay, preventing them from performing their ablutions, or going through any of their religious ceremonies at Amritsar."—*Page* 53.

ones are in and about Amritsir; the money collected in these places is distributed either yearly or every six months, among a certain number who have a claim to it. One full share in one of the chief Bungas in Amritsir I have known to amount to 200 rupees in one year;—and sometimes 1,000 or 1,200 shares are thus distributed.

NOTE.

"The Shahid and *Nirmala*, two other religious tribes among the Sikhs."—*Page* 53.

Generally pronounced *Nee-Maal* Sing, or a Sing who wears a low turban; Nee being an abbreviation of the word "Neevee" Low and "Maala," Turban or Head-dress, and often applied to the long head of hair of a Sikh when tied up in a knot above his forehead:—thus when a Sikh has become an Akalee and wears his hair and turban or head-dress after this manner, he is said to "Nee-Maala wencha Kytha," or he has raised his turban.

NOTE.

"The Muhammedans who have become Sikhs, and their descendants are in the Punjab jargon, termed Mezhebi Sing." —*Page* 56.

The *Bangee* or men of the *Sweeper caste* are the only people called *Muzubee Sing*, generally pronounced Mujbee for abbreviation; there is *no term* that I know of to particularize *a Mahommedan become Sikh*; but no Sikh would make any objection in respect of eating or drinking with a person of the latter description. But with a Mujbee there certainly would be an objection made; however very few Mahommedans have ever become proselytes to the Sikh religion.

NOTE.

"In the collection of the revenue in the Punjab, it is stated to be a general rule, that the chiefs to whom the territories belong, should receive one half

The state of the Rhyate, or Zeemindaurs, is far different from this statement at present.

of the produce, and the farmer the other: but the chief never levies the whole of his share, and in no country perhaps is the Ryot, or cultivator, treated with more indulgence."—*Page* 57.

"The use of opium to intoxicate, is very common with the Sikhs as with most of the military tribes of India. They also take B'hang, another inebriating drug."—*Page* 63.

NOTE.

B'hang is now in usual and daily use by the lower classes, while opium is mostly used by the higher;—and there are few who do not use either one or the other. Liquors are used only occasionally.

"The conduct of the Sikhs to their women differs in no material respect from that of the tribes of Hindus or Muhammedans, from whom they are descended. Their moral character with regard to women, and indeed in most other points, may, from the freedom of their habits, generally be considered as much more lax than that of their ancestors." —*Page*

NOTE.

Here I will give a few anecdotes characteristic of Sikh morals, of facts that I have myself witnessed: 1. A Sikh soldier got married, and shortly after went to Peshawar, whence he returned after eight years absence, during which he had regularly sent whatever he could save of his pay to his wife for her subsistence. On his return he felt a little astonished to find his wife with four fine lads running after her; but he merely asked her to whom they belonged, and the woman, without a blush, answered "*they are yours.*" Pleased by this answer the fellow took up one of the children and patted it, and told her it was all well, but that she must make the world believe what she had affirmed, adding "it satisfies me to be considered, at least, the father," &c. &c.

2. Another soldier, who was absent from his home in the Mahjri country for *five years*, returned, and heard from his neighbours that his wife had two children during his absence; he merely answered, "She is quite right, they will do well for minding the plough, and looking after the cattle." But, some time after, her paramour taking away the children, the husband entered into a lawsuit with him for the possession of them; and the woman was brought before one of the chief Sirdars of the country, where also her husband and paramour were present. There she actually squabbled in favour of the paramour's taking away the children as his rightful property; on which her husband rebuked her, saying "I am astonished at your taking his

part!" "Pooh" said she "drop the affair and let him take away the children, we will have plenty more."—However the husband paid about 40 rupees as a Nuzzur and got the children, and he now treats them as his own.

3. Runjeet Sing had a little Harkarah who was remarkable not only for his lean body and thin legs but for his pedestrian powers. He would go from Lahore to Peshawar, and return in fourteen days. For these exploits he was called Challee Koa, which signified him capable of walking forty coss, sixty miles, a day. This man was married to a young woman by the particular desire of Runjeet Sing himself:—but, about five months after their marriage she was delivered of a son—when Challee Koa went to complain to Runjeet, and his own words were "They call me Challee Koa, and I thought no one could go swifter than myself, but my wife has beat me completely."

4. Chund Kour the mother of No Nehal Sing, was notorious for her loose conduct, even during the life time of Runjeet, who more than once imprisoned some of her paramours. A Frash or Boag, well known by the name of *Minoo* (from his large eyes) was once imprisoned and even heavily ironed in a bastion that stood in the city outside the Hazooree Baug. General Ventura strongly interceded with Runjeet for his release; and I believe he would have been pardoned by his means, had it not been found out that Chund Kour actually was in the habit of paying him visits in the disguise of a *Kunchenee,* or dancing girl of the town, even while thus in close confinement. She was however the means of his being released at last, by her publicly remonstrating with Runjeet himself—and actually wishing to convince him of the imbecility of his son, and making other shameful exposures not at a *private* Durbar, but in the presence of eight or ten of the chief Sirdars of the country—where she even threatened to murder herself and her son should her lover Minoo not be released. It is well known that had No Nehal Singh lived but for a few months longer he would have murdered her. The manner in which she has been known to send written Purwanahs, or orders to any person she might take a fancy to, to present themselves at her own private apartment was notorious.

From Prinsep's Life of Runjeet Sing.

"The family boasts of no antiquity, the first of whom any

NOTE.

His *name* was *not* Deesoo but Budda, and on his becoming

traditionary recollection is preserved was a petty Zumeendar, *named Deesoo,* a Jath of the Sansee tribe, who resided in a village of the district of Manjah called Sookur-Chuk."—*Chap.* 2, *p.* 22.

a Seik he took the name of Boodh Sing.

"His patrimony was confined to three ploughs and a well, and *little is known of him,* except that he was the father of Nodh Sing, whose son Churut Sing founded the fortunes of the family by establishing a Surdaree or Chieftainship, which his descendants, Maha Sing and Runjeet, have improved into the Sovereignty over a wide and fertile territory."—*Chapter* 2, *page* 22.

NOTE.

I have heard *much* regarding Budda and understand he was famous in his day.

"Nodh Sing was *the first of the family who embraced* the *Sikh religion;* he sought in marriage the daughter of Goolab Sing, a Zumeendar of Mejithia, who was already initiated in the rites of that faith. And the Pahul was proposed as the condition of the nuptials."—*Chap.* 2, *p.* 22.

NOTE.

Nodh Sing's *father* was the *first* of the family who embraced the Seik religion, and even Bara his grand-father used to *read the Grunth* and was called Bii Bara.

"Churut Sing following his father's courses, but disdaining to serve in a subordinate capacity, associated with himself his *brothers-in-law Dul Sing and Jodh Sing,* and with their help raised some followers, whom he maintained and kept together by successful predatory enterprizes."—*Chapter* 2, *Page* 22.

NOTE.

In the Punjaub Adventurer Dhul Sing and Jodh Sing are mentioned as the *brothers* of Churut Sing, but they were as here stated his brothers *in law* and sons of Ameer Sing Gujerawalla.

"He left a widow, Desan by name, with two sons and a daughter, called respectively, Maha Sing, Suhuj Sing and Raj *Koonwar.*"—*Chap.* 3, *p.* 39.

NOTE.

Koonwar means a Prince; a Princess is Kour, according to Gilchrist; thus Churut Sing's daughter should have been called Raj *Kour,* she married Saheb Sing of Goojrut.—*(Editor.)*

"Captain Wade differs from Captain Murray in the date assigned to the birth of Maha Sing. Captain W. places it in 1757, making him fourteen years old in 1771, when Churut Sing died, according to his version. Captain Murray fixes it in 1764, making him ten years old in 1774."—*Note p.* 40.

NOTE.

I believe that Maha Sing was born in 1759, and that Churut Sing was killed in 1774, as stated by Capt. Murray.

"The nuptials of Maha Sing were celebrated in 1776 with the daughter of Gujput Sing of *Jeend,* to whom he had previously been betrothed."—*Chap.* 3, *p.* 41.

NOTE.

In the Punjaub Adventurer it is stated she was the daughter of Gujput Sing of *Scind;* Jeend is correct.

"Jy Sing had set his hopes on the promise afforded by the character of his son Goor Bukhsh Sing."—*Chap.* 3, *p.* 46.

Vide Genealogical Table.

In that year Goojur Sing, the Sikh Chief of Goojrat, died, and Saheb Sing, his son, succeeded to the Sirdaree.

"*The sister of Maha Sing, had been given in marriage to Saheb Sing by Churut Sing.*"—*Chap.* 3, *p.* 47.

Vide Genealogical Table.

"The Regent mother was accused of having led a life of profligate indulgence, the late Dewan being not the only paramour admitted to her favours. Upon receiving evidence of this, it is said that Runjeet Sing gave his sanction to, or at least connived at, her being put to death; and the old Chief, *Dul Sing, is designated as the perpetrator of the act by means of poison.*"—*Chap.* 3, *p.* 49.

NOTE.

My account of this affair states that Runjeet Sing put her to death with *his own hands,* and I have seen pictures *representing it thus* sold at Lahore.—*(Editor.)*

"In December 1807, Runjeet Sing returned to Lahore and was presented by his wife Mehtab Koonwur, with twins. The boys were named Sheer Sing and Tara Sing, *but Runjeet Sing has never fully acknowledged them as his own offspring.* Mehtab Koonwur's fidelity had for some time been

NOTE.

Sheer Sing was the son of a Mahometan washerman named Allee Buksh in the service of Suda Kour. Tara Sing was the son of a carpenter named Dural Sing.

suspected by her husband, and she had, in consequence, been living with her mother, Suda Koonwur. The report ran, *that the boys were procured by the latter from a Carpenter and Weaver, and were produced as born to her daughter*, the public having for some time previously been prepared for the birth by reports circulated of Mehtab being with child."—*Chap*. 4, *p*. 63.

"Suda Koonwur alone was not present; indisposition was assigned as the reason of her non-attendance on the occasion; but *her dissatisfaction at the failure of an attempt to procure from Runjeet Sing, her son-in-law, the public acknowledgement during these ceremonies, of the two boys she had brought up as twins born to her daughter*, was generally believed to be the true cause of her absence."—*Chap*. 6, *p*. 90.

This corroborates what I have stated that Runjeet would not even acknowledge Sheer Sing as his *son*.—(*Editor*.)

From the Punjaub Adventurer.

"Dyan Sing, though *slightly lame*, is a fine looking man, of a noble presence, polite and affable, of winning manners and modest speech. He sits on the ground, and rather behind the Maharajah, while the others, his inferiors in every way, are seated on chairs. The Raja decidedly is, next to his master, the ablest man in the Punjab; though like him so illiterate *a sscarcely to be able to sign his name*."—*Chap*. 2, *p*. 17.

NOTE.

Dehan Sing was *not in the least lame*, and so active that I have seen him leap over an object *six feet high*, and he was one of the *best and quickest writers* I ever saw.

"Kharak Sing, the eldest, is *an imbecile*, and effects the religieux. Sher Sing, the second is far from clever, but he is prudent; he is fond of imitating the Military and Europeans. Tara Sing, the third, is a dissolute *Vagabond*, leading the most reckless life in the common bazars. None of them appear much at Durbars, and *the two latter are known not to be really sons of the Maharajah*, who perhaps keeps quiet the mystery of their birth, as a check against any possible designs of his acknowledged son.—*Chap*. 2, *p*. 22.

NOTE.

I never considered Kurruck Sing as *imbecile until he was made so by the poison given him*. Tara Sing cannot I think be called a *Vagabond* but a *simpleton or fool*. I have before stated that Sheer Sing was the son of a washerman and Tara Sing the son of a carpenter.

" Of late years such has been the audacity, ability, and influence of the brotherhood, or rather of the two elder, that no year has passed without an extension of their territorial acquisitions; a fair sample of their doings is the fact, that the first intimation Runjeet Sing received of operations on the Ladâk frontier, was the announcement of the occupation of Ladâk itself by Zorawar Sing, the general of Golâb Sing's troops."—*Note, p.* 26.

NOTE.

This man's name was *Zoroveroo*, a Dogra of *low cast*, and he added the *Sing* when made a general by Goolaub.

"There are good men present, Bellasis, said Runjeet, evidently urging me on. 'Yes,' said Tej Sing, *a great huge fellow*, calling himself general and nephew of Khashyal Sing."—*Chap.* 3, *p.* 35.

NOTE.

His name is *Teja* Sing, and he is any thing but a great *huge fellow*, being *hardly middle sized.*

"On the top of the *Rajoaree* pass [*or at the addhe-tuk or Dukke, a height above Bheembur*] I saw a gibbet with two cages containing the skulls of Shams and his nephew, the chiefs of Poonch, who had for a long time *(three months)* resisted the encroachments of the Jammu family. A price was set upon their heads by Golâb Sing, but from their known bravery no one dared attack them openly; and they were at last killed, while asleep, and their heads carried to Golâb Sing, who ordered them to be suspended from the Bheembur pass."—(Adda Tuk).—*Note, p.* 73.

NOTE.

I have inserted the words that are in *italics;* the name of the Poonch chief was pronounced *Shumsh.*

" Nodh Sing, therefore, on his marriage, forsook his peaceful occupations and joined, as a trooper, the *Misal* of Kapur Sing of Gujarat, called the Fyzoollapureen *Misal;* he died in 1750, leaving *three sons*, when the eldest, Charat Sing, joining with *his brothers, Dull and Jodh Sing,* raised a banner of their own."—*Chap.* 9, *p.* 120.

NOTE.

Nodh Sing died in 1752, and had *four* sons. Churut Sing had a brother named Dull Sing, but *Jodh Sing was his brother-in-law*, and the famous Dull Sing was his *brother-in-law also;* little is known of his brother Dull Sing.

"In the end of 1840, the poor cypher of a Maharajah died; whether fairly or not, is not known; the court went out to the funeral solemnities, and the ambitious Prince was in all the glory of his new title, *when the train re-entered the city of Lahore.* There was a narrow gateway, the crowd was great, and made a rush to seize the money, scattered on such occasions among the populace. *The elephant on which No Nihal was seated, was pushed close to the wall, the building gave way, a beam fell and killed both the new Maharajah and Udam Sing, who was seated on the same elephant.*"—*Note, p.* 146.

NOTE.

No Nihal Sing was *not seated on an elephant,* but was *on foot,* and it was not *a beam* that fell, but some brick bats, and the Prince was not *killed on the spot:* I was present.

"Then, tell me, *man,* why you think so?"—*Chap.* 12, *p.* 163.

NOTE.

Runjeet Sing, in familiar conversation, used the word bii, or brother, and never *admee* or man.

"Bas, bas, *faqeer,* interrupted the King."—*Chap.* 12, *p.* 165.

NOTE.

Runjeet Sing in speaking to the faqeer, always addressed him *faqeer saheb,* or *fayeer jee.*

"The *menial* shrunk at the retort, and still more at the glance of his master, who was not, he saw, in a mood to be trifled with, he therefore answered respectfully, "the ladies are honourably tended, Rajah *ji.*"—*Chap.* 12, *p.* 172.

NOTE.

No menial would presume to address the Rajah, Rajah *ji;* he would say, Maharajh, or Rajah Saheb.

"Golab Sing is the elder brother, and in the family pact he has charge of their conquered territories in the hills; while he manages those of Dhyan Sing, he yearly adds to his own by conquest, or by the terror of his name. He has overrun the whole district between Kashmir and Attock; and

NOTE.

Sudan is the name of their *cast,* not of their *country;* the Sudan race were a tribe of Sud Bramins, the Sattis were Seths or Chetrees, who were compelled to embrace the Mahometan religion a little before, and during, the reign of Arungzeeb.

inflicted such terrible vengeance on the people of Sudân (a large district south east of Mozaffarabad *cutting up, maiming, flaying, to the amount, it is said, of* 12,000 *persons*, that the men of Dundi and Satti, two adjoining territories, sent in their submission, but begged *not to see his face*."—*Page* 182.

NOTE.

"In the Punjab, intoxication is common, and Dhyan Sing himself, though not a Sikh, *frequently drank hard*."—*Chap.* 14, *p.* 186.

Dehan Sing never tasted liquor known to be of an intoxicating quality, he seemed to dread it; and only after very long marches or when sitting up all night would he take a *manjorm* made purposely for him.

NOTE.

"The faqueer called for *his elephant*, and I mounting my good steed, Chanda."—*Chap.* 14, *p.* 192.

The faqueer never did or would ride any animal, even a horse; he always used a palankeen, forty years old, and not worth five rupees.

NOTE.

"Perhaps one of the passengers would be a Brahmin traveller, with his quiet, sly, subdued countenance, and white beard, as strong a contrast to the overbearing air, and *black mane* of the Sings, (who *mostly dye their beard when it begins to grizzle*.")—*Chap.* 15, *p.* 204.

The Seiks by their tenets are strictly *forbidden to dye their hair*, and you never see an *old* Seik with a *black beard.*

NOTE.

"One part or other of Northern Hindustan, has been continually exposed to the sword, but all the invaders passed through the Punjaub; it has therefore suffered the most, and bears to this day in almost every quarter, testimony to the blighting effects of war, and its train of ills, pestilence and famine among them."—*Chap.* 20, *p.* 263.

I have made a list of all the ruins I have seen and know to exist; this list enumerates 3,756, and I speak only of the tract of country between the Indus and the Ravee.

NOTE.

"A curious illustration of this remark is, that Rajah Suchet Sing has been three times married, and has no children;

Goolaub Sing has only been married *once* and had *three* sons by his wife and *two* illegitimate children but not one by while his brothers, who have *each been four times married, have each but two sons;* the name of Jowahir. Dehan Sing had *three sons.* those of Dhyan Sing, being the well-known Hera Sing and Jowar Sing:—those of Golab Sing were, Udam Sing, killed by the fall of a gateway, when No Nihal Sing also perished, and *Jowahir Sing* now alive."—*Note, p.* 275.

From Colonel Steinbach's Work.

"Most of the towns are surrounded by a mud or brick wall of frail quality; Lahore itself is so defended, with the addition of a dry moat, which, *on emergency, could be filled with water* from the neighbouring Ravee. But, *the mud walls* would afford no protection against artillery. *They were originally constructed by the inhabitants.*"—*Page* 3.

NOTE.

The dry moat, or ditch of Lahore, could only be supplied with water from the Ravee, at considerable trouble and expense, as there is *no water course, or canal of any kind for that* purpose; and, during eight or nine months out of the twelve, the nearest point of the River is at least two, or two and a half miles from the walls of the Fort.

The present walls as every body may see are of *brick work;* and, were originally erected by *the Emperor Akbar, and not by the inhabitants;* and not only the walls of the present town, but those of the present fort, were built also by that Emperor. The "moat," "half moon batteries" "*fausse braye,*" &c., were formed by Runjeet, and the walls themselves underwent considerable repairs during his reign, &c. &c.

"Umritzur, situated between the rivers "Beas" and "Ravee," is of somewhat larger extent than Lahore, and from *having been the capital,* when Runjeet Sing exercised dominion over the Punjaub, is now a place of great commercial importance."—*Page* 4.

NOTE.

Umritsir was *never considered the capital.* However, in comparing the two cities, Lahore may be considered *the seat of Government* and military depôt, and the original capital of the country; but of late years, or since the accession to power of Runjeet, and consequently Hindu supremacy, Umritsir has not only rivalled it, but far surpassed it, in every other respect, so that at present, Umritsir may be called the "Mart" and "Trading Capital" of the Punjaub; its wealth, commerce, &c. now far exceeding those of Lahore;—in fact, every commodity sold at Lahore comes from Umritsir. Thus Umritsir may, in a commercial point of view, be considered the wholesale, and Lahore, the retail shop of the Punjaub.

"General *Avitabile*, an European officer, lately in the service of the Sikh Government, who *spent much of his accumulated wealth in decorating and improving the locality of his residence*."—*Page* 5.

NOTE.

General Avitabile is not supposed to have ever spent any but the state money, in erecting buildings, or improving the locality of any place, even his own residence;—Generals Allard and Ventura, though they received some large sums from Runjeet to enable them to build up and decorate their residence of *Anarkullee*, still *they did*, it is believed, *spend some of their own private money*, on the completion of that object.

"*The upper part* of the Jeylum *runs through the vale of Kashmir*, which is likewise watered by several broad and beautiful Lakes, one of which is twenty miles in length, and nine in width."—*Page* 6.

NOTE.

The upper part of the river Jeelum *cannot be said to run through the Vale of Cashmere*; as the most northern stream and main source of the Jeelum, rises in the holy tank, or holy precincts of the shrine of Mutter, *beyond the high range of the Thibet mountains*, that run north of Cashmere. It is the second or lesser and southern stream, which may be put down as but a tributary stream, that rises in the Peer Punjaub range, about S. E. of Cashmere, and runs through the valley, and joins the main stream a little below Mozuffurabad.

"It was with *some difficulty* that the Rajah Dhyan Sing (Runjeet's minister,) under strong excitement, was *prevented from throwing himself into the flames. Considerable doubt has been thrown over the sincerity of this intended act* of self devotion; but the *general opinion was, that he fully intended it*, from the apparent absence of any motive for *hypocrisy*."—*Page* 19.

NOTE.

Very few in the Punjaub, if any, who were acquainted with the character of Rajah Dehan Sing, ever *doubted the hypocrisy* of this act, and it was indeed *far from being the general opinion, that he fully intended to burn himself* with the body of Runjeet. His motive for playing this farce, was any thing but misunderstood, by all those who *knew him*.

"About this time the son of Kurruck Sing, the Prince No Nehal Sing, returned to Lahore from Peshawur."—*Page* 21.

NOTE.

Rajah Dehan Sing wrote to Rajah Goolaub Sing his brother, then at Peshawur, giving him a daily and full account of how matters stood at Lahore, and requesting of him to reach Lahore with the young Prince quickly, whom the elder brother had well tutored, and made ready to become his tool, even before they had arrived at Lahore.

"Public report, indeed, accused, Kurruck Sing of *scandalous improprieties*, with his favourite Cheyt Sing."—*Page* 22.

NOTE.

Those public reports were all *groundless*, and only got up, and *spread by the Dogra Faction*.

"The elephant on which No Nehal Sing was seated, in passing through the gate of the palace, pushed against the *brick work*, when the whole came down, killing the Rajah Dhyan Sing's nephew, who was seated upon the same elephant, upon the spot, *and fracturing the skull* of No Nehal Sing *so dreadfully*, that *he never spoke afterwards*, and expired in a few hours. The incident is generally supposed, to have been premeditated, and not the effect of accident, as stated by the Government; but the whole affair was so enveloped in mystery, that even to the present day it has been found impossible to attach suspicion to any party, and the matter has now long since ceased to occupy men's thoughts."—*Page* 25.

NOTE.

This account is nearly the same as that in the Punjaub Adventurer, which I have mentioned as being incorrect. Colonel Steinbach is right, however, in stating it was the *brick work* that came down. When No Nehal Sing's body was *produced* by Rajah Dehan Sing, his skull certainly *was* dreadfully fractured, *but, it did not appear to me to be the case when he fell*; on the contrary, I saw but *little blood* on his forehead; *he struggled, and tried to get up*, and I would not undertake to say *he never spoke afterwards*.

"*It was at length decided, by the advice of Dhyan Sing, to offer the crown to the Prince Shere Sing*, a twin son of Runjeet Sing, by his wife Mehtab. Considerable

NOTE.

No consultation took place on No Nehal Sing's death; but when Rajah Dehan Sing announced it to the mother, Chund Kour, he promised *her* she should succeed to the objection was at first offered by the Sikh Sirdars, upon the ground of his alleged illegitimacy, Runjeet Sing never having fully acknowledged the twins as his offspring.

The opposition, however, was for the time overcome, and a messenger dispatched to Shere Sing with the glad tidings."—*Pages* 26-27.

Rajh, but he had sent off a messenger to Sheer Sing who, according to *previous agreement*, soon made his appearance at the capital, and *then his succession was opposed* by the Sindiawalla and other Sirdars, and it was *not* overcome.

"The Prince Shere Sing, seeing the overthrow of his hopes, returned to his country seat; and Dhyan Sing, without assigning any particular reason, also shortly after withdrew from Lahore to his own possessions,—a mountainous country called Jummoo, leaving his elder brother, the Rajah Goolab Sing, in the post of Prime minister to the Queen Regent."—*Page* 27.

NOTE.

Sheer Sing and Rajah Dehan Sing's withdrawal from Lahore was a preconcerted measure, and even the elder Rajah was in the secret. It was Dehan Sing, and Goolaub Sing's policy to send Sheer Sing away, while their minions, particularly those of Rajah Dehan Sing, in his name instigated by promises of great reward the Sikh troops, to act the part they afterwards did, on the return of Sheer Sing.

"In the meantime, Ajeet Sing, after the committal of this atrocity, directed his steps towards the city; but meeting the Rajah Dhyan Sing *in his carriage*, he dismounted and got into it, with the intention of returning together. It appears that a dispute took place, between them, respecting the future form of Government, but which was quickly terminated by Ajeet Sing's *stabbing* the Rajah to the heart. He afterwards caused *his head to be cut off*, and sent it to his son, the Rajah Heera Sing, of whom

NOTE.

Ajeet Sing did *not stab* Dehan Sing, nor was *his head cut off;* but when he was killed his body was thrown into the pit of the gun foundry. Dehan Sing was *not in his carriage*, but on horseback, and Ajeet Sing did *not cause the whole of Sheer Sing's family to be murdered; Shah Dehu, the infant alluded to,* I suppose, is, *still alive*, though he was rather more than *one day old*.

further mention will be made. Ajeet Sing, after having caused *the whole of the late Maharajah's family to be murdered, even to an infant born in the Zenana the day previous,* then shut himself up with his followers in the citadel."—*Page* 35.

"Upon Soochet Sing's arrival at Lahore, he did not find himself joined by a single soldier. Seeing this unexpected and desperate state of affairs, aware also that *Heerah Sing had secured the passage of the river* and that *flight* was consequently *impossible,* he shut himself up with his followers in a temple, about three miles distant from Lahore."—*Page* 37.

NOTE.

Heera Sing *did not secure the passage of the river,* but even sent twice to *persuade his uncle to retrace his steps* to the hills.

"Heera Sing soon became aware of the combination formed against him; his first step was *to enlist a large body of Hill-men,* from Jummoo, as a guard to his personal safety."—*Page* 39.

NOTE.

Heera Sing, at this time time *did not enlist any hill-men,* but, on the contrary, a short time before his death he sent away to Jesrota his hill troops, and *they were not recalled.*

"Jowahir Sing proceeded, at the head of a party of the Khalsa Troops, to the *minister's house, when a conflict took place.*"—*Page* 40.

NOTE.

Jowahir Sing did not proceed with any force to attack Heera Sing at his house.

"They, (the Sikh Infantry,) are capable of enduring the fatigue of long marches for several days in succession, (the author having on one occasion marched with his regiment a distance of 300 miles within twelve days,) and are, generally speaking, so hardy, that exposure to oppressive heats or heavy rains has little effect upon them."—*Pages* 63-64.

NOTE.

A little before Cheyt Sing's murder, I myself, started from Peshawar, with the Prince No Nehal Sing, Rajah Goolaub Sing, and about 3,000 troops, horse and foot, and 12 guns. The Prince and the Rajah, with a few horsemen, reached Lahore on the evening of the fifth day, and I, with 900 infantry reached Lahore on the 7th in the morning, and on the 9th day the whole force that left Peshawur reached

Lahore. A Sikh has often been known to travel on foot, from Lahore to Peshawur, in five days; and I had a Sikh in my corps of artillery who repeatedly went on foot from Jummoo to Lahore, and I have known him bring back dispatches in somewhat less than 36 hours; the distance is 60 Punjaub coss, or about 90 miles from Lahore to Jummoo, which makes 180 miles to be travelled in 36 hours; but there are several Sikh soldiers who would, even for a small consideration, go 40 coss, or 60 miles daily, for 12 or 15 days together.

NOTE.

"The one who turns King's evidence is allowed to escape with impunity, and to retain his share of the spoil in all cases of stolen cattle."—*Page* 73.

The King's evidence, or murkei, is never questioned as to what part of the booty he has received himself; he only has to shew, or point out, or even tell the place or spot where the property is, and then he receives from the owner a stipulated sum; and in case of cattle, &c. the thief, though he may be in possession of the cattle at the time, very seldom returns the same, but gives others in lieu of those stolen; and those he gives in this manner, generally turn out to be the stolen property of others. But a murkei is always ready and sure to go and inform the owners (for a certain sum) and immediately a long law suit commences between the parties: nor are these matters ever finished until the murkei has received large sums, equal to the amount of property, when, to prevent any further strife, or through fear, the whole of the property is returned by the thief, he having a previous understanding with the murkei, as to the amount of money raised by this kind of swindling, which generally proves to the sufferers far more injurious and expensive than the plain robbery itself.

NOTE.

"The day for them (the Faqueers) has gone by; *they* have done their work, and are *gathered to their fathers*."—*Page* 100.

The youngest brother is *still alive* and well, and at present most active in all negotiations of consequence, between the British Authorities and the Lahore Durbar.

---

c

From the Medical and Literary Journal for January, 1845.

"*Returning* from the last ceremonies performed to the remains of his father, *he was seated on an elephant* with Oodum Sing, the son of Rajah Golab Sing of Jummoo, and as the animal was passing through one of the gateways *the beam supporting it fell*, and the two youths were killed on the spot."—*Page* 212.

NOTE.

This is *all* quite *incorrect*, as may be seen by the note on the same statement in the Punjaub Adventurer.—*(Editor.)*

"Not only was Sheer Sing murdered, but his son, the young Pertaub Sing, *and another heir, an infant*. The only person now left to succeed to the throne of Lahore, was a boy named Dhuleep Sing, the reputed son of Runjeet, and who had been concealed along *with his mother, a Kashmeree by birth, at Jummoo, under the protection of Golab Sing*."—*Page* 213.

NOTE.

The said infant, Shah Dehu, is still alive. Duleep Sing was *never taken to Jummoo*, and when he was sent to Umritsir, his mother *did not accompany him*. She is not a *Cashmeeree*.

"At Roopur, in 1831, a treaty of firm alliance was made between Runjeet Sing and the late Governor-General, Lord William Bentinck. By this the two Governments *pledged their mutual assistance to each other against all enemies*."—*Page* 215.

NOTE.

If this is the case we were bound to have supported the Government of *Chund Koor*. —*(Editor.)*

From the Calcutta Review for August, 1844.

"Uttur Sing, the eldest surviving brother, was considered a respectable man and one well versed in politics. He was a remnant of Runjeet Sing's school and, as such, drew around him the genuine Khalsa, and those who held the memory of the great Maharajah in reverence. But

NOTE.

Uttur Sing was the *second* son of Ameer Sing, and Bhood Sing was the *third*, and had not Uttur Sing taken refuge in the Company's Territory, he would of course have been put in prison with his brother Lena Sing, and as he never would have acted the part, that Sirdar did, he would have remained in while Uttur Sing shewed, as a soldier, much of the spirit of *his elder brother, Boodh Singh,* he wanted the political boldness requisite for a Punjaub Leader and Reformer; he wanted also tact, and never was worse advised than when *he took refuge within the Sutlej,* and gave his enemies the opportunity of placarding him as sold to the Feringhees. In person Uttur Sing was *middle sized, of stout build, and of plain unmarked countenance."—Page* 495.

confinement. He was a *slight, thin,* mean-looking man, with a grey beard, and *marked with the small pox.—(Editor.)*

"A writer in Blackwood's Magazine includes the Fakeer Azeezoodeen *among the conspirators against Sheer Singh; but he had no concern in the atrocity.* The Fakeer was an able, and honest, but, at the same time a timid Councillor of Runjeet Singh."—*Page* 496.

NOTE.

The Fakeer certainly was at least aware that some revolution was about to take place, as he wrote to his son, Cheragoo-deen, the Vakeel at Ferozpore, telling him as much.—*(Editor.)*

"We have stated that the Scindawallas had been favourably received at Lahore by all parties. The Maharajah doubtless hoping that his benevolences would gain their hearts, and the Rajahs hoping to make tools of them against the Maharajah. Sheer Singh was naturally open-hearted and indolent. He was content to be monarch and to leave the reins of Government with the Rajahs, if they gave him his will in the patronage and promotion of his favorites, and did not otherwise molest him or disturb him in his fiddling and hunting pursuits. But he soon began to find himself watched; to perceive the fate that systematically befel his friends and protégés, and at last he heard that Dulleep Singh, a child of eight or nine years of age, recognized by Runjeet Sing as his son, though in full knowledge of his not being so, *was at Jummoo.* His fears awakened, he made various efforts to throw off the yoke. For a time, Dhyan Sing, affecting disgust, would retire from the court,

NOTE.

Uttur Sing never went to Lahore, and never would acknowledge Sheer Sing. Ajeet Sing went, as I have stated elsewhere, on purpose to put Sheer Sing to death.—*(Editor.)*

NOTE.

Dulleep Sing never was taken *to Jummoo.*

and after one of these absences he brought Dulleep Sing with him to Lahore."—*Page* 498.

" How long an alliance had been formed by the Rajahs with the Scindawallas is uncertain; but, from the cautious tactics of the former, *it is supposed that having ingratiated themselves with Lena Sing and Ajeet Sing, they suddenly hinted, with every appearance of friendly sincerity, that Sheer Sing had only lured them to Lahore for the purpose of destroying the family* at a blow; that, alarmed at the intelligence, they at once entered into the plot to cut off Sheer Sing *and his children.*"—*Page* 499.

NOTE.

The very reverse appears to have been the case; and Ajeet Sing, upon this occasion, it would seem, was even too deep for the wily minister. The writer has also fallen into the common error that *all* Sheer Sing's children *were destroyed,* though only Pertaub Sing was put to death.

" Our Newspapers call Kashmera and Peshora Sing, *Princes;* but, until Sheer Sing's death, they were only recognized as *petty Sirdars.* Although Runjeet Sing had not objected to people *calling them his sons,* they were never treated as such, *in the same manner as Sheer Sing.*"—*Page* 502.

NOTE.

They were styled *Koonwur,* and that means *Prince;* and if they were not treated in the same manner as Sheer Sing, *neither was Tara Sing,* whom he *called his twin brother.* The Governor-General, as may be seen by the following extract from his letter to the Court of Directors, styled Peshora Sing, Koonwur.—*(Ed.)*

" There seems to be very little doubt that Sirdar Chutter Singh Attareewalla did, after much hesitation, enter into the views of the Wuzeer Jowahir Singh, and cause the Koonwur Peshora Singh to be put to death on his way from Attock to Lahore."

" The Prince's (now Maharajah's) cavalcade attended by all the Jumboo family, except Golab Sing, and by all the Seikh Sirdars at the capital, had *returned* from performing the last ceremonies over the

NOTE.

This is the fourth writer who has given an *incorrect* account of the death of Nao Nihal Sing; he is correct however in stating that it was the *brick parapet wall that fell* and not a *beam;* he is also correct in body of Khurnck Sing, when, *as the elephant on which Nao Nihal sat,* attended by Meean Oodum Sing, the son of Rajah Golab Sing, was passing under the gateway of the Lahore citadel, *the brick parapet wall fell* and crushed both the Maharajah and his companion. Oodum Sing was killed on the spot, and Nao Nihal Sing was *carried insensible into the palace,* and never spoke again. The wily minister affected that the young sovereign had only received a slight injury, and would soon recover, but for twenty-four hours *prevented all but his own partizans from seeing him.* Rajah Dhyan Sing at once despatched a trusty messenger with a true account of occurrences to Rajah Golab Sing, sending to the father the bloody garments of his son and heir, to enable the widows of the latter to perform Suttee. *At the same time another messenger was sent to Sheer Sing,* at Bettala, about seventy miles from Lahore, telling him that *if he would be ruler of the Punjaub, he must reach Lahore within twenty-four hours.*"—*Calcutta Review, No.* 2, *p.* 481-82.

stating that Dehan Sing would not allow any *but his own party to see the Prince;* he is correct, too, in stating, that Sheer Sing was immediately sent for.—*(Editor.)*

"In Chund Kour's *intrigues* the name of the British Government was much used; and it was currently believed that the Punjaub was sold by her and the Sindawallas, and six annas in the rupee offered to the English; probably such was the case, but the offer only *injured their cause with their own countrymen,* and does not seem to have mended it with the British, whose authorities summarily stopped the recruiting."—*Page* 490.

NOTE.

I dont see how it can be said that Chund Kour *intrigued* because she sent her Vakeel with proposals to the British Government; but she certainly *injured her cause with the Sikhs,* and so did *the Scindawallas* who supported her.—*(Editor.)*

"On Sheer Sing's accession, the Sindawallas fled; but Lena Sing being apprehended, *was thrown into irons, and kept in close confinement.* Uttur Sing and Ajeet Sing *intrigued* on the British border, and alarmed the Durbar."—*Page* 495.

NOTE.

Here the word *intrigue* is again made use of, but we are not told *how* the Scindawallas intrigued, or *who* they intrigued with.—*(Editor.)*

THE PRODUCTIONS OF THE PUNJAUB, AND OF THOSE HILL STATES, &c. DEPENDANT ON IT.

(m) is put for Medicinal as used in the Punjaub.

Native Appellations.	*English Names.*	*Places where Produced.*
Reshum, *m*	Silk, Tonic	Cashmeer.
Busma	Indigo Plant	Throughout the whole Punjaub.
Hoffeem, Narcotic, *m*	Opium and Seed	Ditto ditto.
Kaisir, Carminative, *m* ..	Saffron	Cashmeer & the Hills, &c.
Audrek, Stimulant and Carminative, *m*	Ginger.............	Ditto and in different parts of the Hills.
Hurdell, Astringent, *m*....	Turmeric	Throughout the whole Hills, Low range.
Kuth, Astringent, &c. *m* ..	....	Cashmeer and high Kussall, &c.
Maindee, ditto ditto, *m* ..	Henna	Punjaub in general.
Mejeett, ditto ditto, *m*	Madder	Kolatchee & Dera Ismûl Khan.
Kosumba Seed, *m*	Safflower	Punjaub in general, &c.
Kuppah	Cotton and Plant....	Ditto ditto.
Konuck, 3 sorts..........	Wheat, 3 kinds	Ditto ditto & the Hills, &c.
Jow	Oats...............	Ditto ditto ditto.
Mekei	Indian Wheat	Ditto ditto ditto.
Bogera	....	Ditto ditto ditto.
Chola	Gram	Ditto ditto ditto.
Musser	Ditto	Ditto ditto ditto.
Mung	Ditto	Ditto ditto ditto.
Singara, Bread made from it..............	....	Cashmeer and the Hills.
Trumba, ditto ditto	....	Ditto ditto ditto.
Istik Pecha, *m*	Purgative, good......	Ditto ditto ditto.
Benufsha, *m*	Violet—Laxative, good	Hills in general.
Kau Zeebbaum, *m*	Carminative.	Ditto and Cashmeer, &c.
Jeera, *m*	Ditto	Ditto ditto ditto.
Koul doda	Sedative	Ditto ditto ditto.
Ecrote	Wallnuts	Ditto ditto ditto.
Tangee	Hazell Nutt	Ditto ditto ditto.
Sew, 4 sorts	Apples............	Ditto ditto ditto.
Noc, 5 sorts	Pears	Ditto ditto ditto.
Angour	Grapes	Ditto ditto ditto.
Goth e Boogoo	Large Pear........	Ditto ditto Cashmeer.
Glasse	....	Ditto ditto ditto.
Aloocha	....	Ditto ditto and the Punjaub, &c. &c.
Aumul thash, *m*	Cassia fistularies, Purgative and Laxative	Hills in general.
Aûla, *m*	Tonic	Ditto ditto.
Behera, *m*	Ditto	Ditto ditto.
Hareere, *m*............	Ditto	Ditto ditto.
Kour, bitter, *m*	Ditto	Ditto ditto.
Mol Kungenee, *m*........	....	Ditto ditto and Punjaub.
Jeeree, bitter, *m*........	Ditto	Ditto ditto ditto.
Baang, *m*	Henbane, Narcotic Soporific	Ditto ditto ditto.

Native Appellations.	*English Names.*	*Places where Produced.*
Datura, *m*	Datura, Narcotic	Hills & Punjaub.
Buttung	Sweet Pear	Ditto ditto.
Simloo	Fruit	Ditto ditto.
Akeree	Ditto	Ditto ditto.
Chereitha, *m*	Worm seed Plants bitter Tonic	
Emlook	Fruit	Hills in general.
Aunjeer, *m*	Ditto	Ditto ditto and Punjaub.
Anaub, *m*	Purgative ditto	Ditto ditto.
Kokko	Ditto	Ditto ditto.
Dheruneh	Ditto	Ditto ditto.
Mokeree	Ditto	Ditto ditto.
Chinottoo	Ditto	Ditto ditto.
Thun—a yellow dye		Ditto ditto.
Mullett, *m*	Liquorice Root	Attock and Scinde Banks of, &c. &c.
Chuara, *m*	Sudorific	Punjaub, &c. &c.
Gutahee, *m*	Astringent	Hills & Cashmeer, &c.&c.
Sirroo		Punjaub in general, &c.
Hulsee, *m*	Linseed, Emollient	Ditto ditto ditto.
Shetooth		Ditto ditto ditto.
Aum Seed, *m*	Mangoes, Astringent	Ditto ditto ditto.
Aroo		Ditto ditto ditto.
Anaar, Astringent, *m*	Pomegranite	Ditto ditto ditto.
Bee Seed, *m*	Emollient	Ditto ditto and Hills.
Nimboo, *m*	Lemons	Ditto ditto ditto.
Nouringee, *m*	Oranges	Ditto ditto ditto.
Mitta		Ditto ditto ditto.
Kutta		Ditto ditto ditto.
Gol Gol		Ditto ditto ditto.
Cheko Derra		Ditto ditto ditto.
Therevee, *m*	Colycinth, Purgative	Ditto ditto ditto.
Thooma Root, *m*	Purgative	Ditto ditto ditto.
Kela	Plaintains	Punjaub in general, &c.
Kerbooja Seed, *m*	Melons	Ditto ditto ditto.
Therbooja ditto, *m*	Water ditto	Ditto ditto ditto.
Therrah ditto, *m*		Ditto ditto ditto.
Keera ditto, *m*		Ditto ditto ditto.
Metree ditto, *m*		Ditto ditto ditto.
Polluck	Spinage	Ditto ditto ditto.
Tomoccoo	Tobacco	Ditto ditto ditto.
Bere		Ditto ditto ditto.
Souf, *m*	Caroway Seed, Carminative	Ditto ditto ditto.
Jeweine, *m*	Aniseed, Carminative	Ditto ditto ditto.
Haalloo, *m*		Ditto ditto ditto.
Kaajoor	Dates	Ditto ditto ditto.
Pirnee		Ditto ditto ditto.
Falsa, Astringent, *m*	Fruit	Ditto ditto ditto.
Aroo	Ditto	Ditto ditto ditto.
Chumba	Flower	Ditto ditto ditto.
Rebele	Ditto	Ditto ditto ditto.
Mothee	Ditto	Ditto ditto ditto.
Gulaub, *m*	Rose, red, 3 kinds	Ditto ditto ditto.
Kulfa, *m*	Cooling, sedative	Ditto ditto ditto.
Churaall		Ditto ditto ditto.
Dock, Astringent, *m*	Wild Grape, &c.	Ditto ditto ditto.

Native Appellations.	*English Names.*	*Places where Produced.*
Zoe Seed, Emetic, *m*	**De obstruent**	**Punjaub in general, &c.**
Piaze	**Onion**	**Ditto ditto ditto.**
Thome, Stimulant, *m*	**Garlic, Paralysis**	**Ditto ditto ditto.**
Buthony		**Ditto ditto ditto.**
Dunnia, Carminative, *m*	**Coriander Seed**	
Gol Viree, *m*	**Purgative**	
Kuddoo Seed, *m*	**Emollient**	**Throughout the whole Punjaub.**
Tinda		**Ditto ditto ditto.**
Choul	**Rice, 4 sorts**	**Ditto ditto ditto.**
Jewar		**Ditto ditto ditto.**
Mah, *m*	**Emollient, Nutritive**	**Ditto ditto ditto.**
Mung, *m*	**Light Nutritive**	**Ditto ditto ditto.**
Thill, *m*		**Ditto ditto ditto.**
Muddull		**Ditto ditto ditto.**
Cheena		**Ditto ditto ditto.**
Kungenee		**Ditto ditto ditto.**
Swank		**Ditto ditto ditto.**
Kodera		**Ditto ditto ditto.**
Kumaade	**Sugar Cane**	**Ditto ditto ditto.**
Thoria		**Ditto ditto ditto.**
Bede Musk, *m*	**Willow, Sedative & Carminative**	**Ditto ditto ditto.**
Gool Abaassee, *m*		**Ditto ditto ditto.**
Saath Verg, *m*		**Ditto ditto ditto.**
Gool Vergup, *m*		**Ditto ditto ditto.**
Maalthee		**Ditto ditto ditto.**
Gungeloo Seed, *m*	**Turnips, Emetic**	**Ditto ditto ditto.**
Moolee Seed, *m*	**Raddish, Emetic, good**	**Ditto ditto ditto.**
Gaajer	**Parsnips**	**Ditto ditto ditto.**
Arebee	**Carrots**	**Ditto ditto ditto.**
Suker Kundee		**Ditto ditto ditto.**
Bajera		**Ditto ditto ditto.**
Sunn	**Hemp**	**Ditto ditto ditto.**
Sun Kukkeree	**Flax**	**Ditto ditto ditto.**
Tei, Stimulant, *m*	**Mustard**	
Kow, *m*	**Cooling, Sedative, &c.**	**Punjaub in general.**
Kulfa	**Astringent, Cooling**	**Ditto ditto.**
Kasence,	**Cooling, Sedative**	**Ditto ditto.**
Kurm		**Ditto ditto.**
Quaar Gundul, *m*	**Aloes**	**Ditto ditto.**
Poodhena,	**Peppermint**	**Ditto ditto.**
Neaz Bo, *m*	**Mint**	**Ditto ditto.**
Baboona, *m*	**Camomile**	**Ditto ditto.**
Lassoora		**Ditto ditto.**
Pugwara		**Ditto ditto.**
Kutch Naar, *m*	**Astringent**	**Ditto ditto.**
Hirrind Tele, *m*	**Castor Oil**	**Ditto ditto and Hills.**
Lac Dye	**Lac**	**Ditto ditto ditto.**
Telia, black and white, *m*	**Escarotic & Virulent Poison**	**Ditto ditto ditto.**
Nirbubsy, *m*		**Ditto ditto ditto.**
Tulsee, *m*	**Mint**	**Ditto ditto ditto.**
Meroon, *m*	**Mint**	**Ditto ditto ditto.**
Beedana, *m*	**Emollient**	**Ditto ditto ditto.**
Main Pull, *m*	**Emetic, good**	**Ditto ditto ditto.**
Castooree, *m*	**Castor**	**Kúbett.**

Native Appellations.	*English Names.*	*Places where Produced.*
Pum, Pushmeena........	....	Ledock — Thibet — Ooskoordoo.
Hermull, *m*	Wild Rue Seed	Kameele—Wormwood.
Thulsee, Carminative, *m* ..	Sweet Basil	Aangeer—Fig.
Nerbissee, *m*	Zedoary	Bee—Citron.
Lobia	Cabbage	
Neel o Phir, *m*	Water Lily	
Gool Kyra, *m*...........	Lily of the Valley	
Jaipull, *m*	Nutmeg	
Jemaall Gota, *m*	Croton, Cathartic	
Googull, *m*	Gum Bedillium......	
Noc Chikkun, *m*	Euphorbium	

TREES AND SHRUBS.

Bore		
Peepull		
Burna		
Thunn		
Cheell .... }	Fir Dale	
Bear .... }		
Purwa..................		
Vun....................		
Jund		
Kereer Seed, *m*..........	Astringent	
Kikker, *m*	Ditto	
Tallee	Sissoo	
Kutch Naul*		
Swaingena Seed, *m*		
Ferm Kikker		
Saffedha	White Poplar	
Chunara		
Cymbull		
Gool Nesthur...........		
Emlee, Astringent, *m*	Tamarind	
Aum*	Mangoe	
Jummoo		
Bere,* Nutritive, *m*	Emollient	
Lesoora		
Aula*		
Kou.................. }	A kind of Box Wood	
Lou .... }		
Pullaih		
Behera*		
Hareere*		
Kire...................		
Gondee		
Pona		
Dreke,* *m*	Bitter Tonic	Hills.
Nim,* *m*	Ditto ditto	
Jainthe	....	Punjaub.
Birmimee	....	Hills.
Ecrote*		
Emlook		
Pugwara*		

Native Appellations.	*English Names.*	*Places where Produced.*
Bedam, *m*	Almonds, Emollient..	Punjaub.
Anar,* *m*	Pomgranite	Ditto.
Pull		Hills.
Mojenoo		Punjaub.
Eeroo		Hills.
Hor Singaar		Punjaub.
Gool Cheen		Hills.
Reroo		Punjaub.
Kameela, *m*	Seed is Purgative	Hills.
Kukera		Ditto.
Gurria		Ditto.
Sirree		Punjaub and Hills.
Bere Lac		Punjaub, &c.
Ikker		Hills.
Gurna		Ditto.

MINERALOGICAL PRODUCTIONS.

Coal, of 4 sorts	Hills, n. and w.
Galena, 3 kinds, &c. &c	Hills, in different parts
Iron, 5 kinds, &c.	Hills, the entire north, &c.
Salt-rock, 3 kinds	Salt ranges
Alum, Kolabang	Kolabang & salt range
Borax, Ledok, &c. &c.	Thibett
Sulphur, Mineral, &c.	Cashmeer, Kurwar and salt range
Sulphate of Iron	Hills, n. & salt range
Pyritees, Iron	Ditto ditto ditto
Ditto, Copper and Iron	Ditto ditto ditto
Crystal rock	Kustwar and Hills
Sulphate, Copper Mineral, Gilghit	Thibet and Gilghit
Copper Mines, Ooskurdoo and Gilghit	
Gold, sand* and native†	* All the Rivers. †Thibet, Leddoack, &c.
Manganese, Black and Grey Ox	Hills, Jummoo
Antimony, Sulphuret	Kaagaam, Gilghit
Saltpetre, or Nitrate of Potass fields, &c.	Punjaub and Bar
Muriate of Amonia	Lahore, m. and Thibet, native
Lapis Lazuli, Gilghit	
Nickel Pyrites	Hills, n. salt range
Cobalt ditto	Ditto ditto ditto.
Mica, 3 sorts	N. Hills

MANUFACTURES OF THE PUNJAUB, AND IN THE STATES DEPENDANT ON IT.

Plain tanned Leather, of all sorts, &c.
Green, Red, Black, &c., dyed Goat and Calf Skins.
Choumuct or Grained Ass Leather.
Chamois Leather, dressed, &c. &c.
Indigo, Moultan and Jummoo, &c.
Opium, Panjaub in general.
Shawl and Pushmeena, &c., Panjaub and Cashmeer, &c.
Chintz, Saubu and the Hills.
Gool Buddun, or Striped Silk Stuffs.
Derü, or Plain Silk Stuff.
Silk, &c., Scarfs, Moultan, &c., embroidered.
Coarse Woollen Cloths, Kunla-Looe, &c.
Camel Hair Cloth.
Fine and Coarse Cotton Cloths.
Glass and Glass Beads.
Paper of different sorts.
Fine Date and Straw Net, &c., Work.
Vinegar, from Grapes, &c.
Needles.
Lahore, famous for its bow and arrows.
Gold and silver and Tin and Zinc Wire Lace and Leaf.
Damasked and plain Iron Matchlocks and Swords, &c. Daggers, &c.
Steel and Iron Chain Armour.
Famous Snuff of Peshawar.
Sulphuric, Nitric, Muriate and Nitro Muriate, &c. &c. Acids.
Muriate of Amonia.
Saltpetre or Nitre.
Alum.
Potass.
Soda.
Ivory Work, made and dyed, of all sorts and colours.
Sulphate of Copper, Lahore.
Super Acetate of ditto ditto.
Borax, purified, &c.
Soap.
Purified Wax and Yellow Candles.
Cinnibar, Lahore.

A LIST OF THE DIFFERENT CASTES IN THE PUNJAUB.

h for Hindoo—m for Mahomedan, and sks. for Seik.

Rajpoot or 1st Class.

Soorj boonse, *h.*
Chunder Bunse, *h.*
Jumwall, *h.*
Chumiall, *h.*
Samiall, *h.*
Menass, *h.*
Salire, *h.* and *m.*
Rekwall, *h.*
Bow, *h.* and *m.*
Chib, *m.* and *h.*
Jelall, ditto ditto.
Chundraall, ditto ditto.
Suddun, *m.*
Suttee, *m.*
Dhoonde, *m.*
Chittreall, *m.*
Pethour, *m.* and *h.*
Chouhan, *m.* and *h.*
Kukka, *m.*
Bomba, *m.*
Goree, *m.* and *h.*
Rungur, *m.*
Thoor, *m.*
Pidaall, *m.*
Sukker, *m.*
Naroo, *m.*
Koker, *m.*
Buttee, *m.*
Johei, *m.*
Pavaan, *m.*
Kotouche, *h.*——31.

Kotthree or Chetree, 2nd Class.

Kunneh, 2½ Ghura, } 4 great Families, *h.*
Kopoor, ... }
Seth, ... }
Medouthere, ... }
Jagull, *h.*
Choperat, *h.*
Vadoun, *h.*
Lack Vurria, *h.*
Saami ock, *h.*
Thoolee, *h.*
Thalwar, *h.*
Maatheh, *h.*
Puree, *h.*
Mundeh, *h.*
Mundra joga, *h.*
Anund, *h.*
Nigereth, *h.*
Chouger, *h.*
Kochen, *h.*
Doogull, *h.*
Siothereh, *h.*
Kokeh, *h.*

Bolle wallia, *h.* all Hindoos.
Bobera.
Soe.
Chheddeh.
Rora.
Baunia.——28.

Jate, or 3rd Class.

Bojooa, *sks.*
Veeruk, *sks.*
Gill, *sks.*
Avan, *sks.* and *m.* few.
Duluck, *sks.*
Kukker, ditto.
Lollee, ditto.
Akaulee, ditto.
Gudger, *m.*
Eer, *h.* Itinerate.
Harrei, *m.*
Cheema, *sks.*
Chetta, *m.* and *h.*
Chaïl, ditto ditto.
Doogull, ditto ditto.
Rathaves, ditto ditto.
Saü, ditto ditto.
Goudull, *sks.* and *m.*
Ranja, *m.* and *h.*
Seetra, *sks.* and *m.*
Seecale, ditto ditto.
Trigur, ditto ditto.
Theheem, ditto ditto
Lack, ditto ditto.
Nichun, ditto ditto.
Mingeu, ditto ditto.
Tewanna, *m.*
Jelother, ditto.
Kotia, ditto.
Herl, ditto.
Curl, ditto.
Gurai, *m.*
Buugu, *sks.*
Behere, *sks.*
Naugere, *sks.*
Sole, *sks.*
Doul, *sks.*
Deu, *sks.*
Dèthe, *sks.*
Saawull, *sks.*
Cheder, *sks.*
Dulloo, *m.* and *sks.*
Dother, *sks.* and *m.*
Jurah, ditto ditto.
Surah, ditto ditto.
Athar, ditto ditto.
Hathar, ditto ditto.
Buter, ditto ditto.
Raah, ditto.
Maun, *sks.*
Buller, *sks.* and *m.*
Hère, *sks.*
Tharer, *sks.* and *m.*
Veraich, *m.* and *sks.*
Lidder, *m.* and *sks.*
Mongeth, ditto ditto.
Hanjerah, ditto ditto.
Monèse, *m.* and *sks.*
Hase, ditto ditto.
Vuttoo, ditto ditto.
Dilloo, *sks.* and *m.*
Mollee, ditto ditto.
Busserah, ditto ditto.
Vaise, *sks.* &c. few *m.*
Somret, *m.* and few *sks.*
Soomraah, *m.* mostly.
Saatheh, *m.* ditto.
Ootherah, *m.*
Vaunder, *m.*
Tinset, *m.*
Shopel, *m.* mostly.
Sundoo, *sks.* and *m.*
Sindoo, ditto ditto.
Vunon, ditto ditto.
Saungreh, ditto ditto.
Tuddy, ditto ditto.
Merolet, ditto ditto.
Velainche, *sks.* and few *m.*
Lilleh, *sks.*
Kellassun, *sks.* and *m.*
Thauriwall, ditto ditto.——81.

Koomeen, or 4th Class.

Telia, *m.*
Mochee, *m.*
Maachee, *m.*
Maskee, *m.*
Mire, *h.*
Jeur, *h.*
Chunger, *m.*
Kirkira, *m.*
Perpunja, *m.*
Doby, *m.*
Berwala, *m.*
Nü, *sks.* and *m.*
Doom, *m.*
Bramin, *h.*
Putt, *h.* and *m.* Itinerate.
Merassee, *m.*
Kunger, *h.* and *m.*
Kainchen, ditto ditto.
Sutt Kunger, ditto, Itinerate.
Maithum, *m.*
Gorekuud, *m.*
Nutt, *m.* Itinerate.
Baazyghur, *h.* Itinerate.
Molla, *m.* and *h.*
Marwaree, *h.*
Kelunder, *m.*
Thurkaan, *sks.* and *m.*
Sovar, ditto ditto.
Mussellee, *m.*
Mudjbee, *sks.*
Soniar, *sks.* *h.* and *m.*

Naria, *m.*
Tatiar, *h. sks.* and *m.*
Kummiar, *m.*
Kolloll, *m.* and *h.*
Kukkazye, *m.*
Jogee, *m.* and *h.*
Decount, *h.*
Acharjee, *h.*
Koja, *m.*
Gogerat, *m.* and partly itinerate.——41.

Bramin Castes.

Kolia.
Gour.
Gottuck.
Chibber.
Tuk.
Rickea.
Motera.
Acharjee.——8.

The Four great classes of Mahometans.

Seid.
Sheik.
Mogull.
Patann.
Khoresee.

The Lowest Class.

Churah, partly itinerate.
Saansee, itinerate.
Gondehlah, ditto.
Bouria, ditto,
Bungee, partly ditto.
Butwall, partly ditto.
Meg, partly ditto.
Berhera, itinerate.
Gogera Cheera, ditto.——9.
Jinsee.
Mauthom.
Baroopia.
Sepaida.
Godeela.
Hollol Kore.——15.

AN ESTIMATE OF THE POPULATION OF DIFFERENT CITIES IN THE PUNJAUB.

3,000	Shops	Lahore.
14,500	Families	
72,500	Inhabitants	
4,500	Shops	Umritsir.
12,000	Families	
60,000	Inhabitants	
2,500	Shops	Cashmeer.
12,000	Families	
65,000	Inhabitants	
1,800	Shops	Moulthan.
9,000	Families	
45,000	Inhabitants	
2,000	Shops	Peshawer.
10,000	Families	
55,000	Inhabitants	
300	Shops	Ismeil Kanko Dera.
1,500	Families	
8,000	Inhabitants	
250	Shops	Jummoo.
1,600	Families	
10,000	Inhabitants	

AN ESTIMATE OF THE POPULATION OF THE DIFFERENT DISTRICTS AND COUNTRIES OF THE PUNJAUB.

The whole valley of Cashmeer, including the City itself, and the New Possession of Ghilghit Kukka Bomba and Kaagaan Mozeffrebad	550,000

Moultan, including the whole of the dependencies within Ko Kote—and all along the East Bank of the Indus—with the Baar and Kurl Courtage, &c. &c....................................	750,000
Peshawer, including all its dependencies across the Indus, with Eusophzye and North of the Loonda Quart, &c. &c............	600,000
Ismeil Khan Ke Dera, including all its dependencies on the West of the Indus, Dera Gazee Khan Bunnoo—Kolabauz Tank—Kolatchee, &c.	450,000
Jummoo, including the whole and entire northern range of Hill Country, from the Setledge to the Indus—with Lehdock and its dependencies and Doskoordso, &c. and Little Thibet—Jeskard. But excepting Chauba and all other independent states, as also Cashmeer and its dependencies	1,100,000
Lahore, including all the Tract of Country, &c. and districts not before mentioned, but including Umritsur and the Manju Country—and all other dependencies except the Dooab, and the former Protected Sikh States on the East Bank of the Setledge, &c. &c.	1,900,000
Total Inhabitants of the Punjaub at present	53,50,000

LIST OF SIRDARS AND CHIEFS.

The following is a list of the Sirdars and Chiefs, who have been killed since the death of Runjeet Sing.

1. Chete Sing, murdered by Dehan Sing.
2. Maharajah Kurruck Sing, poisoned by ditto.
3. Maharajah Nonihal Sing, made away with by ditto, but in what way not known.
4. Omeer Sing, (Alloowallah,) drowned by Maharajah Sheer Sing.
5. Chund Kour, wife of Kurruck Sing, and mother of Nonihal Sing, stoned to death by order of Sheer Sing.
6. Mahtab Sing, (Kootooa,) killed by Rajah Dehan Sing.
7. Juwallah Sing, (Jeur,) ditto ditto.
8. Maharajah Sheer Sing, shot by Ajeet Sing, (Scindiawallah.)
9. Sirdar Bhood Sing, (Jeur,) killed by Ajeet Sing's people.
10. Pertaub Sing, eldest son of Sheer Sing, killed by Lena Sing, (Scindia-wallah.)
11. Dehan Sing, shot by one of Ajeet Sing's sowars.
12. Lena Sing, (Scindiawallah,) killed in fight with Heera Sing.
13. Ajeet Sing, killed in fight with Heera Sing.
14. Beldam Sing, killed by order of Heera Sing.
15. Bely Ram Misser, killed by order of Heera Sing.
16. Miser Ram Kissen, his brother, ditto.
17. Bhaiee Gurmuck Sing, killed by order of Heera Sing.
18. Rajah Suchet Sing, killed by order of Heera Sing.
19. Kesera Sing, killed by order of Heera Sing.
20. Dewan Bheem Sing, killed by order of Heera Sing.
21. Baba Beer Sing, killed in fight with Heera Sing's Troops.
22. Cashmera Sing, killed in fight with Heera Sing's Troops.
23. Utter Sing, (Scindiawallah,) killed in fight with Heera Sing's Troops.
24. General Goolaub Sing, shot by Utter Sing, (Scindiawallah.)
25. Rajah Heera Sing, killed in fight with the Khalsa Troops.
26. Pundit Julla, ditto ditto.
27. Meean Laub Sing, ditto ditto.
28. Meean Sone Sing, ditto ditto.
29. Nikka Dewan Chund, ditto ditto.
30. Futty Sing, (Maun,) killed by Goolaub Sing's people.

31. Ruthonoo Chonderee, and Visier to Heera Sing, killed by Goolaub Sing's people.
32. Dewan Gunputt, ditto ditto.
33. Prince Peshora Sing, ditto ditto
34. Jowahir Sing, ditto ditto.
35. Baba Ruttone Sing, ditto ditto.
36. Bii Chetha Sing, ditto ditto.

Chiefs and Sirdars that have died natural deaths since the death of Runjeet Sing.

1. Jemadar Kooseeall Sing.
2. Jewan Sing, (Mookul.)
3. Colonel Donkal Sing.
4. Ameer Sing, (Maun.)—Leg broke by accident.
5. Faqueer Shah Ooddeen, (son of Uzezoodden.)
6. Gen. Ram Sing, (son of Kooseal Sing.)
7. Faqueer Azez Ooddeen.

Sirdars and Chiefs killed in the late actions with the British.

1. Chutter Sing, (Khollawallah,) at Ferozeshah.
2. Gunda Sing, (Koonjea,) ditto.
3. Goolaub Sing, (Kapta,) ditto.
4. Sham Sing, (Attareewallah,) at Sobraon.
5. Kishan Sing, (son of Kooseeall Sing,) ditto.
6. Mavor Sing Majeeteea, ditto.
7. General Maka Khan, ditto.
8. Colonel Imaum Shah, ditto.
9. Mungloo (brother of Mungola,) ditto.
10. Heera Sing, (Topee,) ditto.
11. Hookum Sing (Mulwaye,) ditto.
12. Dewan Ramdetha, ditto.

List of Chiefs and Sirdars at present living at Lahore.

1. Rajah Lall Sing, a Brahmin, who has risen from the rank of Muleeteer to be Minister of State.

2. Sirdar Teja Sing, (commonly called Tej Sing,) Commander-in-Chief.

3. Dewan Deenanauth, a clever, cool-headed man.

4. Utter Sing, Kholawallah, (brother of Chutter Sing, killed at Ferozeshah,) cold in manner, and timid, but well meaning.

5. Chutter Sing, Attareewallah, (cousin of Sham Sing, Attareewallah,) and father of Sheer Sing, Governor of Peshawer.) He is crafty, designing, and intriguing.

6. Kaer Sing, Scindiawallah, (son of Utter Sing, deceased.) He is a good, well meaning young man.

7. Shumsheer Sing, Scindiawallah, (son of the famous Bhood Sing, deceased, and cousin of the above :)—a man of more talent and more tact than any of his family.

8. Buggut Ram, one who has enriched himself and family by bribes.

9. Bii Ram Sing, seemingly a cunning, quiet, harmless person.

10. Dewan Jawahir Mull, a man of no character whatsoever.

11. Dewan Huckeem Ra, a deep, unprincipled intriguer.

ABSTRACT,

SHOWING THE DISPOSITION OF THE SIKH ARMY, 1ST JULY, 1844.

STATION.	Infantry.	Cavalry.	Artillery.		
			Men.	Guns.	Swivels.
Lahore	16,820	14,675	2,475	238	395
On furlough	19,600	5,300	560	50	50
Mitha Towana, (Dera Ismael Khan)	2,500	1,500	20	4	....
Jummoo Hills	8,000	2,750	600	50	300
Poonch Hills	500	....	....	....	....
Bhimbur Hills	500	....	....	....	....
Nowshehra Hills	1,500	....	40	10	....
Reeasee Hills	3,000	....	100	22	....
Ludakh	2,000	....	40	10	....
Syed Ghur, (foot of hills)	2,000	500	30	10	....
Pind Dadun Khan, (on Jhelum)	500	....	....	....	....
Ramnugger Hills	2,000	....	30	8	....
Samba Hills	3,000	400	60	8	25
Jesrota Hills	5,000	500	60	8	....
Jalundhur Doab, Beas and Sutlej	1,000	200	40	4	....
Cashmeer	2,300	400	100	14	....
Muzzufferabad, (near to Cashmeer)	500	....	....	....	....
Hussoora, (N. W. of Cashmeer)	500	....	....	....	....
Ghilghit	1,000	....	20	4	....
Shahdura, (Lahore)	100	100	....	....	....
Attok	....	100	....	....	....
Hussun Ubdal, (near Attok)	....	900	60	....	50
Peshawer	5,700	400	140	14	....
Yoosufzaees, (N. E. of Peshawer)	400	100	60	6	....
Huzara, (E. of Attok)	3,100	....	80	8	....
Tank, (Dera Ismael Khan)	1,500	400	30	....	25
Mooltan	3,500	500	235	40	70
Kote Mithun, (Junction of Indus and Sutlej)	500	....	....	....	....
Rojhan, (near Sukkur)	500	....	....	....	....
Syedwallah, } near DeraGhazee }	....	250	....	....	....
Sunghur, } Khan }	400	250	....	....	....
In the neighbourhood of Mooltan	1,500	500	....	....	....
Koonjah, (near Vuzeerabad)	200	300	20	4	....
Kohat, (Peshawer)	600	500	45	4	25
Dooaba, (near Peshawer)	500	300	25	2	15
Hushtnuggur, (Peshawer)	600	400	40	8	15
In the Kangra Hills	5,000	....	....	....	....
Suraj, (Kooloo Hills)	1,000	....	....	....	....
Mujethea, (Umritsir)	....	400	15	2	....
Teelook Nath, (Hills)	200	....	....	....	....
With Sirdar Lena Sing Mujeetheea	200	100	....	....	....
Adeena Nuggur, (Hills)	200	....	....	....	....
Kussoor, (opposite Ferozepore)	200	....	60	8	....
Azaree, (near Umritsir)	200	100	10	2	....
Kupoorthulla, (near the Beas)	2,000	1,300	120	12	....
Sultanpore, (ditto)	200	....	45	2	25
On the Ferries of the Sutlej	500	800	....	....	....

(Signed) J. D. CUNNINGHAM,

Assist.-Agent, Governor-General, N. W. Frontier.

THE BOUNDARY OF THE PUNJAUB IN 1845.

On the North-west to the village and small fort of Ookole, about twelve miles N. of Booloosliere, and about twenty-five miles of N. W. of Gilghit, two years ago taken and governed by the Suba of Cashmeer. Thence N. E. towards Chaolooa, a small fort to the north boundary of Bultheestan, and but twelve miles south of the Khara Koorum range; thence E. S. E. to Peeka the N. boundary of Koofaloon; thence E. towards Taupuphaun N. of Nobra or Loobraun or Lubra; thence S. E. towards the Thoongleeng pass, N. E. of Juskaur; thence to Pautoo, N. E. boundary of Chumba; thence along the N. boundary of Kooloo, which forms the N. E. angle; thence winding down S. towards Sookethe, a little to the S. or S. E. of which the river forms the boundary; thence following the whole line of the river S. and S. W. to Mitten ko Kote, or Nawan, which forms the S. extremity; thence turning upwards N. W. towards Hadjeghur or the Rowant pass; thence N. along the east but of the Soolymaun range towards Sailpe or Sungur; thence along the E. base of the visier range to Serveur Ghur, fifteen or sixteen miles W. of Taunk; thence again N. towards Dhelass Khan ko Ghurree, the W. boundary of Bunnoo; thence N. to Thelumber, a fort on the N. boundary of Bunnoo; thence again S. E. back to Kharabaug, a fort on the W. bank of the Indus; thence N. along the E. bank to Neelaub ko Putthon, or (improperly) Putton; thence to Zaareth or Kooma, twelve miles W. of the Attock fort; thence W. towards Koopaut; thence N. towards Futtyghur, a fort at or near the Khyber Pass; thence to Mitchenee, and thence to Loonquoor, and thence E. along the base of the Eusophzye range to Maa Bunn and Der or Dherbund; thence it may be said to run northward along the E. bank of the range to Sooghoor, or where it may join the Ghilghit district.

e

A LIST OF THE PRINCIPAL SIRDARS AND CHIEFS IN THE PUNJAUB, CLASSED ACCORDING TO THE PARTY THEY WERE SUPPOSED TO SIDE WITH AFTER THE DEATH OF SHERE SING.

Dulleep Sing, on the Guddee.
Rajah Heera Sing, Minister.

Dogeras or Rajpoots, &c. { The Chumba Rajah, Chumba.
Ditto Seeba ditto, Seeba.
Ditto Patankote ditto, Patankote. }

* Sirdar Nihal Sing, Alloowalla, Kopoorthella.
* Ditto Kishen Sing, Kooshall Sing's son, Lahore.
\+ Ditto Teja Sing, Governor of Peshawer.
* Ditto Futty Sing Mann, Peshawer.
* Ditto Lena Sing Majeeteea, at present absent, Benares.
\+ Ditto Rungore Sing, ditto, younger brother, Hills.
* Ditto Sham Sing, Attareewalla, Kussoor.
\+ Ditto Shumshere Sing, Scindawalla, Peshawer.
\+ Ditto Utter Sing, Kollewalla, Umritsir.
* Bela Sing, Nekei, Lahore.
\+ Gunda Sing, Busthenee, Rammuggur or Russool, ditto.
* Gooroo Sadoo Sing, Katharpooria.
* All the rest of the Gooroos, Babas, &c. &c.
* Gunda Sing, Molwahi.
\+ Utter Sing, Nerena, or Kolloowallah.
* Jewar Sing, uncle to the Maha Rajah.
\+ Lol Sing, Treasurer or Thoshokonia.
\+ Faqueer Azoozoo Deen, invalided, Lahore.
\+ Ditto Nooroo Deen his younger brother, Lahore.
Nehal Sing, Visier to the late Rajah Suchet Sing.
\+ Bii Ram Sing, on a mission to Jummoo.
\+ Mungall Sing, brother in-law to No Nehal Sing.
\+ Boor Sing, Shere Sing's Mucktear and Kordar, &c.
\+ Eeseraa Sing, Mucktear of Rajah Suchet Sing.
\+ Sown Mull, Governor of Moultan, if alive.
\+ The Sons and family of ditto.
\+ All or most of the Generals and other officers of the Army.

Dogeras or Rajpoots. { Rajah Goolaub Sing.
Meean Jewar Sing, brother to Rajah Heera Sing.
Ditto Sone Sing, present eldest son of Rajah Goolab Sing, Jumboo.
Ditto Peenoo or Runbeer Sing, younger do.—Samba and Rammugger
Ditto Etoowa illegitimate son of do.—Putwar.
Ditto Laub Sing and son—Lahore and Jumboo.
Ditto Urbela Sing, Guzerat Chinaub.
Ditto Jewar Sing—Ra Kesree Sing's son. }

* Rajah Haree Mula Khan, Rajouree.
* Ex Rajah Deall Sing, Chimnee.
* Ex Do. Fyzull Daol Khan, Rentass and Doomiein.
* Do. Do. { Shaw Velly Khan Guekker of Greek descent.
* Do. Do. Futty Alli Khan ditto, Perwalla and Kohoutty.
* Do. Do. Ali Gouh Khan ditto, Godera and Rowel Pindee. }

These three are descendents of the original Princes of the entire Putwarr, Dhonnee and Gebe countries, and as far North as Mozeffrabad. Rajah Hodee, Rajah Sir Cop, and Rajah Labow, &c. &c. &c. were all Gukkers, &c. &c. on the Indus.

* Ex Rajah Fyzull Shaw, Dhunnee.
* Do. Do. Mamood Khan, Gebee.
* Do. Do. Seeunder Khan, Mokudd.
* Do. Do. Sultan Zubber Dost, Mozeffrabad.
* Do. Do. Ali Mamoud, Gool Teree.

* Ex Rajah Sher Bazz, Poonah.
* Do. Do. Ameer Khan, Soorumthee.
* Do. Do. Shums Khan, Perl and Sudun.
* Do. Do. other numerous Mahomedan Rajahs.
* Amed Shaw ex King of little Thibet or Buthcestan, a prisoner or Hostage, Custwar, or dead.
* Nawoor Seen, son of the late Rajah of Ledock, Jumboo, or Custwar.
Ex Rajah Murthezar Khan, Kuddy Kuddi Aly.
\+ Shaik Goolam Mia deen, Governor of Cashmeer, and family, son, &c.
\+ Chettur Sing, Attareewalla.
\+ Jewar Sing Kolollwalla.
\+ Chunda Sing, Chowvindia.
} Dewan Deena Naut.
} Do. Jewar Mull.

---

* This mark points out those persons that (should they dare) would be the acknowledged and rancorous enemies of both Rajah Heera Sing, and Rajah Goolaub Sing, and all their Family. These may be called the Anti-Dogra Faction.

\+ Those marked thus are supposed from wisdom, fear or other reasons to appear as much as possible neutral in all respects, but were always in fact found to be the very people that have done and continue to do more injury than any other—as they are never on one side but always sure to be trifling and deeply intriguing on both sides of every matter and question. They are always and in reality unconnected with any party, but in fact at the bottom instigating in both or every party.—It may be said that they are even unconnected among themselves, and each, to forward his own private ends, would sacrifice his nearest of kin; and, it is remarkable, that those very people always, at least to the present moment, contrived and so managed their policy, that while they benefitted themselves during all the disturbances, well feathered their nests—still not one of them ever has been a sufferer in any of the disturbances.

Should any fair or proper opportunity offer—there would be three acknowledged Parties or Factions.

Each avowed enemies to the other, viz. {
The Seik, impolitic and careless.
The Dogra or Hill Rajpoot, the richest, fewest, but most politic.
The Mahomedan, the most numerous, but poorest.

THE NUMERICAL FORCE OF THE STANDING ARMY OF THE PUNJAUB, IN 1845.]

Battalions.	
8	at Peshawer, relieved every two years.
2	at Hazara, ditto ditto.
2	at Cashmeer, stationary.
2	at Moultan, ditto.
20	gone on operations against Rajah Goolaub Sing.
16	at present at the seat of Government.
50	
600	strong each.
30,000	Total regulars belonging to the state.

Sirdars, Battalions.

Battalions.	
2	Meean Jewar Sing, Nowsheira.
8	Rajah Goolaub Sing, Jummoo.
6	Rajah Heera Sing, including two of the late minister.
2	Rajah Suchet Sing, Samba.
2	Ra Kesree Sing, Samba.
1	Meean Laub Sing.
21	all Dogra or Hill men.

These computations were made in April and May, 1845.

2	Lena Sing Majeeteea, Lahore.	These computations were made in April and May, 1845.
2	Alloo Alleea, Kapoo Thella.	
25		
600	each.	
15,000	Total.	
15,000	add to this the above.	
30,000		
45,000	Total regular infantry of the Punjaub.	

Regular Horse.

8	Regiments.
500	each.
4,000	Total, Regulars.

Irregular Horse or Gorechers.

4000	Chariaree Dera.
3000	Mothee Ram ko Dera.
2000	Wooda Gorechars.
2000	Orderly ko dera.
11000	To these Camps may be added
11000	more, including all Stragglers, Missuldaurs and Jageerdaurs.
22,000	Total Irregular Cavalry.

In all Horse and Foot 67,000, with 276 pieces of Ordnance, 163 of which are Horse Artillery.

The entire armed population of the country at present does not exceed 1,50,000, of all casts and religions, &c. &c. &c. It could not produce more, this is the highest average or estimation.

(These computations were made in April and May, 1845.)

OFFICERS WHO HAVE BEEN OR ARE IN THE SEIK SERVICE.

Alvarine	Italian	Infantry	Died at Lahore.
Gordon	Anglo-Indian.	Cavalry	Ditto.
Ventura	Italian	Infantry	Left.
Allard	French	Cavalry	Died at Peshawur.
Court	Ditto	Artillery	Left.
Avitabile	Italian	Infantry	Ditto.
Hommus	Spaniard	Ditto	Died at Lahore.
Vochen	Russian	Ditto	Left.
Honigberger	German	Medical	Still in the service.
Dottenwise	Ditto	Engineer	Left.
Harlan	American	Civil	Left.
De l'Ust	French	Infantry	Left.
Holmes	Anglo-Indian	Ditto	Still in the Service.
Dubignon	French	Ditto	At present a Merchant at Lahore.
Hest	Greek	Ditto	Killed at Lahore.
Hurelcek	Ditto	Ditto	Left.
McPherson	English	Ditto	Ditto.
Gardner	American	Artillery	Ditto.

Kunarah	American....	Artillery....	Still in the Service.
Cortlandt	Anglo-Indian.	Infantry....	Ditto.
Fitzroy	Ditto	Ditto	Left.
Barlow	Ditto	Ditto	Ditto.
Mouton..........	French	Cavalry	Ditto.
Steinbach..........	German	Infantry....	At present in Golab Sing's Service.
De la Roche........	French	Ditto	Killed by a fall from his horse.
De la Font, 1st.....	Ditto	Ditto	Left the Service.
De la Font, 2nd.....	Ditto	Ditto	Ditto.
Foulkes	English	Cavalry	Killed by the Seiks.
Hurbon	Spaniard	Engineers..	Left the Service.
Leslie	Anglo-Indian.	Infantry....	Ditto ditto.
Martindale	Ditto	Ditto	Ditto.
Ford	English	Ditto	Died by wounds, &c. received from the Sikhs.
De Fasheye	French	Cavalry	Died at Lahore.
Ditto, Son..........	Ditto	Ditto	Left the Service.
Dr. Harvey..........	Scotch......	Medical....	Ditto.
Jervais..........	French......	Infantry....	Ditto.
Mœrvious	Prussian	Ditto	Ditto.
Bianchi..........	Italian......	Ditto	Ditto.
Argou..........	French......	Ditto	Ditto.

AMOUNT OF REVENUE OR MONEY PAID INTO THE TREASURY, FOR 1844.

Lacks.	
36	from Moultan.
12½	do. Cashmeer.
2¼	do. Dooab.
9	Nuseerabad.
15	Barr and Lena Mundee.
7	Moukera.
1	Bunnoo.
1	Lena Sing, for the Hill Provinces.
11	Tazes and Tolls, &c.
22	from different other small districts, &c. &c. &c.
116¾	Total in Lacks, received.
5	Hoffroee, or Toxeer are made.
121¾	Total.*

Total expense of all the troops at the present rate of 11½ rupees to each Infantry man, and 30 per mensem to all horse, including all officer's pay, commissariat, and other expenses.

30,000 Infantry .... Rs.	6,422,000
15,000 Horse; the remainder being Jageerdaurs	5,400,000
Artillery, total expense, cattle, &c. &c.	1,000,000
	12,822,000

Or about 128 lacks.

* The entire or total revenue of all the territories, &c., within the boundary line mentioned, including all Jageerdars, Grants of Lands, Theumurts or Benefices, &c. &c. would amount, if properly governed or managed, to upwards of four crores of rupees, or about four millions of English money,

PRODUCTS AND MANUFACTURES.

A List of the products and manufactures, especially the Hills north of the Punjaub, Cashmere, Ledock, Doskoordoo, Bulthistan, or Little Thibett, Gilghitt, Bhothan, &c. &c.—which might be made to constitute part of the commerce between those parts and the surrounding countries, or between northern Asia in general and Lower Scinde, Kurratchee, or Bombay—by means of the River Indus and its tributary streams, or rivers Cheenaub, Ghelum, &c. &c.

Agate.
Alabaster.
Almonds.
Aloes.
Aniseed.
Arsenic.
Asphaltum.
Apples.
Aumulthrape.
Alum—Putkeree, Kholabarry—2½-3.

Bamboo.
Barilla, Barr, Sedjee—1-1½.
Bears' Skins, Grease, Hams, &c.
Beaver.
Beryl.
Black Lead, or Plumbago.
Boœ Wood.
Beherah.
Benuflita, Borax or Borete of Soda.

Cantharides.
Caraway Seed.
Casia.
Castor Oil.
Catechu Gum and Wood—Kuth.
Chamois Skins, Leather, &c.
Civet.
Cork-wood.
Copper—from the mine in the Hills.
Coral—Russian, Siberian and Chinese.
Coriander Seeds.
Cotton—*raw and manufactured.—*5-6-7-8.
Crystal—Rock.
Camel Hair—raw and manufactured.
Coal—Mineral, of various sorts.
Charcoal—Cobal tore—Chernss—Carthamus. 10-12.

Deals—in Planks or Logs of different sorts—5-6 per Beam.
Dragon's Blood.
Diamonds found in the Mundee District.

Ebony-wood.
Emery.
Ermine.

Figs.
Flax—1-1½-2.
Fuller's Earth.
Furs of various sorts.
Fustic—Okell Beer.

Galls.
Garnett.
Gentian.
Ginger
Gold—Dust, and Ingots, &c.
Grapes.
Guiacum—8-10.
Gum, Glue—Grain of various sorts.
Gypsum.
Ghoots—Galena, Argentiferous, &c. &c. &c.

Horses—Honey—4-5-6.
Hemp—2-2½-3—Thread 2½-3—maund.
Hareere.
Herbs—medicinal and dyes of various sorts.
Horns of various kinds and animals—1-5 koree.

Indian Wheat—Maize, &c. &c.
Indigo.
Ipecacuanha.
Iron—3-4-5-6.

Jalap.
Jasper.
Jet.

Kei or Sulpate of Iron-crude, &c. ½ 1—Kholabang.
Kuth or Ruth—Catechus wood—Kussumba.

Lac.
Lapis Lazuli.
Lemons.
Lignum vitæ.
Limes.
Loadstone.
Logwood.
Leather of various sorts—Bussee—8 10-12 koree.
Lead, from the mines.

Madder 2½-3-4—Bunnoo, Taunk 3½ 3

Magnetic Iron-ore, &c. of different kinds. Pyrites, &c.
Mahogony, Indian.
Maize.
Manganese, Black and grey Oxides from the mines.
Marble, of various sorts and colours.
Molasses—2-2½-3—Doaba—Umritsir.
Mica.
Musk.
Mules.

Naphtha.
Natron.
Nitre—1 Rupee—Man—Nekah—Bara—Sheerah.

Onyx.
Opium.
Oranges.
Orpiment.
Ottar of Roses.
Oulah.
Okellbeer.

Papyrus.
Pearl Ash.
Potass, Carbonate.
Petroleum.
Pitch—4-5.
Platina.
Plantain, Gum seed, Fruit.
Pine-apple seed, wood, &c.
Plumbago.
Pomegranite—rind, seed, fruit.
Porphyry, of various sorts and colours, &c. &c.
Peshum—Raw and manufactured of various kinds.
Pyrites—Iron and Copper, &c. &c.
Paper—Cashmeer and Tartary, &c. &c.

Quassia—Indian.

Raisins.
Resins of various sorts.
Rice—Bara, scented, &c. &c., 3-4 to 7.
Rock Salt—½-1.
Rose Wood.

Sable.
Saleld—root, &c.
Saffron—Kaisie—9-10-11-12 — Sago — Hill.
Sal Ammoniac.
Saltpetre—2-2½-3 Shurah
Sandal Wood.
Sardonyx.
Sarsaparilla Root.
Shagreen—Indian.
Silk, * raw and manufactured * 9-10—Bokara 2-4-6.
Silver—from mines & Chinese Crooses.
Sugar—Cond 4-5-6.
Sulphur—4-6.
Sissoo or Seesum Wood.
Skins—raw, &c. &c. Hides of various sorts—6-7-8—Barr Koree *Dherup* seeds of various sorts.

Tar.
Tea—Brick, Kekei, &c.—1-2-4.
Tin—from the mines.
Timber of various sorts and species.
Tobacco—2-2½ maund.
Treacle.
Topaz.
Tripoli.
Turmeric.
Turpentine—3-4 maund—Hills—Broza.
Turquoise—from the N. mines.

Yabboo.

Wool—raw and manufactured of various sorts, &c. &c.
Wax, 15-20.
Weld.

Zinc.

ARTICLES PROCURABLE IN THE PUNJAB AT THE STATED PRICES, PUKKA RUPEES PER MAUND.

Alum—Putteree Kholabaugh—2-2½-3.
Barilla—Sedjee—Barr—½-1-1½.
Borax—Swaga—8-10-12—Hills.
Catechu Wood Keith.
Cotton—Reo—Dooaba Malwa—5-6-8.
Deals—in Logs—5-6-7 each, or 12 to 20 each large Tree.
Flax, Raw—1-1½-2.
Fustic—Okell Beer.
Ghee—Shrese—7-8-10—Lahore, &c.
Honey—3-4-6—Saith Hills.
Hemp, Raw—1-1½-2.
Horn, Sing—Dherup, &c.—1-5 Koree or 100.
Iron—3-4-5.
Kei, Sulphate of Iron ½-1—Kholabarry.
Leather, Tanned, Chum—7-9-12 Koree.
Madder—Megeeth—Bunnoo, &c.—2½-3-4.
Manganese Ore—Ingenee—2-4—Hills, Mines, &c.
Molasses—Goord, Dooabe, &c.—2-2½-3.
Nitre Sharah—½-1-1½—Barr.
Rice—2½-4-6.
Rock Salt—Nimock-½-1—Ko Pint—Daden Kha.
Saffron—Kaissir—8-10-12—Cashmeer.
Silk, Raw, Rephem—8-9-10 seer, Hindostan 2-4 seer.
Tobacco—1½-2-2½.
Tea—2-3-4 seer—Cashmeer.
Turmeric.
Wool Raw 2—2½-3-*Oon*—Barr.
Wax—Moom—Hills-10-12-15.

Gold Dust—Bulthistan and along the Upper Banks of the Indus—can be procured sometimes even in large quantities at from 9, 10, 12 and 14 Cashmeeree Rupees the Tholah—These Rupees are but about 9 or 9½ annas each.

From Prinsep's Life of Runjeet Singh, (omitted in the proper place.)

"He was content, therefore, to accept a promise of the revenue of the four districts, Pursuvon, Goojrat, Seal kote and Aurungabad."—*C.* 1, *page* 10.

NOTE.

At present there were districts under the name of Aurungabad. Runjeet did away as much as possible with all the Mahometan names of districts, towns and even villages. Thus Russoolnugger, on the south bank of the Cheenaub, was ordered by him to be named Ramnugger, in default of which many fines and punishments have been awarded.

"Early in the morning, therefore, of the 12th April, 1752, this army moved from its lines and took up ground on an elevated spot marked by an old brick kiln. They prepared immediately for action."—*C.* 1, *page* 12.

NOTE.

There was no brick kiln near the scene of this action. As the engagement was fought on a fine open plain, just on the high road between the present small village of Gunja and Lahore, and about 5 miles E. N. E. of the latter, and E. of the village of Mamood Butee. On the field of battle some tombs may be seen at the present day of some of the principle chiefs and leaders that fell on both sides. Among them is Kaorna Mull's tomb, he having been interred on the very spot where he fell and died.

"The family boasts of no antiquity, the first of whom any traditionary recollection is preserved, was a petty zemindar named Deesoo, a Jath of the Sansee tribe, who resided in a village of the Manjha district called Sookur Chuk."—*C.* 2, *page* 22.

NOTE.

Sooker Chuk is not a village in the Manjha district. It is in the vicinity of Guzerawalla, and about 13 or 14 miles E. of the Cheenaub from Wesierabad.

"The Ghunneya Missel headed by Jy Singh, a Jath of Ghunnee, which lies also east of Lahore."—*C.* 2, *page* 29.

NOTE.

The Ghunneya Missul did not take its name from the village of Ghunnee, but from the name of the original or acknowledged head of that Family and Missul, whose name was plain Khunia at first, but taking the Paahul, changed it into Khunia Singh. He is said to be the grandfather of Jy Singh, and remarkable for the boldness of his exploits as a marauder. Thus in early life he acquired sufficient riches and power to enable him to establish and become the head of a Missul.

NOTE.

"If dissatisfied with his Chief a Misuldar might transfer himself with his possessions to another, under whose protection or countenance he might prefer to continue."—*C.* 2, *page* 635.

This practice has been the main and principle cause of the dilapidation of the strong and united Sikh Missul establishment or system, the fall or breaking up of which was chiefly brought about by the Missuldary and individual members, always in late years seeking to serve and join those they considered the strongest, most active, bold, and ready to assist and protect them and their interests, or screen and shelter them from the punishment due on account of their numerous and outrageous acts. Thus Cherut Sing, and his son Mah Sing, by their great boasting; large promises added to a quick, ready, active, bold and unflinching depredating system, found means to swell their ranks and increase their own power and interest at the expense of their brother chiefs; thus by a wily policy, erecting a strong fabric of their own on the fallen and falling ruins, and with the very materials of their unsuspecting friends and neighbours.

NOTE.

"The two armies lay encamped on opposite sides of the Busuntee, and in a particular skirmish between the Sikh auxiliaries, Churut Singh was killed by the bursting of his own matchlock."—*C.* 3, *page* 30.

Churut Singh was not killed on the banks of the Bussunther, which is some 12 or 14 miles E. or S. E. of Jummoo, but close to a place called Thilloo Kan Thalan, about 1½ or 2 miles S. W. of Jummoo.

NOTE.

"Dewan Lukoo was dispatched on an Expedition to Kitas, where he was slain, &c. &c."—*C.* 3, *page* 49.

Not to Kitass, which is W. of the Ghelum and in the Salt range, and at that period not in the possession of the Sukerchuk Family. But to Kodrabad on the W. Bank of the Cheenaub.

NOTE.

"Runjeet Singh returned to his capital and detached Moh-

Bhao and Chibh are two different tribes, and are spread

kum Chund Dewan to enforce the collection of tribute, and to complete arrangements in the Hills, where the Rajas of Bhimbhur and Rajcoree and the tribe of Chibh Bhao were refractory."—*C.* 5, *page* 82.

over a large tract of the lower ranges. They are equally strong and powerful. Their famous strongholds and large villages of *Deva* and Vettala are well known, as capable of producing at least 10 or 12,000 well armed and hardy mountaineers.

"Ram Lol returned for his brother's sake and ultimately received the Pahul or Sikh initiation and changed his name to Ram Singh."—*C.* 7, *page* 114.

NOTE.

Ram Lol never took the Pahul or became a Sikh—or was his name ever changed to Ram Singh.

"This individual was originally a petty officer of horse in the service of Ameer Khan." —*C.* 9, *page* 145.

NOTE.

The Seyd was originally at Peshawer in the service of Sirdar Pheer Mamood Khan as a foot soldier on a monthly salary of 4 or 5 rupees.

"He (Runjeet Singh) holds besides Kashmeer and the entire hill country to the snowy range and even Ludak beyond the Heemelaya. For though many of the Rajahs of this tract still remain in their possessions, they have been reduced to the character of subjects, paying tribute equal to their utmost means and contributing men to the armies of Lahore whenever called upon." —*C.* 11, *page* 183.

NOTE.

Ludak, Iskurdoo, &c. were invaded and subjugated by Goolab Singh and the Dogra Family, without previous instruction or the knowledge of Runjeet, and when he was informed by them of any thing of the kind, it was in a tenor and manner merely to serve their own ends. Nor did ever any part of the revenue of those states enter the Lahore Treasury. The country being represented to him as an unproductive wild and desert Tract.

INDEX.

A.

B.

C.

INDEX.